The Church
as
Woman and
Mother

The Church as Woman and Mother

Historical and Theological Foundations

CRISTINA LLEDO GOMEZ

Foreword by Tina Beattie

Paulist Press
New York / Mahwah, NJ

Cover images—Front: Thirteenth-century Deesis mosaic in Hagia Sophia (Istanbul, Turkey). Retouched photograph by Myrabella / Wikimedia Commons / CC BY-SA 3.0. Used with permission. Background texture photo by nopparatz/ depositphotos.com.
Cover design by Tamian Wood
Book design by Sharyn Banks

Library of Congress Cataloging-in-Publication Data

Names: Gomez, Cristina Lledo, author.
Title: The church as woman and mother : historical and theological foundations / Cristina Lledo Gomez.
Description: New York : Paulist Press, 2018. | Includes bibliographical references and index.
Identifiers: LCCN 2017061012 (print) | LCCN 2018021203 (ebook) | ISBN 9781587686948 (e-book) | ISBN 9780809153329 (pbk. : alk. paper)
Subjects: LCSH: Church. | Motherhood—Religious aspects—Catholic Church. | Catholic Church—Doctrines.
Classification: LCC BX1746 (ebook) | LCC BX1746 .G564 2018 (print) | DDC 262/.7—dc23
LC record available at https://lccn.loc.gov/2017061012

ISBN 978-0-8091-5332-9 (paperback)
ISBN 978-1-58768-694-8 (e-book)

Published by Paulist Press
997 Macarthur Boulevard
Mahwah, New Jersey 07430

www.paulistpress.com

Printed and bound in the United States of America

For Sophia, Julian, and Adrian

Contents

List of Illustrations

FOREWORD

TINA BEATTIE

I met Cristina Lledo Gomez when she was beginning her PhD. My own doctoral research had been a feminist reading of Marian theology in patristic and contemporary Catholic thought, so we shared many interests and perspectives. We were also both mothers who knew what it was like to juggle academic studies with raising young children, and that too gave us common ground.

Cristina spoke with passion about her research interests, but she also lamented how difficult it was to find a supervisor who would accommodate a feminist theological perspective. She was being encouraged to adopt a more conservative scholarly approach by analyzing patristic sources for arguments and insights regarding maternal ecclesiology and setting aside any specifically feminist methodology or arguments. I shared her frustration about this resistance to feminism, but when I read her thesis some years later as an external examiner, I realized that she had managed to combine deep scholarly rigor with creative feminist flair. The result is an impressive study of patristic and postconciliar theology that addresses fundamental questions about the role and representation of women in the Catholic Church today. This is a study that shows that feminist scholars can hold their own among the brightest and best of modern systematic theologians, while bringing a freshness and an energy to their task of excavating neglected treasures from the earliest traditions of the church.

Feminist theology is a dynamic school of thought that is constantly redrawing its boundaries and revising its methods as new questions emerge from different contexts and cultures. One might compare it, not with the sclerotic weariness of some theological methods that have yet to shake off the legacy of neoscholasticism, but with the searching vision and excitement of the patristic era, when Christians had to argue for the legitimacy of their claims in intellectual cultures and social environments that were often suspicious of or hostile toward them. Today, feminist theologians face similar challenges as they seek to transform tradition and nurture new visions and hopes, while having to navigate a precarious path between secular feminist hostility and mainstream theological suspicion. These pressures have proved to be a source of much creative energy and a stimulus to scholarly inquiry, as this book so eloquently demonstrates. Gomez's work shows that the premodern and the postmodern can be fertile partners in theological inquiry and doctrinal development.

There is still a tendency to tokenism in many undergraduate theology curricula, when a chapter from a book by Mary Daly or Rosemary Radford Ruether suffices to ward off critics who might complain about the lack of women authors or feminist perspectives. Yet feminist scholars today have moved far beyond these early sources, which had their roots in the pragmatism of liberal American theology, focusing on issues of politics and social justice and rejecting many of the more symbolic and sacramental approaches of the Catholic theological tradition. Feminist theologians coming from that liberal end of the spectrum still tend to be dismissive of ecclesiological language that refers to the church as woman, bride, virgin, and mother, seeing it as the legacy of an anachronistic patriarchal system that should be discarded in favor of more modern and progressive images of Christian discipleship. Gomez shows how wrong they are.

While an abstract concept of "woman" has been associated with idealized projections of society and nature across many cultures and eras, Gomez goes beyond these problematic stereotypes to delve more deeply into how such feminized terms were used in the early church. Returning to patristic sources of the first five centuries of the church in the West, she shows how the description of the church as a woman and a mother drew its inspiration from embodied social and domestic realities. While such realities were filtered through a metaphorical lens—the church was like but also not like these maternal models—there was a resonance between them. In language that she borrows from theologian Janet Martin Soskice, Gomez argues that they were "living metaphors." They were culturally resonant because the "Roman woman," even if idealized, made sense to the numerous countries that formed the Roman Empire. The modern church uses these same Roman metaphors, but they have no resonance in a multicultural context with many different concepts of what it means to be a woman.

By way of meticulous research, Gomez argues that the idea of the maternal church should not be discarded but reanimated by reconnecting maternal metaphors with relevant and familiar images of maternal life. Patristic ecclesiology appealed to well-known examples of motherhood and womanhood in Roman society, in a complex symbolic relationship that was critically and constructively shaped by familiar social models and adapted over time to fit changing cultural contexts. Gomez shows that this flexible approach to symbolism and interpretation is not relativism but a sign of a living tradition that seeks to retain its relevance by remaining connected to the social realities that are mediated through its symbols and signs.

In arguing this, she situates patristic authors in their cultural contexts, drawing not only on textual evidence but on a wide range of artefacts such as coins, clothing, and effigies. Rather than projecting back onto these ancient authors some abstract concept of maternal femininity, she seeks to recreate their own culturally embedded perspectives to ask what evolving references to the church as woman, mother, bride, and virgin might have meant in the context of authors such as Irenaeus, Tertullian, Ambrose, and Augustine. Through this careful work of contextualizing various feminized images that emerged during the formative years of Christian ecclesiology, Gomez argues convincingly that:

> By the time Augustine used female metaphors for the church, his predecessors had already set the stage. Every female recognized and respected in the surrounding Roman and pagan culture and in Scripture was for Augustine's picking—the daughter, bride, virgin, queen, wife, mother, and widow. (p. 113)

These "living metaphors" served to affirm the significance and relevance of Christian doctrine, while resisting the various heresies that threatened the cohesion of the early church.

Gomez contrasts this with the feminized ecclesiology that emerged in the era before and after the Second Vatican Council, up to and including Pope Francis, in which references to the church as mother and woman are often idealized and divorced from the experiential realities of women in modern society. The language tends to alienate people because it fails to resonate with the various meanings that attach to motherhood in different cultures and contexts. In tracing these ecclesiological concepts to their roots in scripture and Roman society of the first five centuries, Gomez offers a theological response to the challenges of late modernity that is historically discerning, rooted in tradition, and attentive to the questions that face the church today, not only regarding the role of women but more widely what it means to witness to the kingdom of God in today's societies.

To reclaim a viable maternal ecclesiology entails being attentive to cultural expressions and experiences of mothering. It also entails separating the idea of the church as woman from too close an association with the church as Mary. Gomez's exploration of the social context of Vatican II suggests that the surge in Marian apparitions and popular devotions during the traumas of twentieth-century life led to an infantilizing concept of motherhood in which the Marian church provided refuge for the faithful and shielded them from the harsh realities of life.* She argues for a maternal ecclesiology that learns from women what it means to mother children at various stages of life, as they themselves mature and offer maternal love and care to others. While Marian devotion remains a crucial factor in this, it cannot be the defining characteristic of the transformative world order that emerges when the church offers a mature response to the maternal vocation to care for the vulnerable and to nurture qualities of forgiveness, mercy, and love toward others.

In its supple and irenic treatment of patristic sources, Gomez's study is an exemplary model of scholarship sharpened by feminist

---

* Cf. Cristina Lledo Gomez, "From Infants to Mothers: Recovering the Call to the People of God to Become Mother Church in *Lumen Gentium*," *Ecclesiology* 11, no.1, (January 2015): 32–62; and "The Motherhood of the Church: Mary, the Quotidian, and the People of God," in *Catholic Women Speak: Bringing Our Gifts to the Table*, Catholic Women Speak Network, eds. (Mahwah, NJ: Paulist Press, 2015).

insights, but also disciplined by the rigors of sound historical and theological scholarship. It is, however, in the chapter on Bergoglio (Pope Francis) that she brings a feminist flourish to her study by treating this contemporary pope in exactly the same way in which she treated his patristic forebears. Who were the women who influenced him personally? What was the cultural context in which his ideas of maternal femininity were formed? How have these two factors influenced his theological formation?

Gomez describes the women who influenced him in his family and among his friendships. She then widens the lens to analyze the construction of idealized womanhood in the decades preceding the Second Vatican Council, particularly in the 1950s, when she argues that "natural" concepts of marriage and family life had to be shored up against a rapidly changing environment regarding gender and relationships. She situates Francis's understanding of "woman" as ambivalently positioned between the lingering idealization of motherhood and "feminine genius" that recurs in preconciliar and postconciliar documents on the one hand, and his pastoral awareness of the realities of women's lives, aspirations, and maternal struggles on the other. She argues that, although inconsistent, this attentiveness to the experiential dimension of mothering in some of his theological reflections is slowly beginning to repair the rupture between the idealized language of maternal ecclesiology and the realities of maternal life. Gomez's own work is an important part of this healing process in which Holy Mother Church might find a revitalized identity by listening to and learning from wholly human mothers.

This book makes a fine contribution to understanding the Catholic Church in its historical and contemporary struggles around the language of gender and identity. It should be required reading in seminaries and courses on ecclesiology, but it will be of interest to all who wish to understand more about how language and culture are woven together in the making of theology, and how the most relevant theological insights emerge when the bonds between the two are respected.

Preface

"Why is the church a woman?"
"Why is it called a mother?" "Do we have to call it
a mother?"
"What does the pope mean when he says the church
is la Chiesa, *not* il Chiesa*?"*

It was October 1, 2015. I was in Rome at the Pontifical University Antonianum, sitting on a panel with fellow contributors to the book *Catholic Women Speak: Bringing Our Gifts to the Table*, which was being launched in time for the Synod on the Family, held October 4 to 25 that year. The book was written as a living source for the cardinals, bishops, and *periti*, evidencing the realities of various women's lives in their rich diversity. We wanted to ensure that "woman" or family was not idealized or spoken of in abstract ways at the synod. So the book was published in record time, and we made sure it found its way into the hands and, hopefully, minds of the bishops, *periti*, and cardinals.

At the launch, I spoke of why I wrote my chapter, "The Motherhood of the Church: Mary, the Quotidian, and the People of God"—that is, because the "Good Mother" myth still exists today, even in so-called advanced Western democratic societies that claim to have moved on from Simone de Beauvoir's *Second Sex* (1949) and Betty Friedan's *Feminine Mystique* (1963). I pointed out that this Good Mother myth exists through Mary as the perfect virgin-mother to infant Jesus, or as *mater dolorosa* hovering over the dead body of Jesus à la *pietà* images, or in church documents, where womanhood is often collapsed into motherhood, and motherhood is sentimentalized and viewed narrowly as simply birthing, comforting, teaching, and loving sacrifice. Further, I reflected that the Good Mother myth, which may appear harmless, has in fact affected and continues to affect women all over the world in insidious but also overtly dangerous ways, as evidenced by the stories of my fellow coauthors and panel presenters.

To counter the Good Mother/Good Woman myth, my chapter called for a revision of the image of the church as a woman, specifically as a mother. I suggested that if the image was going to be used, then it should take seriously the realities of daily mothering in its complexities and challenges. The image should also take into consideration that mothering is not only toward infants but also toward growing and adult children. By doing this, there would be a better chance of viewing mothers in an unsentimental way, as human beings with needs and hopes for themselves and their world; and it would question the reduction of womanhood into motherhood. At the same time, the revision would also encourage a way of being church, where members would take up their baptismal call to participate in the church's mission by growing up and becoming mothers to others themselves. This idea is not something new, but is mined from the writings of the early Latin church fathers who used the image of the church as a woman as part of their own rhetoric directed toward predominantly ancient Roman audiences. I showed that the need to relook at the church imagined as a woman and mother was not only imperative for women, but also for men, and ultimately for the mission of the church itself.

At question time, the two questions I received constantly were essentially these: "Why is the church a woman?" "Why is it called a mother?" At the time of the launch, I was in the middle of a research fellowship at Boston College's School of Theology and Ministry. I had just completed my doctorate on the uses of "Mother Church" at the Second Vatican Council and in the writings of early church fathers. The fellowship allowed me to turn my hard-earned four years of research into a book. I had a book plan that I was following, which was what I had proposed to Boston College when I had applied for a fellowship there. But that day of the launch of *Catholic Women Speak*, when I repeatedly received those two questions, I knew I had to write a different book from the one I had originally envisaged.

Hopefully, I have provided some solid answers to those two questions here. I hope, too, that the current book addresses the issue of language use and culturally resonant imaging when communicating to specific audiences—showing that using language simply out of supposed respect for tradition and without consideration of the culture(s) of the people one is addressing alienates others, dividing them between those who are in the know and those who are not.

Writing this book has been a mammoth task that would not have been possible had it not been for the help and guidance of so many people. First, I'd like to thank Boston College, School of Theology and Ministry (STM), for giving me the space and resources to write. Thank you to my research assistant, Storm Obuchowski, for his thoroughness, efficiency, and friendship. Thank you too to the eminent scholars at the STM, who gave me their encouragement and generous feedback. I am particularly grateful to the early patristic scholar Brian Dunkle, SJ, for helping me to refine and give direction to my book, specifically the chapters on Tertullian, Cyprian, and Ambrose. Also, I thank the library staff at the college, especially Virginia Greeley and Stephen Dalton, who continued to provide copies of texts I needed even after I had returned to Australia.

Thank you to the scholars beyond the STM who have been generous with their feedback. The following people have read various drafts of all or parts of the book: Denis Minns, OP, the part concerning Irenaeus; Francine Cardman, concerning Tertullian; Raymond F. Canning, Augustine; Andrew R. Davis, biblical and prebiblical precedents; and Ruth Sheridan, the exegesis of Galatians and Revelation. They have not been privy to final copies of my chapters, so any errors found within the present volume are solely my own. Thank you also to the librarians, Michael McAteer, Siobhan Dib, and Margaret Watts, at the Catholic Institute of Sydney's Veech Library, for their very generous assistance with their library's ancient sources collection; to Gerard Moore, my doctoral supervisor, who continues to be a sounding board beyond the PhD; and to Tina Beattie, for encouraging me to publish this book after reading it as an external marker for my doctorate. Some women believe the metaphor of "mother" for the church should be discarded, but Tina and I believe there is something recoverable about the metaphor that can be liberating for everybody.

Thank you very much to Richard Lennan, who instilled in me a love for the church and Karl Rahner, and who encouraged me to pursue studies to the PhD level. It was serendipitous as well as humbling to find myself no longer the student but a colleague to my mentor, whom I admire and hold in high esteem. I thank Richard for his ongoing support, and for reading the draft chapters and offering me his advice.

Thank you to the other institutions and religious orders who have provided both financial and moral support. Thank you to the Sisters of Mercy Australia and Papua New Guinea, particularly Sister Veronica Lawson, who heard me speak about "Mother Church" at Grace College's Women's Theology Conference (GCWTC) in 2015. I thank them for their gift of $5000 to help with costs as I began my fellowship in Boston. Thank you to Charles Sturt University's Public and Contextual Theology Research Centre. The centre helped me, as one of their research fellows, to access library material and grants to attend conferences. Thank you to the Dominican Sisters of Australia, especially Sister Patricia Madigan, who gave $1500 to encourage me to continue undertaking and sharing my research.

I also wish to thank Mark Elkington for photographing the Livia statue held in the National Archaeological Museum of Spain, in Madrid, and for giving permission to reproduce the photo that appears as figure 3.2 (see p. 57) in this volume. Thank you also to the Classical Numismatic Group, Inc. (www.cngcoins.com), which gave me permission to reproduce the photos in figure 3.3 (see p. 58). Further, in-depth bibliographic information regarding the ancient sources I used in this book can be found in appendix 2. Thank you to Gerard Kelly, president of the Catholic Institute of Sydney (2004–17), who gave me a room in the college to enable me to focus on finishing my PhD thesis in its final months. To Christopher Brennan, thank you for your stellar job with editing. And thank you to my publisher, Paulist Press, particularly Paul McMahon. You believed in this book and were excited about publishing it.

Finally, I thank my friends, family, and work colleagues who have helped in numerous ways, through either babysitting, making meals, or providing moral support, as I carved out the time and space to finish the manuscript. There have been many times I doubted this book would come to fruition, but they just told me to keep going. Thank you especially to Sarah Massa, and my mother-in-law, May Gomez, on this count. I'd also like to thank my fellow

Australian theologians Natalie Lindner L'huillier and Rohan Curnow for their indispensable friendship. A special thank you goes to my two children, Sophia and Julian, who not only had to put up with a parent doing a doctorate but also with one who was writing a book. I hope they have enjoyed at least part of the journey by experiencing a few months of another culture in the United States. I hope too that I have modeled for them how to look beyond the immediate horizon and how always to expand their vision through listening to the stirrings of their hearts, rather than simply to societal convention. Finally, to the love of my life, Adrian, who has been on a rollercoaster ride with me with the doctorate, research fellowship, this book, and our entire marriage. Thank you. Words do not suffice.

Abbreviations

ACW   Ancient Christian Writers Series

         ACW 6: *The Didache, the Epistle of Barnabus, the Epistles and the Martyrdom of St. Polycarp, the Fragments of Papias, the Epistle to Diognetus.* Translated and annotated by James A. Kleist. Mahwah, NJ: Newman Press, 1961.

         ACW 26: *Origen: The Song of Songs Commentary and Homilies.* Translated and annotated by R. P. Lawson. Mahwah, NJ: Newman Press, 1957.

ANCL   Alexander Roberts and James Donaldson eds. *Ante-Nicene Christian Library: Translations of the Writings of the Fathers down to A.D. 325.* Edinburgh: T&T Clark 1867–.

ANF   Alexander Roberts and James Donaldson, ed. and trans. *The Ante-Nicene Fathers: Translations of the Writings of the Fathers Down to A.D. 325.* Edinburgh: T&T Clark, 1885–, reprint 1978.

Bévenot   Cyprian. *Cyprian: De Lapsis and De Ecclesiae Catholicae Unitate: Text and Translation.* Translated by Maurice Bévenot. Oxford: Clarendon, 1971.

CCSL   Corpus Christianorum Latina Series. Turnholti: Brepols, 1953–.

Christie   A. J. Christie. *On Holy Virginity: With a Brief Account of the Life of St. Ambrose.* Oxford: John Henry Parker, 1843.

FC   Roy J. Deferrari, ed. The Fathers of the Church. Washington, DC: Catholic University Press, 1947–.

LCL   Loeb Classical Library. Cambridge, MA: Harvard University Press, 1912–.

Lightfoot *The Apostolic Fathers.* Vol. 3, by J.B. Lightfoot, edited and completed by J.R. Harmer. Grand Rapids, MI: Baker Book House, 1976.

NPNF   *A Select Library of the Nicene and Post-Nicene Fathers of the Christian Church.* Grand Rapids, MI: William B. Eerdmans, 1887–. *NPNF1*: Series 1; *NPNF2*: Series 2.

OECT   Oxford Early Christian Texts Series. Oxford: Oxford University Press, 1980–.

PG   P. J. Migne, ed. Patrologia Graeca. Paris: Librairie de Paris, 1844–64.

PL   P. J. Migne, ed. Patrologia Latina. Paris: Librairie de Paris, 1844–64.

PO   K. Mekerttschian and S. G. Wilson, trans. and eds. Patrologia Orientalis. Paris: Librairie de Paris, 1907–88.

VigChr   *Vigiliae Christianae: A Review of Early Christian Life and Language.*

WSA   J. E. Rotelle, ed. The Works of Saint Augustine: A Translation for the 21st Century. New York: New City, 1990–.

Introduction

Why write a book on the church as a woman, and specifically as a mother? Apart from wanting to provide solid answers to audiences who have often asked why the church is a woman, as noted in the preface, it is because the very mention of "Mother Church" elicits the response "Oh, your topic is about Mary." While Mary, the mother of Jesus, holds a special place in my heart, especially since my orphaned mother adopted her as her own, I demonstrate that the portrayal of the church as a woman developed in response to various church issues and for purposes separate from the imagination of the church as Mary.

When the image of the church as a mother is collapsed into the image of Mary as a mother, it promotes a passivity contradicting the Christian baptismal calling to be priest, prophet, and king. For the long association of Mary with devotion and piety, which reached its heights in her miraculous appearances in various world locations during the twentieth century (coinciding with all the instability of the world wars and fiscal depression), leads to a tendency to put oneself under Mary's mantle, as passive infants simply receiving the care of a mother. In contrast, the patristic writers of the early church invite us to understand that the church is us, the baptized, and that we are called to grow up and "mother others." This mothering church is to be the explicit presence of a different world order, God's kingdom—where the poor and the marginalized are the priority, where love, forgiveness, and mercy are the default responses toward others. This is not to say we cannot ask Mary to place us under her mantle and pray for us. The Catholic maxim applies: it is not "either/or" but "both/and." In other words, it is necessary to emphasize also that we the baptized are called to adult faith and to build community, through witness, accompaniment, and proclaiming the good news, which is the underpinning vision for all Christian activity.

1

In demonstrating the solid foundations of the image of the church as mother, the bulk of the book is devoted to the first five centuries, when this female metaphor for the church was being developed in the West. The Eastern Christian churches also imagine the church as a woman, but this lies outside the scope of this investigation. This book is written through the lenses of a systematic theologian, not through those of an early patristic scholar or biblical expert. Hence, while primary sources have been examined and referenced, I have often used reputable translations and only applied my own when no equivalent and appropriate English texts were easily accessible. Moreover, I owe a great debt to the extensive research and guidance of early patristic and biblical scholars. The goal has not been to add to the scholarship of each area but to weave together all the recent and compelling findings as a systematician and as one specializing in the study of the church (ecclesiology), and to hold up the findings against teachings of the church as found in recent papal and conciliar documents that utilize the metaphor of "mother" for the church.

Consequently, my aim is not only to untangle Mother Church from Mary as mother, such that we recognize that each exist with their own merit and trajectories, but also to put a spotlight on the rhetoric we use in the church in order to ask the following: Does our language connect with or alienate people? Should we be maintaining the use of traditional language and imagery when their meanings have shifted or been lost over time, or, worse still, now have negative associations? Do we work to retrieve or reappropriate such language, or is it our challenge to develop new imagery that better resonates with our contemporary contexts? Even the word *mother* now has different connotations and implications intertwined with the many diverse cultural milieus within which it is employed.

In the first chapter, we examine the pre-Christian history of this imagery, noting the factors that contributed to the imagination of the church as a woman, before the early church fathers began to call it a mother. This began with the idea of the city perceived as a woman, which in turn explains how Jerusalem/Zion is presented as a female, particularly as a mother, daughter, widow, and even whore in the Hebrew Scriptures. We consider, then, the New Testament passages that traditionally have been justifications for our understanding of Mother Church as the Christian Church superseding the Jewish faith. Yet, in fact, these scriptural texts align more with a vision of "Mother Church" as the kingdom of God, where Jews, Christians, and all people of goodwill live together. By the time the early church fathers, like Irenaeus, began to imagine the church as a woman, the martyrdoms within the church began to be associated with its "birthing" function, that is, its ability to make new Christians or to renew the commitment of old members of the Christian Church. The maternal image of the church began to be utilized as a response to various heresies inside and outside of the church.

In the next four chapters, we argue that when the Catholic Church is explicitly named "Mother Church," it calls upon the image of the ancient Roman mother, herself a projection of the ideal woman embodying the values of Roman society. More specifically, in chapter 2, we note that Tertullian's pairing of Mother Church with Father God is reflective of his cultural context, where the Roman family was composed of mother, father, and children, and to be without a mother is to be without a family. This has life and death implications for the Christian Roman and thus acts as an invaluable rhetorical tool for Tertullian.

In chapter 3, we examine Cyprian's initial uses of the metaphor for the church, which sought to tap into the picture of the mother as unifying and stabilizing for the Christian community, amid the third-century crisis. However, we demonstrate that Cyprian later presents the church as a bride, rather than as a mother, because rebaptisms continued to be an issue for the church, and the rebaptism issue began to be a matter of urgency. We observe parallels between Cyprian's and Origen's imagination of the church as a bride that has implications for the tradition of the church imagined as a female. While Origen's picture of the church as a bride was in fact an affirmation of creation, a response to floating religious ideas that rejected the body, this picture, unfortunately, reinforces the patriarchal relationship between man and woman. This has had an adverse effect upon the tradition of the church imagined as a woman and on the perception of women in the church. However, it is problematic to abandon the church as a bride image since this scriptural metaphor communicates something significant in terms of the church's relationship with Jesus.

Where "Mother Church" had her own purpose separate from the imagination of Mary as mother in Tertullian's and Cyprian's texts, in chapter 4, we see that Ambrose imposes the idea of Mary as mother onto the church, to work with Roman values attached to womanhood, motherhood, and the family. More specifically, by showing that virginity in the church fulfills the double Roman calling for women to become mothers and virgins for Rome, Ambrose found a way to convince Roman women to enter ecclesial virginity. In fact, Ambrose presents Mary and the church as models of motherhood and virginity to justify the call for virgin-mothers for the church.

In chapter 5, we explore Augustine utilizing various female images for the church and not just Mary as a mother and virgin, but also as a model for the church as virgin and mother. I demonstrate that the female imagery was applied in response to various heresies and uncertainties, which in turn questioned the relevance of female metaphors for the church. All metaphors have their strengths and limitations and consequently, the virgin-mother church as modeled in Mary, although it communicated vital teachings regarding salvation, the church, and Jesus, did, in fact, leave unresolved tensions for Augustine.

The last chapter moves to the twentieth and twenty-first centuries, where we investigate Pope Francis's uses of female church language in light of the Second Vatican Council's imagination of the church as *Mater et Magistra* (mother and teacher). This chapter explores the contemporary relevance of the investigation of the foundations of the church imagined as a woman. While Francis's idea of the woman is grounded in loving relationships with real women, there remain elements of idealism that are present in Vatican II and post–Vatican II papal documents. This chapter outlines the context for Francis's use of language about women and the church, particularly for examples that have been viewed as controversial or offensive, such as his reference to female theologians as "strawberries on the cake." Furthermore, I ask whether there is something that Pope Francis and his papal predecessors are responding to when they refer to the church as a "woman as mother," just as the early church fathers referred to the "mother church" or "bridal church" in response to new or longstanding heresies. In the end, we hope for new possibilities for the tradition of the church as mother, bride, virgin, and queen, and the church's imagination of woman becoming more reflective of realities through Francis's priority to respond to real persons. This surely includes the realities of women in their varying contexts.

In conclusion, we examine the implications of this exploration of the female church in the texts of the early church fathers as well as in those from Vatican II and subsequent popes. While the current volume has direct relevance for Christian audiences, especially those curious about its feminine imagery, hopefully, non-Christian scholars will also find interest in its historical and sociological explorations. Personally, it has been fascinating to enter the ancient Roman world and its ideals regarding woman that were then reflected onto the church presented as a woman. Nearly two thousand years later, we find the same processes at work wherein the Catholic Church adopts its own idea of "woman" to communicate something about the nature of the church. This has implications not only for women's place in the church, but also for the effectiveness of symbols and language currently used in church thought and practice.

1

The City as a Woman, Faith as a Mother

As a mother comforts her child,
so I will comfort you;
you shall be comforted in Jerusalem.

—Isaiah 66:13

In this passage from the Hebrew Scriptures, the prophet Isaiah paints a poignant portrait of what God would be like as a mother. Here, Jerusalem embraces and enfolds a devastated and worn-out, returning Israelite community, the community having earlier been sent away from their beloved city and now returning from exile, faced with the destruction of their temple (the first temple). But Jerusalem was more than a city to the Israelites. It was a nation, a people, and their history—embodied here as a mother—providing consolation to her hurting and disoriented child. Centuries before the Christian Church was symbolized as a woman and mother, Jerusalem was scripturally pictured as a mother—and a daughter, virgin, wife, widow, queen, and even as a whore. Going further back, other ancient cultures also used the imagery of womanhood as a way of constructing the meaning and character of their cities and their relationship with their inhabitants.

In this chapter, we investigate various historical components that have contributed to the depiction of the church as a woman and mother. First, we look at cultural precedents from the ancient Near East, such as Sumer, Akkadia, Babylon, and Phrygia, where cities were envisioned as women. Second, we explore Jewish biblical imagery whereby Jerusalem or Zion city was pictured as a woman. Understanding these backgrounds will assist us in interpreting New Testament texts, such as Galatians 4:26 and Revelation 12:17, that are used to justify the image of the Christian Church as a mother.

7

Zion city (also known as Jerusalem) as a mother forms the background of these texts that can lead us to a more nuanced interpretation in which "mother" refers not simply to the church but to the kingdom of God. Such an emphasis differs from traditional readings of these biblical texts. Finally, we examine early patristic writings that allude to the church as a woman, mother, bride, and virgin. The first instance of the metaphor of mother being applied to the living Christian community is found in the martyrdom texts attributed to Irenaeus of Lyons. Irenaeus's development of the images of the church as woman and mother are foundational to the later patristic elaboration of this symbolism that we will explore in more detail.

THE CITY AS A WOMAN

When biblical scholars explore the origins of the personification of Jerusalem/Zion as a woman, they often refer to the work of Aloysius Fitzgerald, who has examined the considerable influence of the ancient Near East.[1] This area included Mesopotamia, Ancient Egypt, and Anatolia/Asia Minor. It is in this area where history shows the earliest records of civilization, with the first city-states established by 3200 BCE.[2] The earliest set of texts from there that can be "effectively read" date from around 2500 BCE.[3] Fitzgerald has theorized that in the ancient Near East–West Semitic area, capital cities were portrayed as goddesses, who were married to the patron deity of their respective city.[4] He argues that since these Near Eastern cities were portrayed as the patron goddess, they were deified, and this cultural context presents the foundation for the imaging of Jerusalem/Zion as a woman. While Fitzgerald's thesis on deification has been criticized,[5] he still has a highly significant point that in ancient societies, cities were portrayed as women. One such example that Fitzgerald provides relates to Phoenician coins from the later Hellenistic period that portray *Tychē Poleōs* as a woman with a walled or turreted crown, representing a city via the goddess *Tychē* (of fortune or fate). While this evidence does not necessarily lead to the conclusion that cities were deified, it does support the idea that they were imagined as women.[6] A counterexample, however, can be seen in the Assyro-Babylonian/Akkadian language (which is the earliest form of Semitic),[7] in which the word for "city" (*ālu*) is usually gendered masculine, and therefore names of cities (and countries) in this language also tend to be masculine.[8] However, "the Canaanite scribes who wrote the Akkadian of the Amarna letters, which were to be read in the Egyptian court, made the city [i.e., cities in general] feminine."[9] This evidence demonstrates the association of cities with the imagery of womanhood in the ancient Near Eastern imagination.[10] This is the case for Zion/Jerusalem as it is portrayed in the Hebrew Scriptures.

ZION/JERUSALEM AS A WOMAN

In Hebrew, the word for "city," *'ir*, is feminine, thus leading to an understanding of the city as a woman from a linguistic point of view. The city of Jerusalem personified as a woman represents a nation, its people, and their historical relationship with YHWH. For example, in Ezekiel 16, Jerusalem city is depicted as an individual with a history, personality, and a future: from abandoned baby girl, "thrown out in the open field"; through childhood and adolescence, "you grew up...and arrived at full womanhood"; to bride, "I pledged myself to you and entered into a covenant with you"; to queen, "you grew exceedingly beautiful, fit to be a queen"; to mother, "your sons and your daughters, whom you had borne to me"; and to covenant-breaking whore, "But you trusted in your beauty, and played the whore because of your fame...offering yourself to every passer-by, and multiplying your whoring" (Ezek 16:5, 7, 8, 13, 20, 15, 25).

The personification of Jerusalem played upon the audience's understanding of an affinity between female roles (such as mother, wife, and daughter) and the relationships between the city, its ruler, and its inhabitants. For "cities like women can be desired, conquered, protected, and governed by men."[11] And like a mother, cities can also be regarded as providing nourishment, shelter, security, instruction, and identity.

The Hebrew Scriptures take for granted the picture of Zion as a mother, frequently referring to the Israelite people as "daughter Zion" or the "daughters of Zion" (e.g., Jer 4:31; 6:2, 23; Isa 3:16–26). Zion literally designates three successive places of religious and historical significance within Jerusalem—originally the City of David on Jerusalem's lower eastern hill, then the Temple Mount on the upper eastern hill, and finally, following the destruction of Jerusalem, it was misattributed to its current site, on the western hill. Despite these physical moves, the religious significance of Zion, as symbolizing the seat of David's power and the earthly dwelling place of YHWH, remains constant.

While having this distinctive meaning, the Bible often uses Zion by way of metonymy to refer to the whole city of Jerusalem together with its residents (e.g., Pss 50:2; 84:7), and following the destruction of the city in 587 BCE, it came to represent the entire people of Israel (e.g., Isa 10:24; 30:19; Lam 2:8–10). Like Jerusalem, Zion is referred to not just as a physical space but also as a woman who represents the inhabitants of that space. As a woman, Zion is presented as a daughter, bride, widow, wife, and even as a whore (see, e.g., Isa 1:8; Jer 2:2; Lam 1; Jer 3:1; Ezek 16).

Reflecting on the impact of the destruction of the first temple on Mount Zion and the subsequent exile of an entire nation from their beloved Jerusalem city, Isaiah presents a theology of Zion to ask, where is God in these experiences of destruction, despair, and alienation? To bring hope to a devastated people, the writer of Isaiah envisions a future "victorious reign of God,"[12] which will, in due course, parallel Christianity's own vision of the kingdom of God. Deutero-Isaiah (Isa 40—55) reflects on the impact of the first exile by imagining Zion as a "perpetual place of peace, protection and prosperity."[13] This was an expression of the hopes of a people longing to return to their "mother city" and hoping to rebuild their temple. Subsequently, Trito-Isaiah (Isa 56—66) was written after the exiles had returned to Jerusalem, during the rebuilding of the second temple, which was completed circa 516 BCE (but was destroyed later, in 70 CE). Severe hardships were endured in this rebuilding. Therefore, while the exiles had returned to their mother city in a physical sense, Zion as a place of peace was yet to be fulfilled. It was a "vision still await[ing] fulfillment and [was] eventually pushed to an eschatological end in later literature."[14] The ultimate vision of Zion, pushed to an eschatological end or eternally existing, results from the destruction of the second temple, and a circumstance in which a nation needed to believe in a Jerusalem/Zion that could never be destroyed.

From Zion theology, we then have projections of Zion as a daughter, an image frequently used in Scripture to symbolize the people of the city, making it possible to personify their relationship with their city's patron deity, YHWH (e.g., Zech 9:9; Zeph 3:14; Jer 6:2; Mic 4:8; Isa 1:8; Ps 9:14). The utility of the daughter metaphor rests on ideas surrounding Zion's election (the Israelites as God's chosen people) and the idea that it is at Mount Zion that God dwells. In Israelite society, the "daughter" was to be protected, but she was also dependent upon the father; her virginity was to be kept intact, as it reflected directly upon the family, its head, and their honor. By imagining Zion as a daughter, the metaphor enabled the use of cultural-familial ideas surrounding the concept of daughter.

In contrast to the "beloved and protected" people of Zion as daughter, Jerusalem is also presented in the Scriptures as a whore, as found in Isaiah (e.g., 1:21), Jeremiah (e.g., 3:1–2), and Ezekiel (e.g., 16:44–48). This tradition of imagery has its foundations in God's relationship with God's people portrayed as a marriage in Hosea. In Hosea, God took issue with the people's belief in the Canaanite god Baal. By speaking of the people's relationship with YHWH in nuptial terms, the writer of Hosea contextualized the command against idolatry, which is the first among the commandments of the Decalogue/Ten Commandments. Similarly, to speak of the city as a whore communicated a breach in the covenantal relationship between the city and its deity. Thus, Zion as a whore communicated the Israelite people's wrongdoing toward their God, YHWH.[15]

In the epigraph of this chapter, we have already seen Zion/Jerusalem also portrayed as a mother. But her image is not univocal. The maternal metaphor varies in the Hebrew Scriptures according to the situation of the people of Israel. For example, Jerusalem as the lamenting woman "expresses the bodily pain and inner distress of the city's population in a situation of war," and she advocates for her children to YHWH.[16] As deserted and inebriated mother, she expresses feelings of being overwhelmed by the experience of destruction and exile (Isa 51:17–20). In contrast, as birthing mother without suffering or labor (Isa 66:7–14), Zion represents hope and promise, comfort and security, and food and shelter, with a renewed relationship with YHWH. As the mother in Psalm 87, Zion/Jerusalem is a symbol of peace and salvation. Overall, these variations on the mother image of Zion/Jerusalem portray the city as experiencing hope and suffering with its people, in turn strengthening the people's survival and their ties to the city.

The parallels are clear between the image of Zion/Jerusalem city as a woman and the Christian vision of the church as a mother, queen, bride, or other female figure, even if there are no direct scriptural links between the two. The female Zion as its people, their history, the dwelling place of God, and Zion's future, the place of salvation, can be viewed as paralleling the female church as its people, their history, a place to worship God, and the locus of salvation. The concept of the future Zion and its role as mediator of salvation resonates with the concept of the present Christian Church and its picture at the end of time. It has been argued that the prophetic visions regarding the future Zion in the Book of Isaiah are not only "taken up and expanded in Jewish-Hellenistic writings (4 Ezra 9:26—10:59; 1 Enoch 90; Psalms of Solomon 11; 17)" but also occur in New Testament texts such as Hebrews 12:22–23 and Revelation 21.[17] In these visions, "Jerusalem is simultaneously described as mediator of salvation and as the place in which salvation starts."[18]

Like Mother Zion, in the early centuries, Mother Church will appear as lamenting or mourning, gathering, feeding and caring for her children, as sole wife to God through Christ, and as a place of comfort and salvation. And these characteristics of the Christian Church will be heightened in a context of persecution and martyrdom, as we will see in later chapters.

A significant question to reflect upon here is whether it is meaningful for the church today to be imagined as mother, bride, virgin, queen, or another female figure. Do these metaphors continue to be relevant when considering the relationship of members of the church to the church itself, or when considering the relationship of the church to the trinitarian God? In many contemporary cultures, the understanding of womanhood has shifted; women are no longer necessarily seen as dependent upon male authority figures or as the sole providers of the nurturing and raising of children. Further, the utilization of the expression "mother" by the prophets was in the sense that Zion provided solidarity, intercession, and eventually comfort and promise in a context of devastation, despair, and rebuilding. In what context are the mother metaphor and the other female metaphors used for the church today? At the Second Vatican Council, the scriptural justifications for the church as a female, particularly as a mother, were presented as Galatians 4:26 and Revelation 12:17 (see *Lumen Gentium* 6). Let us now examine these justifications.

THE MAIN NEW TESTAMENT FOUNDATIONS

Galatians 4:26

In Galatians 4:21–31, Paul uses the motherhood of Hagar and Sarah to represent the slavery that comes from a particular interpretation of the Sinai covenant and the freedom that comes from the reinterpretation of that covenant. This reinterpretation is part of a new belief, which is in Jesus as the Son of God and his proclamation of the good news of God's kingdom.

Galatians is one of Paul's earliest letters, and is fraught with tension over the threat that Paul perceives from so-called Judaizers,[19] who have won over a section of his Gentile (non-Jewish) Christian community. It is considering this sociohistorical situation that scholars typically read Paul's discussion of the role of the law in Galatians 4:21–31. Paul recalls that two sons were born to Abraham: Isaac was born through Sarah, who is called the "free woman," and Ishmael was born through Hagar, the "slave woman." Isaac was born according to the "promise" and Ishmael according to the "flesh." Paul draws upon the common Jewish eschatological (end-time) trope of the "new/heavenly Jerusalem" to illustrate his point. Hagar represents "Mount Sinai," which continues to birth children into slavery, while Sarah represents "the Jerusalem above; [that] is free, and [that] is our mother," who births children into freedom.

But Sarah had been a barren woman for many years. At Galatians 4:27, then, Paul cites Isaiah 54:1, a text offering a message of divine consolation to a barren and desolate woman, later named as Israel. This woman, like Sarah, is invited to rejoice, for her children will be more numerous than the children of the woman who has a husband. The fully restored New Jerusalem in this Deutero-Isaian text is imagined as set with precious jewels (Isa 54:11–12) and is to become the center from which all the children of Israel will be taught by the Lord (Isa 54:13). The city will be at peace and established in righteousness, and terror or war will no longer plague its inhabitants (Isa 54:13–14). Paul then identifies himself and his Christian community in this Galatians text as the children of this free woman. Paul cites Genesis 21:10 to the effect that the "slave and her child" (i.e., Hagar/Sinai/present Jerusalem and the Judaizers) must be "drive[n] out," for they cannot inherit with the son of the free woman (Gal 4:30).

While Paul's conclusion to the Hagar-Sarah narrative in Galatians 4:21–31 seems to lead to an exclusionary or supersession-istic reading of the Jewish faith, he is, in fact, aiming to do something else. Instead of making simple associations in which the Christian faith is symbolized as Sarah and the Jewish faith as Hagar, Paul's reference to Hagar is directed at the Judaizers within the community. This group had entered the community just after Paul had left to preach elsewhere, and the Judaizers insisted that all members should follow the law of Moses. For the Judaizers saw themselves as aligned with the true church of Jerusalem, while Paul and his churches were suspect due to a "setback" in Antioch (Gal 2:11–14). That is, Paul's churches did not strictly follow Jewish law, which, for the Judaizers, Christ brought fulfillment to, rather than freedom from. The Pauline Galatian church could consequently be accused of being descendants of Ishmael (i.e., children of the slave woman). But for Paul, the Galatian community was redeemed by faith in Christ, not by nomistic observance. In other words, faith in Christ and not the strict following of Jewish law equates to direct "descent" from Abraham and Sarah.[20]

Central to this faith in Christ is the call to live like Christ—to be crucified and to die with Christ. Through self-giving, the old self is to die to make room for the new self, which images the living

Christ. This is the new freedom and identity in Christ. But such freedom does not open doors to an immoral life. Like the Torah, the cruciform existence is for the benefit of others, entailing certain responsibilities. Paul describes the Galatian community as a womb in which Christ is formed, but he also sees himself as mother and midwife to Christ's birth in saying, "My little children, for whom I am again in the pain of childbirth until Christ is formed in you" (Gal 4:19).

Maggie Low, who explores "Mother Zion" in Deutero-Isaiah, finds a clear reference to Mother Zion in Galatians 4:21–31. The basis of Zion theology is that God is the Creator of all life; in the context of Galatians, "God is the creator of life that gives freedom from slavery," a freedom not "from the demands of righteousness" but from "oppressive requirements."[21] This affirms the idea that it is the legalistic religiosity imposed by Judaizers, and not the entire Jewish faith, that Paul denounces as he calls the Galatians from slavery to freedom. Furthermore, it indicates that the "mother"/ "mother of us all"/"Jerusalem above" of Galatians 4:26 is not to be interpreted as it has traditionally been—as simply the Christian Mother Church. Rather, it is something bigger. It is the kingdom of God, a mother city, where all are called to live in God's freedom. This idea of the mother city as the kingdom of God is reinforced in the other text traditionally used as a basis for the Christian Mother Church, Revelation 12:17.

Revelation 12:17

The imagery-laden Book of Revelation for many people evokes ideas of a future apocalypse heralding the end of the world, along with the return of the Messiah, who comes to save a chosen few. Yet in writing Revelation, John the seer had a different time and audience in mind. It was aimed at the persecuted Christian communities under Roman occupation in the early centuries of the Common Era that he wished to help prepare for further trials. In Revelation, it is not our future but our past that John addresses. As Wes Howard-Brook and Anthony Gwyther elucidate,

The primary struggle for the *ekklēsiai* or Church community at the time was to resist participation or assimilation into the dominant Roman imperial ethos. The issue was whether those *ekklēsiai* who had faithfully resisted Rome would continue in that practice, and whether those who had been co-opted by Rome could be renewed in their resistance.[22]

We also note that members of John's intended audience were Jew or Gentile. Therefore, they were schooled in the narratives of the Old Testament and of Greek/Roman mythology. The significance of this becomes evident when we undertake a close reading of Revelation 12:1–17.

Beginning with Revelation 12:1, the text mentions a "great portent" that appeared in heaven: "a woman clothed with the sun, with the moon under her feet, and on her head a crown of twelve stars." The woman was "pregnant" and "in birth pangs," birthing her child and crying aloud in pain (12:2). As in Galatians 4:26–27, so in Revelation 12:1, Isaiah can be read as a related text (Isa 26:17; 66:7). Revelation's use of the image of the woman in labor participates in a similar interpretive procedure as Galatians 4:26–27, drawing on themes of Jewish apocalyptic thought (see Isa 48:21; 50:1; 66:7–11; Hos 4:5; Bar 4:8–23). In some of the deuterocanonical/intertestamental apocalyptic literature,[23] the image of Israel as a celestial pregnant woman giving birth to the Messiah would become a marked motif (see 4 Ezra 10).

Gordon Fee argues that Revelation 12:1 echoes Joseph's dream, wherein Abraham, Sarah, and the twelve patriarchs of Israel are imaged as the sun, moon, and stars.[24] The identity then of the pregnant woman points not just to Mary, mother to the Messiah Jesus, because the maternal figure of 12:1 is situated within a larger context. That is, it is Mary, but it is also the Jewish nation that gives birth to the Messiah Jesus.

Revelation 12:1 also signals an abrupt change of scene in the text. As the woman labors in heaven, the distinct temporal conditions of pregnancy and birth are collapsed into a brief sequence. It is at this point that another "portent" appears in "heaven": a "great red dragon, with seven heads and ten horns, and seven diadems on his heads" (12:3). The dragon appears before the woman, ready to snatch the child and eat it as soon as she gives birth (12:4). The woman delivers a boy, "a son...who is to rule all the nations with a rod of iron. But her child was snatched away and taken to God and to his throne" (12:5). Meanwhile, the woman "fled into the wilderness, where she has a place prepared by God" (12:6) to be kept safe. In verses 7 to 12, John describes the subsequent war in heaven between Michael and his angels, and the dragon. Verses 13 to 17 then speak of the woman pursued by the dragon, but also of her escape to the wilderness (12:14) and of assistance from the earth (12:16), leading to the dragon's pursuit of her children instead (12:17).

Ancient Greek creation mythologies contain similar elements to the narrative of Revelation 12:1–6. They also tell of births of impending rulers in which incumbent rulers sought to prevent their being deposed by swallowing either the mother or the child.[25] Zeus's birth story, in particular, involves these elements, as well as a woman going into hiding, a cosmic war (between the giants and the gods), and a Mother Earth (Gaia) also at war with the ruler and his allies. The stories differ in sequence and purpose from Revelation 12, but they contain enough elements for John's Gentile audience to have found them familiar.

For scholar Brigitte Kahl, the Book of Revelation's context is the struggle between ancient Roman powers and the early Christian communities (*ekklēsiai*). She interprets the woman pursued by the dragon as not just the heavenly mother who gave birth to the Messiah (12:1–5), but *also* as "the earthly mother of his followers and siblings";[26] that is, the Christian Church as singular, Mother Church (*Mater Ekklesia*), while her children are the various Christian communities (*ekklēsiai*), as seen in 12:17.

In Kahl's view, Mother Church is pursued by the dragon/Roman powers/Caesar because "she is the source and location of the messianic countervision, counterknowledge and counterworship that threaten the dragon's rule. That is the reason she needs to be eliminated."[27] In other words, Mother Church represents the vision of the reign of God, a new way of living, of worshiping, of understanding, that threatens the rule and control of Rome. Rome exempted Jews from pagan worship requirements because of an agreement made under Rome's conditions.[28] In contrast, Rome had no such agreements with Christianity; thus, it posed a threat to the Roman sense of law and order.

Given that the mother of Revelation 12:17 represents a vision of a new kingdom, the kingdom of God, and considering its connections to deuterocanonical texts that image Israel birthing a Messiah, it seems more appropriate to name this woman the "Mother City" rather than the "Mother Church." Like the interpretation made previously regarding the woman of Galatians 4:26, imagining Revelation 12:17 as a mother city points to God's kingdom, which is larger than the initial picture of the woman as being simply the Christian Church. This challenges the old divisive adage, *extra ecclesiam nulla salus* (outside the church there is no salvation), and has great implications for ecumenical religious dialogue and interactions. But this does not take away from Christianity's specific role and duty to reflect the reign of God on earth. Rather, it highlights that, in God's kingdom, Christians, Jews, and all nations are included and called into a new way of relating and being. As Low notes, it is "the realization of God's reign in its totality now experienced by Christians in inaugurated fashion."[29] In one sense, Zion theology's picture of a restored Jerusalem is extended in this vision of the exalted woman, the "Jerusalem above" and "mother of us all" of Revelation 12:17, where all nations are gathered to worship God, and to live in peace.

As Low has read the mother of Galatians 4:26, so she similarly suggests that the mother of Revelation 12:1–17 should be imagined as "Mother City" instead of "Mother Church." To do otherwise would limit the utility of the maternal metaphor for its Revelation audience, who themselves were about to experience a new set of imperial persecutions. Low explains the advantage of this: "Rather than representing the persecuted church, woman Zion as the indomitable kingdom of God would provide a firmer assurance for a people going through tribulations."[30]

In her reflections on the theological implications of seeing the influence of Mother Zion of Second Isaiah in the texts of Galatians 4 and Revelation 12, Low presents a picture of Mother Zion that very much aligns with Christianity's vision of God's

18

kingdom on earth (as present Zion) and at the eschaton (Zion as final resting place):

> Mother Zion is our final and true home where we will find deepest rest and fullest comfort that our earthly homes and biological mothers represent in an imperfect but yet sacramental way. Further, the exaltation of Zion… is not about self-centred nationalism (whether ethnic, religious or political) but about YHWH's sovereignty—a sovereignty that intends to bring peace and righteousness both to Israel (Isaiah 54) and to all the world (Isa 51:4–5 cf. Isa 2:2–4). Present day Zion is a historical symbol of that divine kingship, a kingship whose eschatological fulfillment we can long for and work toward.[31]

Howard-Brook and Gwyther's description for the New Jerusalem in reflecting on Revelation applies just as much here: the new Jerusalem/Zion/mother city "is found wherever human community resists the ways of empire and places God at the centre of its shared life."[32]

EARLY PATRISTIC FOUNDATIONS

Mother Faith, Lady Faith, Eternal Mother

Having explored the portrait of Mother Jerusalem as a scriptural precursor to Mother Church, we now turn to the early patristic writers and their concept of *Mater Pistis* (Mother Faith) as another foundation for the development of *Mater Ecclesia* (Mother Church).

Mater Pistis is evidenced in Polycarp's[33] *Letter to the Philippians* (ca. 120 CE), where faith is described as the "mother of us all."[34] The companion to Justin, Hierax, in his reply to the Roman prefect Rusticus, similarly names "Mother Faith," as recorded in the *Martyrdom of Justin and His Companions* (ca. 165 CE): In Rusticus's own words, he says, "Our true father is Christ, and our mother our faith in him."[35]

In the Shepherd of Hermas (ca. 98–161 CE), rather than "Mother Faith," it is "Lady Faith" who comes to the fore. In fact, "Lady Faith," whom the Shepherd regarded as the pagan goddess Sibyl, is presented as the "church."[36] The Lady herself confirms this description: "The tower which you see being built is myself, the Church, who have appeared to you both now and formerly."[37] Further on, the Lady presents the stones used to build the tower as the various members in the church, as apostles, bishops, teachers, and deacons.[38] Later, the Lady tells the Shepherd that seven women support the tower. These women represent seven virtues, of which "Faith" is the first and "mother" of them all.[39]

These early patristic texts appear to be the first descriptions of the church as its people and as the location of faith personified as a woman and mother. But it is generally understood that the church, which the Shepherd specifically sought to present, was an archetypal preexisting church rather than a living worshiping community.[40] That is, it was a church existing before the creation of the world rather than because of Christ's ministry, death, and resurrection.

But the Shepherd had a purpose in presenting this ecclesial image: a form of Gnosticism had infiltrated the Roman Christian community and the Shepherd wished to establish the necessity of the Christian Church for salvation. For while some Gnostics[41] acknowledged the existence of a church and even called it a woman and mother (e.g., Valentinian Gnosticism), they generally claimed that salvation was through the attainment of special knowledge (*gnosis*) only. This meant that the Shepherd had to present a church that had existed before creation, a spiritual entity that transcended human creation and knowledge. Clement of Alexandria (150–215 CE), a contemporary of the Shepherd, also sought to invalidate Gnosticism by arguing for the necessity of the church for one's own salvation. He did this by presenting a preexisting church just like the "Lady Faith" of the Shepherd's *Visions*.[42]

The Martyrdom Tradition and Irenaeus

Blandina (162–77 CE), a Christian slave girl, was seen as exemplifying the Mother Church as birther, martyr, and intercessor. In the following passage, Blandina is a suffering and yet triumphant figure:

> But the blessed Blandina, last of all, having, like a high-born mother (μήτηρ εὐγενὴς), exhorted her children and sent them forth victorious to the King, travelled herself along the same path of conflicts as they did, and hastened to them, rejoicing and exulting at her departure, like one bidden to a marriage as though invited to a marriage feast rather than cast to the beasts.[43]

We find this Christian martyrdom account and more violent graphic details in the *Letter of the Churches of Vienne and Lyons to the Churches of Asia and Phrygia* (ca. 177 CE, and henceforth, the *Letter*). Some scholars argue that the author of this letter is unknown, while others say the author is the early church father Irenaeus (ca. 125–200 CE).[44]

Irenaeus was the leader of the two churches, Vienne and Lyons, and the images of the church as woman and mother found in the letter are consistent with Irenaeus's own usage in his writings. Regardless of whether he authored the letter, what we find in the account of Blandina are the first allusions to the Christian community as a living human community, as opposed to a preexisting or spiritual church imagined as a mother.

The account of Blandina's martyrdom is representative of Irenaeus's primary image for Mother Church: as a pregnant and birthing mother via the giving of life through martyrdom.[45] The maternal-interceding acts of the martyrs are made clearer in another passage from the same letter from the churches of Lyons and Vienne:

> For they did not boast over the fallen, but from their own abundance supplied with a mother's love [μητρικὰ σπλάγχνα][46] those that needed, and shedding many tears for them to the Father, they prayed for life, and he gave it to them, and they divided it among their neighbours, and then departed to God.[47]

The context of this letter was the persecutions of the Lyons Christian community in the year 177 CE. It began with a general banning of Christians from participation in public activities, which turned into a ban from public places. Christians were accused of atheism because of their refusal to honor the local gods. But to honor the local gods meant recanting the Christian faith. The persecutions were initially enforced by local mobs but became heightened in martyrdom at the public amphitheater.

In both martyrdom accounts, those of Blandina and of the church of Lyons, there is no distinction between the "mother" and the community, her children. In fact, the mother was the community and the experiences of the martyrs became the mother's experiences. Likewise, their feelings and actions were hers too. After being birthed, the children have but two choices: death by recanting their faith, described by the *Letter* as the mother's "abortions," or life, continuing to live the new life from their spiritual birth or being reconceived within the mother's womb, described in the *Letter* as the mother's "quickening," via the martyrdom of others.

In addition, as seen in the account of Blandina, Irenaeus calls the "mother" a "virgin." In this, he was applying the fleshly experience of the martyrs to the church so that it can be called a "virgin-mother." The purity of the fleshly sufferings of the martyrs would intercede for the "aborted" Christians (those who had denied their faith) and thus enable their spiritual rebirth. Here the use of "virgin-mother" communicates that purity is the condition in which new believers are born and saved. At this stage, the oxymoronic image of the virgin-mother, later applied to the church by Ambrose and Augustine, surfaces already with Irenaeus. While Irenaeus uses the imagery to describe the Christian community undergoing martyrdom, he does not explicitly use the concept "virgin-Mother Church" in any of his writings. Such a title will not interest patristic writers like Tertullian and Cyprian, of the second and third centuries. Only in the fourth and fifth centuries, through Ambrose and Augustine, do we see the title resurface. There are good reasons for this, which we explore later.

While the Lyons and Vienne churches had to deal with threats of torture and death by the governing Roman Empire, they were concerned also with losing members to Gnosticism[48] because the latter claimed to be the true version of Christianity. Thus, their falsity needed to be exposed and overthrown since "what appealed to Gnostic converts was the theological synthesis of diverse scriptural passages, along with a secret pattern to hold them together."[49] We have here an equally dominant image of not just the birthing martyr mother but of a mother who is that one true giver of orthodox Christian teaching, leading to real salvation as opposed to the false teachings of the Gnostics:

> For where the church is, there is the Spirit of God; and where the Spirit of God is, there is the church, and every kind of grace; but the Spirit is truth. Those, therefore, who do not partake of Him, are neither nourished into life from the mother's breasts, nor do they enjoy that most limpid fountain which issues from the body of Christ; but they dig for themselves broken cisterns out of earthly trenches, and drink putrid water out of the mire, fleeing from the faith of the church lest they be convicted; and rejecting the Spirit, that they may not be instructed.[50]

This concept of the church, via the breastfeeding image, passing on true knowledge, in contrast to the "food" of "injurious doctrines" offered by Gnosticism, is also seen clearly in another of Irenaeus's texts:

> It befits us, therefore, to avoid their doctrines, and to take care in order to avoid any injury from them; to flee to the Church, and be brought up in her bosom [*et in ejus sinu educari*], and be nourished with the Lord's Scriptures.[51]

In both passages, images of the necessary food of life, a mother's milk, is paralleled with the necessary food of the spiritual life, the orthodox truth handed down from the apostles. Moreover, in ancient Greek culture, it was believed a mother passed on elements of herself to her child through her milk—her knowledge, demeanor, and good character.[52] Similarly, Irenaeus presents Mother Church passing on her "high-born" status to her faithful through the milk of her orthodox teachings.

By presenting this Mother Church as breastfeeding and so imparting true knowledge, Irenaeus was leading his audience away from the Mother Church of the Gnostics and toward their "true" mother, the Catholic Church.[53] In Irenaeus's view, the Gnostic Valentinians called the church their mother as well as various other names, some mimicking significant Christian terms: "This mother they also call Ogdoad, Sophia, Terra, Jerusalem, Holy Spirit, and, with a masculine reference, Lord."[54] But it was not only that Gnosticism mimicked Christian terms; it also created a confusing ecclesiology. Like the mother of Galatians 4:26, the Gnostic Mother Church also "dwells above"[55] and she is explicitly called "ecclesia."[56]

The birthing and breastfeeding Mother Church, made vivid particularly through the martyrdom of members of the Lyons community, and one in competition with the Gnostic mother, is nevertheless dominated by an even more significant feminine image for the church for Irenaeus: the church as bride. This image is particularly significant for Irenaeus, considering the Montanist controversy, which had arisen in the Gallic communities' home origin of Phrygia,[57] for "they were seriously involved in the controversy" and "were extremely conscious of the Church-heresy antithesis, of contamination imperilling the spotless Bride of Christ."[58]

Irenaeus might have been reluctant, however, to use bridal imagery for the church as his Gnostic opponents, the Valentinians, also utilized it for their purposes.[59] They used the nuptial image to project a future where the material realm disappeared and the soul was incorporated into the cosmos. More problematic for Irenaeus, though, was their use of Paul the Apostle's writings to justify their teaching. Irenaeus does not attempt to contrast his nuptial theology with theirs, but he does present "a positive valuation of the created world and…demonstrate[s] the continuity between the gospel of Christ and the revelation of the Creator."[60]

Irenaeus uses bridal imagery when he references Hosea's marriage to a prostitute and Moses's marriage to an Ethiopian woman.[61] The underlying dynamic in these marriages is that "the faithless wife [*infidelem mulierem*] is sanctified by her faithful husband [*viro fideli*]."[62] This then communicates that the faithlessness of a community symbolized through the outsider and the contaminated (the Ethiopian and the prostitute) could be countered with sanctification and salvation by the community symbolized as the spotless bride of Christ—that is, as a virgin and spouse.[63]

While it is argued that Irenaeus's spotless church as bride to Christ is a "profound symbol of redemption and communion with the divine,"[64] something that is quite positive and gives deep meaning to the human community—divine relationship—it also undeniably employs the patriarchal view of woman, where she is to be lorded over and placed into the narrow roles of virgin, faithful wife, or whore to be redeemed. A contemporary challenge lies in portraying this significant covenantal relationship between God and God's people without such a limiting understanding of women.

Irenaeus's setting of the bridal imagery for the church would have ramifications for the visualization of the church as a woman down the ages. Irenaeus is considered the first orthodox Christian to use the nuptial analogy in a sustained manner to express his ideas on the church and salvation.[65] Karl Shuve argues that while Irenaeus "neither cited nor alluded to the Song of Songs" in his writings, he "had an important role to play in establishing the contextual framework according to which the Song would be interpreted by subsequent Christian exegetes."[66] That role involves opening the door to the possibility of utilizing images from the Hebrew Scriptures of bride and bridegroom for theological reflection in the Christian community. Moreover, Shuve argues, Irenaeus set the "typological pattern according to which Old Testament narratives of marriage and courtship were to be read."[67] This was for upholding "the essential goodness of embodied existence." Gnostics and members of similar religious cults believed in a dichotomy between the body and soul and that, through their secret knowledge, only the soul could be saved. In contrast, Irenaeus used bridal imagery to uphold the value of the body and its indelible role in the salvation of the entire human being.

Mary as Mother Church in Irenaeus?

With Irenaeus, we begin to find allusions to mother as a metaphor for the church (having "children"; nourishing from her "bosom"; being a "virgin-mother") but no explicit use of *Mater Ecclesia*. Interestingly, Irenaeus also refused to explicitly call Mary a mother.[68] A number of theologians argue that despite the lack of direct connections made between Mother Church and Mary, the early patristic writers such as Irenaeus had intuited this link, as seen in his description of church as mother, spouse, and virgin, and of Mary as mother and virgin.[69] However, this is doubtful, as there is something contrived about the use of both maternal "breasts"[70] and "womb"[71] for the church, whereas only *womb* is used with Mary and in a different sense from the way *womb* is used for the church. In *Against Heresies*, Irenaeus associated the words "fruit of the belly"[72] and "inheritance of the flesh"[73] with womb images connected to Mary. Meanwhile, for the church, the womb image is found only once in the *Letter*[74] and not at all in *Against Heresies*. As well, the image of the bosom is associated with the maternal church but not with Mary.[75]

Irenaeus sought to refute the Gnostic claim that Christ was the proper son of their "Demiurge" and merely "passed through Mary just as water flows through a tube."[76] He used Mary's mother-hood to confirm Christ's humanity, saying, "Those, therefore, who allege that He took nothing from the Virgin do greatly err, [since] in order that they may cast away the inheritance of the flesh, they also reject the analogy [between him and Adam]."[77] This idea of Mary as mother as a mere container for Jesus would not have been unfamiliar in the ancient Greek world. Garland explains how in *Eumenides of Aeschylus*, Apollo perceives the mother as mere "nurse of the newly-implanted seed" and the father as the true parent.[78] The Gnostics believed that Jesus was fully divine and only appeared human.[79] So, it was quite challenging for the church to claim that Jesus did take on the flesh of Mary, since this opposed the cultural understanding of the role and physiology of a mother. In this way, Mary's purpose as mother differed in purpose from Irenaeus's naming of the church as a mother, which was mainly utilized in *Against Heresies* to contrast with Gnostic claims to privileged knowl-edge of the Christian faith, as we saw earlier. Frances Young also shows that Mary did not equate to the image of Mother Church from the very beginning.[80] As we will discover, it was used only later, when the early Christian Church developed.

CONCLUSION

Long before the Christian Church was portrayed as a woman and mother, ancient societies imagined their cities and countries as women. As seen in their coinage and languages, these portrayals allowed citizens to characterize their relationship with their city and with its patron god and/or goddess. These portrayals provided the context for the biblical portrayal of Jerusalem/Zion city as a woman. Ancient Israelite society viewed women as those who were to be protected or conquered, as providers of comfort, food, and security to children. Similarly, cities were also to be conquered and protected, and their inhabitants needed food and comfort. At various times, different images of women have been used for Jerusalem, depending on concurrent events in Israelite history—from destruction of the first temple, exile and return, to the destruction of the second temple. The lamenting Mother Zion of Lamentations contrasts with the exalted mother of Deutero-Isaiah because each reflects different events and the corresponding needs of the people of those contrasting times.

By the time the mother metaphor is expressed in Galatians 4 and Revelation 12, the context has changed again: from an Israelite nation and its experience of exile to a Christian community negotiating identity and beliefs due to its varying membership (in Galatia) or its persecution and fear (in Revelation). The authors of these texts cater to their audiences: in the case of Galatians, to communicate the requirements of a new identity in Christ; in Revelation, calling upon Jewish and Greek mythological allusions and providing reassurance as the community prepares for a new set of persecutions by the occupying Romans. But in the background of these texts remains the figure of Mother Zion. Thus, we have seen that, in the New Testament, it is more appropriate to understand the mother metaphor as representing the "mother city" or the kingdom of God, where all nations, Jew and Gentile, are called together under the sovereignty of God, rather than as simply the Christian Mother Church.

We have also seen the beginnings of the use of female and maternal ecclesial metaphors among early patristic authors. In Irenaeus, the female church refers to a living community grounded in history rather than one that is a preexisting archetype. This church is an intercessor-martyr for those who seek salvation. She is bride and virgin as true partner of God, representing redemption and the communion of the church. As breastfeeding mother, she is the source of orthodox truth, in contrast to competing Gnostic claims.

Irenaeus's uses of the "mother" imagines her as fulfilling basic functions—birthing and feeding. As bride and virgin, she affirms embodied existence and the intimate relationship between God and God's people. Unreflective use of these metaphors in later times is problematic because they come from a specific time and culture that communicate limiting messages regarding woman's role and place in society, particularly that of woman as mother. Moreover, while bridal imagery in Irenaeus's time was an affirming and clever device used for validating embodied existence, it none-theless opened the way for later patristic writers to speak of the church and its relationship with God as a patriarchal relationship, limiting woman and her role in familial relationships and in society.

Finally, we see in Irenaeus's female church a deliberate dis-tinction between the motherhood of Mary and the motherhood of the church. This distinction has importance in that the community and its function as mother and bride is not collapsed into Mary's motherhood. As we note in the next chapter, it is in the writings of Tertullian that the community members become distinct from the female church.

2

She Is Mother of the Family, Wife to One Man Only

A Christian, indeed, will seek heirs,
disinherited as [s/he] is from the entire world!
[S/he] has brothers and sisters;
[S/he] has the church as [her/his] mother.

—Tertullian, *On Monogamy* 16.3–4

Tertullian (155/160–220 CE), a teacher rather than a priest, was the first to refer explicitly to the church community as *Mater Ecclesia*. Why did Tertullian need to make this reference if the church was already viewed as a woman and mother? It seems there was already a plethora of religious groups and philosophies in those early centuries, with their charismatic leaders and attractive teachings, some even mimicking the Christian faith and its own practices and beliefs. The question, then, for an individual in those times—as it is for us today—was this: Which belief or beliefs should I adhere to, given they all seem to be selling happiness, or providing an explanation of the world, of life's purpose, and of the existence of good and evil? More pointedly, in religious terms, which belief should I adhere to for the salvation of my soul? Belief in the power of the gods and goddesses over the lives of people remained in their psyche centuries after the death of Christ. Enter Tertullian, with his push for the church as a mother partnered with the image of God as Father. By creating this *familia* (family), Tertullian presents a convincing argument for the church to be considered as being a mother by drawing an analogy between belonging to the family of God and belonging to a Roman *familia*. Belonging to this divine family is a life or death issue for the soul, just as belonging to the Roman *familia* implies life or death for the citizen who wishes to engage in Roman civic society.

In this chapter, we see that the pairing of Mother Church with Father God reflected Tertullian's cultural context, where the Roman *materfamilias* was seen by the side of her spouse, the *paterfamilias*, her purpose fulfilled in her duty to her husband through the birthing, nourishing, and supporting of their children. However, we also see that Tertullian was not uncritical in his use of contemporary culture; he applied a method of rejection-appropriation in his imaging of Mother Church, rejecting a certain type of woman, the unvirtuous *matrona*, and appropriating the more virtuous type, the *materfamilias*, for the church. Finally, we briefly discuss the implications of the chapter's findings for the tradition of the church imaged as a bride, holy, a virgin, and a mother.

THE ANCIENT ROMAN
MATERFAMILIAS AND *FAMILIA*

The ancient Roman *materfamilias* was the mother of the family. She was the wife of the *paterfamilias*, the father who was the head of the ancient Roman household. The *paterfamilias*, who must be a Roman citizen, had power over all members of the household (*patria potestas*) to the extent that he could sell them into slavery or take their lives. The household, or *familia*, at a basic level, included parents and unmarried children but could also include slaves and their families, freed men and women (*libertini*), as well as maternal figures such as nurses, foster mothers, and other surrogate mothers. Agnatic descendants and their families living in separate households could have also been associated with the *familia*.

The *paterfamilias* could be a grandfather, son, or other male member of the family, but never a woman. He was head of the household and juridically in control of the family's estate. Therefore, the *materfamilias* could never be the head of her household. When the *pater* died, a mother and her children were no longer under the control of "another" (*alieni iuris*) and became legally independent (*sui iuris*). This meant they were no longer under the guardianship of a *paterfamilias* but could be under the guardianship (*tutela*) of another male. Usually, this role fell to the eldest son or male relative. Women, especially among the upper classes, often found themselves widows since, at an early age, they had married older men.[1]

In his use of familial imagery for the church, Tertullian focused on the *familia* as consisting simply of the *materfamilias*, *paterfamilias*, and *filiusfamilias* (child), and excluded more complex familial relationships such as grandchildren and in-laws. Roman culture emphasized the ties between mother and father. The emperor Augustus promoted the ideal of the *paterfamilias* as having the one spouse at his side and the *materfamilias* as *univira*. It was understood that to be a wife was to be a mother, and vice versa. In fact, women were not honored apart from "being someone's wife, mother or daughter."[2] Family cohesion was sometimes expressed when, in portraits, the wife was represented as taking on some of the physiognomy of her husband. For example, Faustina the Younger (130–176/177 CE) is portrayed with Emperor Marcus Aurelius's (121–80 CE) "prominent brow" and "pronounced almond-shaped eyes."[3]

The ties between a Roman mother and her son were more prominent in the upper classes, where the son could pursue a political career. The Roman mother was expected to support the son's career aspirations by educating him in the necessary subjects at home. In turn, the son showed his appreciation by being loyal to the mother and showing her respect. Sometimes, the support of the mother for her son was so excessive that she was accused of personal ambition—attempting to climb the political ladder through her son. It was expected that a son would keep a close connection with his mother, either by living with her in the family home, or, in the case of a widowed, remarried, or divorced mother, by visiting her regularly.

Roman citizens sought to be in a family because of the many advantages this provided them, including the power to bring legal and social legitimacy to an individual who would otherwise have few ways to make a distinction in society. The family was also the exemplar of moral standards for Roman society, where roles were distinct and characters idealized. Funerary monuments even presented groupings of siblings who were childless, or unrelated individuals, as a family. This enabled "individuals from the same (or even different) *familia* [to] claim for themselves the associated normative values of social respectability while commemorating relationships which fell outside the nuclear family model."[4] In fact, "burial clubs" in ancient Roman society would meet regularly on a social basis, celebrate birthdays of the deceased, and perform kin-like obsequies. The groups were of immense importance for individuals who could not call on ties through kinship or patronage. Further, it was sometimes the case, like Tatianos, son of Bartas, that while his funerary relief "depicts a typical family banqueting scene, with wife, children, a full table, and of course, a dog beneath...the inscription belies the portrait. There is no mention of wife or children; only that his kinsfolk arranged the burial."[5] It seems that Tatianos wanted to present himself as having fulfilled the Roman familial ideal despite the stark opposite reality.

The Julian laws on marriage and adultery (*Lex Juliae de maritandis ordinibus*, 18 BCE, and *Lex Julia de adulteriis coercendi*, 17 BCE) were instituted by Emperor Augustus as part of his moral reforms for the Roman state, highlighting the value of families in the ancient Roman world.[6] The *Papia Poppaea* (9 CE) was introduced later to reinforce the Julian laws. In general, these laws punished bachelors politically, socially, and economically, while rewarding fathers. The childless were also punished. But the more children one had, the more financial and status benefits one received from the state.[7]

A name often considered synonymous with the *materfamilias* is the *matrona*. However, the two may be distinguished as being more representative of the imagery of "woman" or "mother" for Tertullian and Cyprian, respectively. For Tertullian, the mother was the virtuous woman mentioned primarily in relation to her husband. Thus, when Tertullian used the image of Mother Church, it was understood as a *materfamilias* partnered with a *paterfamilias*. For Cyprian, the *matrona* was the celebrated woman in her own right, visually presented in Roman art without the *paterfamilias* by her side, even as it was assumed she was both wife and mother.

Andrew Bierkan, Charles Sherman, and Emile Stocquart, along with Judith Grubbs clarify and affirm these differentiations between the *matrona* and the *materfamilias*.[8] Bierkan, Sherman, and Stocquart explain how the distinctions arose in the first place, arguing that, with the understandings of the power of the *paterfamilias* (*patria potestas*), two systems of marriage (*justae nuptiae*) were established: marriage *cum manu* (under the hand or power of the husband) and marriage *sine manu* (not under the hand or power of the husband). This resulted in two types of legal wives— the *materfamilias*, "who becomes a member of the new family, but only so far as she breaks all her former ties," and the *matrona*, "who, remaining a member of her own family, retains her gods, her own property, merely leaving her father or her agnates."[9] But Grubbs points out that while *materfamilias* was initially understood as "a wife whose marriage brought her *in manu*, that is, under her husband's legal power," by the early third century, *manus* marriage became "obsolete." *Materfamilias* then came to refer to "a respectable matron, whether married or not."[10] Tertullian was a Christian from 193 CE and only became one of the Montanists (a heretical group) in 213 CE. Therefore, these distinctions would have arisen in his time as a Christian teacher and author, and not as a heretic.

Alongside the meaning of being under the legal power of her husband, for the Roman jurist Ulpian, the meaning of *materfamilias* was connected to the character of the woman:

> We ought to understand that a "mother of the family" (*materfamilias*) is she who has not lived dishonorably: for behavior (*mores*) distinguish and separate "mothers of the family" from other women. Therefore, there will be no difference, whether she is married or a widow or divorcée, freeborn or freedwoman: for neither marriage nor birth make a "mother of the family," but rather good behavior (*boni mores*).[11]

Ulpian reiterates this meaning when he says in another part of the legal text just cited, "When you hear '*materfamilias*,' understand a woman of well-known reputation."[12] This affirms Tertullian's own distinctions between certain types of women: the *materfamilias* as a woman of good character and the *matrona*, a mother and wife too, but unvirtuous in his view.

From Ulpian's view, the *materfamilias* was also a title given to the widowed woman. If a widow did not remarry, she became elevated to the status of the *univira*, the ideal Roman woman who has known only one husband, even after his death. In staying true to her husband, the *univira* promoted on an extreme level Roman Emperor Augustus's (63 BCE–14 CE) moral laws on marriage (*Lex Julia de maritandis ordinibus*, 18 BCE) and adultery (*Lex Julia de adulteriis coercendis*, 17 BCE).[13]

The *univira* was part of the idealization of Roman woman as wife, but there were two other concepts associated with this idealization. They were (1) *aeternus* and *sempiternus*, adjectives pointing to the bond of marriage, which lasted for a lifetime, until the death of the wife, and (2) *morem gerere*, a descriptor conveying a woman's absolute obedience to her husband. These ideals were expressed in "the Roman bride's solemn declaration at the marriage ceremony and preceded the formal *dextrarum iunctio*, 'the linking of right hands,' that constituted the sign of marriage and that can be seen represented on many funerary monuments."[14] It is believed that by the end of the third century, this kind of "male ideal of Roman female behavior was already in place."[15]

While the *univira* was presented as the Roman ideal, we also receive from ancient texts an opposing image to the *materfamilias*, the woman of disrepute. Two centuries after Tertullian, Macrobius (ca. 400 CE) looked critically at Julia (39 BCE–14 CE), the daughter of Emperor Augustus. Julia was notorious for her extramarital affairs. Macrobius describes, in *Saturnalia*, an unnamed friend showing surprise at the resemblance between Julia's children and their father, Agrippa (63–12 BCE). Julia wittily replies, "I take on a passenger only when the ship's hold is full,"[16] indicating she had affairs only while pregnant. Whether or not this portrays an accurate record of events, it shows at least that Roman women were presented at opposite extremes, to contrast acceptable (*materfamilias*) and nonacceptable (scheming adulterer) female comportment in ancient Roman societies.

Before a woman became a *materfamilias*, she was a girl under the power (*in manu*) of her father. In her father's household, a girl was expected to remain a virgin. But the idea of virginity was not only tied to the single girl under her father's power. In Roman law, an understanding of "woman" was viewed thusly: "In the name 'woman' (*mulier*) a virgin ready for a man is also included."[17] This means that, in ancient Roman times, womanhood was very much tied to sexual behavior, alongside social propriety, whether a woman acted respectably or not.[18] A woman could be a single virginal girl, a mother, a widow, but also "one ready for a man." These descriptions of womanhood relied on defining her via her relationship to a man, and according to her sexual and social behavior.

A woman could also become a virgin for the Roman state. As early as the age of six, a girl could be "captured" (*captio*) from the "lap" of her father for the "household" of Rome through its father figure, the *pontifex maximus*, the highest priest of the Roman cult. The girl was enrolled as a Roman vestal virgin to serve the Roman goddess, Vesta, and to keep her flame alight day and night.[19] The flame represented the vitality of Rome. Thus, when the vestals neglected this duty, the Romans saw the death of the flame as an omen concerning their beloved city. A vestal virgin did not come under any powers; she was independent or *sui iuris* (i.e., legally independent, with powers over her estate). But if she were to break the duty of virginity for the Roman state, she would fall under the power of the *pontifex maximus*, who had to bury her alive in public as a punishment and as a warning to others.[20]

Additionally, regarding the ancient Roman world and its views on women as mother, wife, or virgin, views of the *materfamilias* changed over time and, in general, the guardianship of women in ancient Rome involved deviations or exceptions.[21] As well, women were imagined in terms of ideals to communicate values and their roles in society, but these ideals did not necessarily reflect reality. As we noted earlier, Roman law could elevate women in their role of bearing children within legitimate marriage, while at the same time Roman literature could condemn her opposite image, the woman who bore children outside of marriage, the whore. However, the information provided so far is consistent with Tertullian's era. His imaging of the church as woman similarly shows no evidence of a concern for the realities of women. Instead, informed by his Christian and Roman background, what he praised and emphasized in the uses of "mother" for the church was communicated through the extreme images of the elevated and the disdained images of woman—that is, as either virtuous *materfamilias* or immoral *matrona*.

TERTULLIAN'S REJECTION AND APPROPRIATION OF ROMAN CULTURE

Clearly, there is evidence Tertullian appropriated ideas of the "mother" from his surrounding culture. On the one hand, he placed no value in the Roman mother-goddess and popular worship of her in her many forms (as the Great Mother, or Ceres, or Flora).[22] In addition, he criticized other cultures' relations with their mothers, accusing the Persians and Macedonians of incest, lust, and adultery:

> Again, who are more incestuous than those whom Jupiter himself has taught? Ctesias records that the Persians have sexual intercourse with their own mothers. The Macedonians, too, are suspect, because on first hearing the tragedy of Oedipus, they ridiculed his grief at the incest of which he had been guilty.[23]

On the other hand, Tertullian accused his Roman audience for not acting within the boundaries of Roman decorum:

> You are always praising antiquity, and yet every day you have novelties in your way of living. From your having failed to maintain what you should, you make it clear, that, while you abandon the good ways of your fathers, you retain and guard the things you ought not.[24]

That Roman decorum is exemplified in the Greek historian and rhetor Dionysius of Halicarnassus's (60 BCE–7 BCE) account of the contrast between Roman worship and "Barbarian" and "Greek" worship that had been imported into Rome:

> No festival is observed by the Romans...any instances of divine possession, Corybantic frenzies, religious begging rituals, Bacchic rites and secret mysteries, all-night vigils of men and women together in temples or any other trickery of this kind....The [Roman] city is extremely cautious with respect to religious customs which are not

native to Rome and regards as inauspicious all pomp and ceremony which lacks decorous behavior.[25]

Similarly, after Tertullian had criticized the Persians and Macedonians on their relationship with their mothers, he commended the Christian choice for chastity: "A persevering and steadfast chastity has protected us from anything like this: keeping as we do from adulteries and all post-matrimonial unfaithfulness, we are not exposed to incestuous mishaps."[26]

Thus, while Tertullian rejected Roman mother worship and the sexual behavior of other cultures concerning their mothers, he was happy to reappropriate certain Roman cultural values, such as "Roman decorum," which rejected inappropriate sexual interaction, to engage with his audience. While there is no direct link corroborating Tertullian's reappropriation of the Roman mother for Christianity, at least we can say that Roman values regarding motherhood and womanhood are evident in Tertullian's portrayal of church as woman and mother.

TERTULLIAN'S REJECTION OF A TYPE OF *MATRONA*

While Tertullian's Mother Church parallels the virtuous *materfamilias-univira*, at the same time, it must be acknowledged that Tertullian does have a reputation for having described women with absolute disdain. Gender stereotyping and dualistic imaging of woman as virtuous or not was common in the ancient Roman world, as we have already seen. Women's business acumen in the ancient world, for example, was questioned, yet they could be accused of being scheming "gold-diggers."[27] We see an example of Tertullian's hostility toward women in *On the Dress of Women*, where he states,

Do you not believe that you are [each] an Eve? The sentence of God on this sex of yours lives on even in our times and so it is necessary that the guilt should live on, also. You are the one who opened the door to the Devil, you are the one who first plucked the fruit of the forbidden tree, you are the first who deserted the divine law; you are the one who persuaded him whom the Devil was not strong enough to attack. All too easily you destroyed the image of God, man. Because of your desert, that is, death, even the Son of God had to die. And you still think of putting adornments over the skins of animals that cover you?[28]

Commenting on the things women desire, such as wool, silk, pearls, rubies, gold, and the mirror (to present an image that lies), Tertullian presents woman as like her ancestor Eve, who after being thrown out of "paradise" was already "dead." As he suggests that Eve would not have desired these "fineries" after being expelled from paradise, so he suggests to the woman to also not desire these fineries if she wishes to "to be restored to life again." Tertullian says that, since the woman did not desire these things when she lived with God, these are mere "trappings appropriate to a woman who was condemned and is dead," displayed as if to glamorize her own funeral.[29]

While Tertullian, here, seemed to be addressing women in general, his judgment was actually upon the superficially adorned *matrona*, with her jewelry, makeup, and clothing. His harsh criticisms were not upon the respectable *materfamilias*, who by the third century also became known as the *matrona*. The virtuous mother and wife was modeled on heralded figures such as Cornelia (190–102 BCE), who was the wife of Tiberius Gracchus the elder (217–154 BCE), and who gave birth to twelve children, of which only three survived. She is celebrated for holding up her children as her adornment. The story is recounted by Valerius Maximus (fl. ca. 27–31 CE), an author from the era of the emperor Tiberius Claudius Nero (42 BCE–37 CE):

> Cornelia, mother of the Gracchi, when a Campanian woman—a guest in her house—held up her jewellery as the most beautiful of the century, drew her out in conversation until her children came back from school. "These," she said, "are my jewels."[30]

When Cornelia's husband died, she refused numerous marriage proposals, including one from Egypt's Ptolemy VIII (182–116 BCE). This, in turn, cemented her memory in Roman history as the ideal *matrona/univira/materfamilias*, having borne many children and having stayed true to one husband even after his death.

The virtuous *materfamilias*, as exemplified in the legend of Cornelia, sits alongside the vestal virgin, who was also seen as representing the highest of Roman virtues; and therefore, both *materfamilias* and *vestale virgine* were the most highly regarded and respected females in ancient Rome. The vestal virgin was meant to appear in public as the virtue that she represented, namely chastity or purity (*castitas* or *pudicitas*). Her purity was seen to be equal to the bride, who was also meant to be pure and virginal, such that they both employed the same hairstyle, the six braids. The vestal's purity was also exhibited in her wearing of a type of tunic called a *stola*. "The stola was restricted to the use of certain citizen class women."[31] Prostitutes, freedwomen, and women divorced by their husbands because of suspicion of adultery were forbidden to wear the *stola*. Only the chaste and pure mother or vestal virgin could thus wear it.

The low regard that Tertullian had for "woman" was then toward the unvirtuous *matrona* who decorated herself with jewelry, makeup, and fine clothing.[32] In his view, her low character was reflected in her preoccupations with these items.[33] In wearing them, she showed conduciveness to anything but integrity (*integritas*),[34] chastity (*castitas*),[35] and the fear of God (*timor dei*),[36] which in contrast were the values exemplified by Roman mothers and virgins. In living a life of indulgence, the shallow and insincere *matrona* evidenced a distorted view of "glory," which she placed upon the wrong things. Only glory in the lacerated flesh, the martyred flesh, is to be upheld, rather than glory in the adorned body—and not even in the body that has died in the process of giving birth, as Tertullian says: "Do not then ask to die on bridal beds, or in miscarriages, or from gentle fevers; rather, seek to die a martyr that He may be glorified who suffered for you."[37]

AN ACCEPTABLE AND RESPECTABLE WOMAN—MOTHER CHURCH AS *MATERFAMILIAS*

In contrast to the rejected woman, the superficial and adorned *matrona*, Tertullian's Mother Church presents the ideals imposed upon the concept of woman. That is, she is made for motherhood and family life, and that is represented in the images of birthing, breastfeeding, and childcare as primary work, and in being the loyal wife to the one husband.

Birthing Mother Church

As the birthing mother, Tertullian's Mother Church spiritually birthed new Christians and consequently (breast)fed them with spiritual teachings.[38] The concept of birthing Christians was no longer associated simply with martyrdom, as with Irenaeus's Mother Church, but was, for Tertullian, also inextricably tied to the ritual of baptism:

> Therefore, blessed [friends], whom the grace of God awaits, when you ascend from that most sacred font of your new birth, and spread your hands for the first time in the house of your mother, together with your brothers and sisters, ask from the Lord, that His own specialties of grace [and] distributions of gifts may be supplied you.[39]

According to Tertullian, the purpose of baptism was to guarantee purity and moral rigor within the church, in turn guaranteeing the presence of the Holy Spirit within.[40] Just as martyrdom was an extreme expression of commitment to the Christian faith, so too was baptism. First, baptism could occur only once in one's lifetime. If a Christian sinned after baptism, it effected the same wrath and judgment as made upon the world in the story of Noah.[41] Second, baptism involved a life toward perfection, which put virginity forward as its highest ideal. It involved a renunciation of the devil and the world. Yet many Christians were often not prepared to reject their attachments to materialism and the values of the world. They had their own ideas of what membership, via baptism, in the Christian community entailed. As Roy Kearsley explains, "Too many Christians fear that in the church they will serve the poor with their wealth. They had been brought into peril by loving this world and its goods too well."[42] But the renunciation required did not involve a hatred of creation and material goods. Rather, it was about a realignment of vision toward justice for the poor.

For Tertullian, baptism was therefore a serious commitment, which even he delayed until later in his life. The labor pains of a human mother easily translate to the analogy of the labor pains of Mother Church as she gives birth to new Christians through martyrdom. But now with the requirements for baptism, the labor pains also involved the giving up of attachments made in the world. Just as acts of martyrdom rebirthed Christians in the human community, so did baptism birth new members for the community. "It is a death before death and closely linked to martyrdom."[43] Tertullian's contemporary, Perpetua (martyred 203 CE), in fact, evidences that "baptism is a martyrdom put into ritual," where "sacrament and martyrdom are 'different expressions of the same desire.'"[44]

The birthing-mother-to-an-infant church image, exemplified in baptism, was reinforced in what appears to be a Christian appropriation of the ancient cultural practice of feeding milk and honey to infants after their birth. As Tertullian describes it,

> After that, we are immersed in the water three times, making a somewhat fuller pledge than the Lord has prescribed in the Gospel. After this, having stepped forth from the font, we are given a taste of a mixture of milk and honey.[45]

The ancient practice of feeding infants with milk and honey is evidenced in the record of an argument between Soranus of Ephesus, a medical theorist, and his contemporary, Damastes. Both argued over whether to feed milk to an infant in its first few days. Soranus rather recommended giving only "honey moderately boiled." When it was time to give milk to the infant, Soranus suggested that anyone but the mother should provide this since the mother's milk was too thick and unsuitable for the digestive system of the child.[46] Likewise, in the *Epistle of Barnabas* (70–131 CE), the ancient infant feeding practice was appropriated to explain, to a certain Christian community influenced by Alexandrian ideas, the significance of "milk" and "honey" received from their faith.[47]

The Breastfeeding Mother

The church as breastfeeding is a powerful image. Ancient Roman culture had such high ideals regarding maternal breastfeeding that author Aulus Gellius (130–80 CE) described a mother who refused her breasts to her child as being similar to one who aborts her own fetus.[48] While in reality it was common that a wet nurse would feed a baby (even in lower-class families),[49] there were concerns that she would not only pass on her poorer quality of milk and therefore less nutrition, but also pass on from her milk her "extraneous moral traits"[50] and her poor grasp of the Latin language.[51]

Tertullian himself provides an idealized image of the mother and child bond through the act of breastfeeding, acknowledging, at the same time, the presence of the wet nurse and other female carers:

> From the very moment of birth [the soul] has to be regarded as endowed with foreknowledge, much more with intelligence. Accordingly by this intuition the babe knows his mother, discerns the nurse, and even recognises the waiting-maid; refusing the breast of another woman, and the cradle that is not his own, and longing only for the arms to which he is accustomed.[52]

In imaging the nurturing Mother Church, Tertullian not only imagined the feeding of "infant" Christian neophytes but also adult Christian "confessors." These were the men and women who openly confessed Christianity under threat of martyrdom but who were not or had not yet been put to death. In this nurturing, Mother Church provides both spiritual and material sustenance, as the confessors (which Tertullian called "Blessed Martyrs Designate") awaited their trial and persecution:

Blessed Martyrs Designate,—Along with the provision which our lady mother the Church from her bountiful breasts, and each brother out of his private means, makes for your bodily wants in the prison, accept also from me some contribution to your spiritual sustenance; for it is not good that the flesh be feasted and the spirit starve: if that which is weak be carefully looked to, it is but right that that which is still weaker should not be neglected.[53]

Tertullian's encouragement here is toward Christian confessors in prison, awaiting trial and execution. He intended to give them spiritual food by stating that they were freer in prison than those living in the world. Tertullian was motivated to write this text by a fear that those in prison "would backslide"—Tertullian's general fear for Christians in the world.[54]

This emphasis on martyrdom in *To the Martyrs* was a reaction to Gnostics, especially the Valentinians, "who questioned the relevance of martyrdom."[55] *To the Martyrs* was a plea to accept martyrdom as the will of God, and a plea that resistance to arrest was going against this will.[56] Tertullian acted as representative of Mother Church himself in the giving of spiritual food through such encouragement of the confessors and in attending to their bodily needs. Apparently, there was a customary practice amongst Carthaginian Christians of ensuring their confessors were well fed and prepared for the bodily tortures that lay ahead of them.[57]

As Mother and Wife, the Roman
Materfamilias-Univira

Alongside the impressions of a birthing and breastfeeding church, Tertullian's Mother Church appears as a similar figure to the *materfamilias* who stands behind her *paterfamilias*. For in Tertullian's texts, Mother Church generally does not appear in isolation: she usually appears paired with Father God as his spouse,[58] or associated with the family altogether, alongside the Father and Son.[59] An example of this is as follows:

Even our mother the Church is not omitted, seeing that in "son" and "father" there is a recognition of "mother": for the name of both father and son has its actuality from her.[60]

For the ancient Romans, belonging to a family was a life and death issue. The significance of recognition in Roman civic life, by belonging to a family, can be seen in the following:

A critical element in the formation of Roman identity and citizenship, the family, provided protection, economic and emotional support, and was the institution through which wealth and property was protected and transmitted. In Roman thought, the strength of the family reflected the stability of the state, making membership in the polity of Rome itself writ small. Belonging to society was especially important for freedmen, who as slaves had been considered property and less than human, and who were eager to display their new status as Roman citizens.[61]

Tertullian's use of the "mother" taps into this concern:

In short, all heresies, when thoroughly investigated, are detected harboring dissent in many particulars even from their own founders. The majority of them have not even churches. Without mother, without home, bereft of faith, and exiles, they wander about in their own essential worthlessness.[62]

The juxtaposition of "without mother," "without home," "bereft of faith," and "exiles" aligns with the picture of the individual repudiated and considered outside recognition of citizenship in Rome—an individual without a family, a home; an alien.[63] To be without a family meant to not have the chance to distinguish oneself via legal and social legitimacy. In other words, it made it hard for the individual to engage in civic exchange. In addition, the individual did not have access to a proper burial without a family, thus making him or her an outsider to Roman social decorum.

Tertullian acknowledged the pervasive idea of family, as promoted by Emperor Augustus's Julian laws (*leges Juliae*):

> What if a man, with thoughts like the eyes of Lot's wife, is anxious about posterity and desires a second marriage because he has had no children by his first? To think that a Christian, one who is disinherited by all the world, should be hunting around for heirs! He has brothers and sisters. He has the Church, his Mother. The case is different, however, if they suppose that the forum of Christ follows the Julian Laws, and if they imagine that unmarried persons and persons without children are prohibited, by a divine decree, from inheriting the full share of their patrimony.[64]

Here, by naming the church as mother, Tertullian gave the Christian a family group and consequently recognition and status. Just as childless individuals and those without family were inserted into family or family-like groups and gained advantages otherwise cut off from them,[65] so in calling the church a mother, the Roman-Carthaginian Christian was inserted into a family where inheritance, status, freedom, and other associated advantages were provided.

There is an ecclesiological explanation for this inside-outside familial rhetoric. For Tertullian, the unity of the church was of the utmost importance and this was ensured through two elements: (1) an intellectual discipline—"doctrinal consensus through the *regula fidei*" (or the rule of faith[66]), where true belief is distinguished from false; and (2) a practical discipline that guarantees and "preserves" the holiness of the church. Baptism was that key ritual that preserved holiness in the church since it also required rejection of the world and the devil, which, in Tertullian's view, led only to idolatry and death. Explorations outside of the *regula fidei* led to heresy. Likewise, those who engaged in "murder, idolatry, fraud, apostasy, blasphemy...adultery and fornication"[67] committed unforgivable sins and were to be excluded. As Tertullian states, "Dogs, sorcerers, fornicators, murderers, out!"[68] Thus, for Tertullian, heretics were motherless, houseless, outsiders, and faithless.[69] This perspective was supported by the cultural reality that to have no mother was to belong to no family, no household, and therefore to have no chance of inheritance, no moral standing, and no support from society.

Applying the concept of the Roman *familia* to the church, whereby it is the *materfamilias*, God the *paterfamilias*, and the child *filiusfamilias* enabled Tertullian to adopt highly valued familial associations such as "inheritance" and "belonging" to reinforce the concept of a church that demarcated between outsiders and insiders to the Christian faith.

RELEVANCE FOR THE TRADITION OF THE CHURCH AS BRIDE, HOLY, VIRGIN, AND MOTHER

With Tertullian's condemnation of the superficially decorated *matrona* (who indulged and gloried in the wrong things) and his praise for the *materfamilias* (who showed conduciveness to chastity, integrity, and fear of God), he had at his disposal a maternal metaphor that could promote his agenda of purity and moral uprightness for the church. The church as mother, *materfamilias*, is the virtuous and devoted *univira* to Father God, the *paterfamilias* of the Christian family. The church as holy, a virgin, a bride-to-be, a woman or *mulier*, as "a virgin ready for a man," promoted Tertullian's purity agenda. Further, with purity as the shared virtue celebrated in both the mother-wife and vestal virgin, it is unsurprising that Tertullian imagined the church as a virgin, true, modest, and holy:

> But it is in the church that this [edict] is read, and in the church that it is pronounced; and [the church] is a virgin! Far, far from Christ's betrothed be such a proclamation! She, the true, the modest, the saintly, shall be free from stain even of her ears. She has none to whom to make such a promise; and if she had, she does not make it; since even the earthly temple of God can sooner have been called by the Lord a "den of robbers," than of adulterers and fornicators.[70]

46

Tertullian's purpose in writing this text was to assert the church's submission and obedience to Christ. Thus, in his view, sinners, the disobedient, and the faithless were to be excluded.[71] Tertullian's presentation of the church as a virgin emphasized its holiness and contrasted with the faith of heretics, who threatened the unity of the church. The unholy/heretics were characterized by "their lack of godly fear, gravity, diligent care, ordered appointment and due discipline."[72]

But Rankin notes that, apart from *Against Marcion* 5.4.8, where Tertullian calls Mother Church "holy" in reclaiming Marcion's reflection on Galatians 4:26, "Tertullian does not appear explicitly to link the 'motherhood' of the church to her holiness."[73] Neither does Tertullian connect the church's motherhood with her virginity.[74] This does not rule out the possibility that his imaging of the church's motherhood precludes an assumption that the church is a "virgin" at the same time. But it is more likely that since motherhood and virginity were distinctive roles, Tertullian used both as separate metaphors for the church. Thus, we have in Tertullian the church as a mother and the church as a virgin, but not the church as simultaneously virgin-mother.

For Tertullian, to use virgin-mother for the church would present either a tautology or an incompatibility. The defining characteristics of both virgin and *materfamilias* were purity and moral uprightness. Therefore, mother-virgin would be tautological, as it would be like Tertullian describing the church as "pure-pure." In terms of incompatibility, it would be like Tertullian saying that the church is both a virgin "ready for a man" and also one who has had a man and children from this man. Such a mismatch would not work for Tertullian.

Even regarding Mary, Tertullian did not consider her as simultaneously virgin and wife. He describes Mary as a virgin only in bearing Christ and only after this does Mary become an *univira*:

> It was a virgin who gave birth to Christ, but after his birth she was married to one man, so that both ideals of holiness [namely, the virginal and married ideals] might be exemplified in Christ's parentage, in the person of a

mother who was both virgin and married to one husband only.[75]

In Roman terms, Mary was at one time a virgin "ready for a man,"
and after birthing Christ, the virtuous *materfamilias-univira*. Her
moral purity was evident as a virgin, and this purity remained when
she became like the virtuous Roman mother. For Tertullian, Mary's
role was to emphasize the humanity of Christ, especially in response
to Marcion's rejection of the body. It was not about characterizing
the church as both perpetual virgin and mother. The concept of
the church as necessarily both virgin and mother became imperative only later, for Ambrose of Milan (340–97 CE), as we will discuss
in chapter 4.

Meanwhile, Mary as "a virgin ready for a man" aligned with the
ancient Greek concept of the woman as a vessel: for a woman to
conceive, her body must be empty or unoccupied. In the ancient
world, while maternity was proven through birth, paternity was not
so easily observable. To establish connection and belonging
between father and child, paternity was "not as much discovered as
it was created or symbolically constructed."[76] Hence myths of origin, medical (scientific) literature, and postnatal rites were used to
contribute to the rhetoric of men giving life. As an example, ancient
Greek myths show male gods birthing other gods, while goddesses
who attempt to similarly birth produce deformed beings. A female
figure still had a role in this birthing, but it was as if her power to
birth was taken from her and handed over to the male god. For
example, in order to birth Athena, Zeus had to swallow Metis. With
Dionysius, Zeus had to remove Semele's embryo and place it into
his thigh. Consequently, from Zeus's head, Athena is born and from
Zeus's thigh, Dionysius is born.[77]

In contrast, the attempts of female goddesses to birth proved
disastrous, as Turid Karlsen Seim describes:

The goddess Hera…in retaliation to Zeus's "do-it-yourself
procreation" attempted a single-handed generation, the
result being the monstrous serpent Typhoeus—a story
not dissimilar to the Sethian tradition about Sophia who

in an attempt at conceiving by herself gave birth to Yaldabaoth.[78]

Seim further explains that, in ancient times, various theories explained the roles of men and women in birthing: the *preformationism/homunculus* theory explained male sperm as containing miniature human beings who simply need to be implanted in a woman's womb to grow and be born, whereas *pangenesis* taught that both men and women produce seed that contributes to the creation of a child. The Hippocratics, whose beliefs on birth and genetics leaned toward the *pangenesis* theory, believed in the supremacy of the male seed over the female seed. The presence of more male seed produced the stronger form, the male, and vice versa, the more female seed provided the weaker sex, female. Seim claims that the Hippocratic writings commonly promoted the primary role of women as ultimately to receive and carry life, while a man's role is to marry a woman to have a family, where offspring can be recognized as legitimate.[79]

The philosopher Aristotle (384–322 BCE), who wrote after the Hippocratics, devised the theory of *epigenesis*. According to this theory, "the male seed, and later the embryo, is a unity of matter and form; it possesses a productive and generative potency that, once present in the material prepared by the female, begins its work, starting with the construction of the heart."[80] This was a development from *preformationism* in that, rather than simply growth, there is gradual transformation. At the same time, Aristotle's theory contrasted with the Hippocratic version of *pangenesis* and proposed that only males contribute seed and that this is the active principle of life. At the same time, women are the impotent and passive principle of life that is awakened only by contact with the male seed.[81]

In these ancient understandings of reproduction, Mary was presented as exemplifying purity through virginity and motherhood as "one ready to receive" the "male seed" of Father God, who provides life, and as one who gives human flesh to Christ from the seed of Father God. Mary was not envisaged as an image of the church but rather to highlight Christ's humanity as understood within the limits of ancient Roman ideas about human reproduction and existence.

In the previous chapter, recall Irenaeus's thought regarding the church as a woman and mother, which contradicts the claim regarding Mother Church as being a virginal mother from its very beginnings. Such a claim is exemplified by Brendan Leahy, who reflects on the distinctive Marian character of the ecclesiology of Hans Urs von Balthasar. Leahy states that "from the time of Justin and Irenaeus, in fact, the concepts 'virgin-Mother-Church' and 'virgin-mother-Mary' are so intertwined that, in a sense, they cannot be separated."[82] For Tertullian, virginity and motherhood were exclusive, independent images for the church.

Regarding the bride analogy for the church, for Tertullian, marriage was not motivated by love but simply something women would "fall into."[83] He concluded, therefore, that as a married woman, the only appropriate behavior and comportment would be found in the model of the church as bride: "if the church as the 'Bride of Christ' is characterized by submissiveness, humility, obedience and discipline, how much more should human brides express these characteristics?"[84] This, in fact, becomes a circular argument—the married woman is to follow the example of the church as a bride, while the church as a bride is improved upon by the acts of the bride.

Surprisingly, Tertullian uses Eve, rather than Mary, as a model for the church. Through the picture of Eve as spouse of Adam, Tertullian parallels the image of the church as spouse to Christ:

> But, presenting to your weakness the gift of the example of His own flesh, the more perfect Adam—that is Christ, more perfect on this account as well [as on others], that He was more entirely pure—stands before you, if you are willing [to copy Him], as a voluntary celibate in the flesh. If, however, you are unequal [to that perfection], He stands before you a monogamist in spirit, having one Church as His spouse, according to the figure of Adam and of Eve, which [figure] the apostle interprets of that great sacrament of Christ and the Church, [teaching that], through the spiritual, it was analogous to the carnal monogamy.[85]

Taking this analogy further, Tertullian reasons that, as Eve was born from the side of Adam (his rib), so the church was born from the wound on Christ's side:

> For as Adam was a figure of Christ, Adam's sleep shadowed out the death of Christ, who was to sleep a mortal slumber, that from the wound inflicted on His side might, in like manner [as Eve was formed], be typified by the church, the true mother of the living.[86]

While Eve is described as mother of all the living in Genesis 3:20, it is the church whom Tertullian names as the *true* mother of the living.

It is clear, therefore, that the hierarchical structure present in the Roman household, with the *paterfamilias* as the head and having power (*potestas*) over all members of the *familia*, has much resonance in the visualization of the church as a woman, mother, and spouse. The church as *materfamilias-univira* or as Eve, following the imaging of woman in ancient Rome, placed in relation to males (Christ, God the Father, Adam), is, in Tertullian,

> never the head, the *paterfamilias*, the male legally in charge of the household;

> never equal to the male in relation; and

> never the one who "births" the male (i.e., neither the church births Christ nor Eve births Adam from her side).

Here, we see Tertullian reflecting the attitudes of his Roman hierarchical familial culture. In fact, he was mindful of his audience by incorporating the values tied to familial concepts of his day in his emphasis on the church as necessarily pure and moral. Further, while Tertullian emphasized the need for purity and moral uprightness in the church through the images of *materfamilias*, virgin, woman (= "virgin ready for a man"), and bride, he did not pursue purity through a rejection of the body, unlike his opponents, the followers of Marcion.[87] In fact Tertullian wrote on the fleshliness of Christ (*On the Body of Christ*) and of the bodily resurrection (*On the Resurrection of the Body*).[88] At the same time, he showed preference for virginity over married life as a way of moving toward a life of moral perfection (see *To His Wife*, ch. 3). Consequently, virginity for Tertullian was not about a hatred or fear of sex and bodies but rather a concern for the cultivation of virtues such as integrity and fear of God.[89]

CONCLUSION

In Tertullian's vision of the church as woman and mother, we find an extension of Irenaeus's birthing and breastfeeding mother images. Tertullian extended the imagery by pairing Mother Church with Father God, paralleling the image of the ancient Roman *materfamilias-univira* by the side of her one spouse, the *paterfamilias*. With this familial image, Tertullian attached to the church highly regarded values associated with family and belonging. Through the family a person could engage in public life and a man could move forward in his career. The importance of belonging to a family extended even to one's death, when such belonging ensured appropriate obsequies were observed.

Therefore, while the Mother Church image had been part of the North African Catholic tradition, and its image grounded in the scriptural text of Galatians 4:26 (as noted in the previous chapter), Tertullian applied a form of rejection-appropriation in the imaging of the ecclesial mother. He rejected the superficially adorned Roman *matrona* but upheld a Roman *materfamilias-univira* and even *virginal* image for the church, enabling his Roman-Carthaginian audience to accept and relate to such an ecclesial mother. He named the church a bride/spouse, a virgin, and holy, but did not present explicit appellations connecting these characteristics or titles with the motherhood of the church.[90] His discrete use of imagery of mother and virgin for the church are not associated directly with a concept of Mary as both mother and virgin.

Tertullian's development of the maternal ecclesial metaphor created a new vision of what the church was and its relationship with God and its members. While he continued the tradition of imaging the church as birthing and breastfeeding, he reenvisioned and clarified its role and essence through such developments as his emphasis on the personification of Mother Church as an entity distinct from its members; in his integration of baptism into the birthing-martyred Mother Church tradition; in his emphasis on following the *regula fidei* and a shared ritual discipline; and in particular, his association of Mother Church, *materfamilias*, with Father God, *paterfamilias*. This was not a case of simply presenting "an old word new tricks—of applying an old label in a new way."[91] Rather, he imaged the church as woman and mother, reflecting Roman cultural values regarding the woman and families, and aligning them with Christian concerns of cultivating virtue and appropriate worship of the Christian God.

3

From Seated Mother with Her Infants to Bride of Christ

I pray that as our Mother the Church
bewails the downfall and the death of very many,
by your joy you may dry her tears,
and by the challenge of your example
you may confirm the resolution
of the rest who yet remain standing.

—Cyprian, *Letter* 10.4.4

Caecilius Cyprianus Thascius (200–258 CE), also known as St. Cyprian, was the bishop of Carthage, North Africa, from 248 or 249 CE. During the persecutions under the Roman emperor, Decius (r. 249–51 CE), who issued an imperial decree in 250 CE to promote imperial unity, Cyprian escaped to the hills and wrote letters to his community. But, without his physical presence, he left his community vulnerable to chaos.[1] On his return when the persecutions ceased, he faced the clergy and confessors who undertook actions that led themselves and others to apostasy and to schism. Amid this crisis in the church, Cyprian employed the mother metaphor to ask those who had left the church or who were thinking of leaving it to return or remain with "her."

Cyprian's reference to the church as woman and mother, specifically as *Mater Ecclesia*, or just *Mater*,[2] is characterized by his emphasis on the demarcation between those inside and those outside the church. This idea is seen most evidently in his famous dictum: "You cannot have God for your Father if you no longer have the Church for your mother,"[3] whereby each of those who has turned her or his back on the church is described as "an alien, a worldling, an enemy."[4] It is a continuation of a tradition established by Tertullian. But, in Cyprian's ecclesial context, the demarcation was more intense as he dealt with a community beset with persecution because of imperial decrees from the Emperors Decius (r. 249–51 CE), Valerian (coemperor 253–60), and his son Gallienus (coemperor 253–60, sole emperor 260–68).

In this chapter, we argue that, initially, Cyprian's presentation of the maternal-feminine church aligned with Roman imperial propaganda, which used the fecund and faithful *matrona* to promote peace and stability within the unsettled empire. Moreover, this *matrona* figure acted as a culturally resonant image for Cyprian's Roman-Carthaginian-Christian audience. Furthermore, to combat persecution and divisive heresy within his church, Cyprian, like the Roman Emperor Augustus (63 BCE–19 CE), pleaded for unity using the image of the *matrona* with her two infants. It is only when this image did not seem to change his church's situation and rebaptisms continued to be an issue that Cyprian then moved on from the Mother Church image to that of the church as the bride of Christ. This bride has resonances with church father Origen's reading of the bride in the Song of Songs and has implications for the tradition of the church imagined as a woman, mother, bride, wife, and virgin. In the last section of this chapter, we briefly explore these implications.

THE ROMAN *MATRONA*, AUGUSTAN PEACE, AND THE *ARA PACIS AUGUSTAE*

Livia Drusilla (59/58 BCE–29 CE), the wife of Roman Emperor Augustus/Octavian (63 BCE–14 CE), and mother to his heir, Tiberius Claudius Nero (42 BCE–37 CE), was used by Augustus to promote his vision of the archetypal *matrona*. For Augustus, Livia was the symbol of ideal Roman womanhood:

> The one whose virtuous behavior and fertility exemplified the tenets of Augustus' moral and marriage legislation…[she] served as a paradigm for all other Roman women. In her portraiture she is represented as beautiful, idealized, and virtuous, with an oval face and classically conceived features; her portraits are based on the images of fifth-century Greek goddesses.[5] (See figs. 3.1 and 3.2.)

As part of the Augustan program of peace, Livia was made to represent fidelity, fertility, and beauty.[6] Additionally, she was also portrayed as representing other revered Roman values such as *justitia* (justice, equity, righteousness, uprightness), *concordia* (an agreeing together, union, harmony, concord), *salus* (safety, salvation, health, welfare), and *pietas* (piety—with respect to the gods; duty, dutifulness, affection, love, loyalty, patriotism, gratitude; or with respect to one's parents, children, relatives, country, and benefactors).[7]

Figure 3.1: Bust of Livia. Copy from the original preserved in Copenhagen. *Ara Pacis* Museum, Rome. Photo © C. Lledo Gomez, October 2, 2015.

Figure 3.2: Statue of Livia in her uncommon seated position. She is wearing the *stola* (toga-like cloth) and *palla* (veil) to convey similarity in virtue with the virgin and mother. They are the exclusive wearers of the *stola* and *palla*. National Archaeological Museum of Spain, Madrid. Photo © Mark Elkington, June 27, 2016.

Numismatic evidence shows Livia representing these Roman revered values of *pietas* (see fig. 3.3), *iustitia, salus,* and *concordia.*

Figure 3.3: Livia as *Pietas.* Such coins were issued under the Roman rule of her son, Tiberius, 22–23 CE. Photos courtesy of Classical Numismatic Group, Inc.[8]

Note that it was often the case that many coins portrayed Livia as Concordia or Pax even when subsequent emperors came to power and the obverse sides of coins changed accordingly.

The image of Livia as the perfect woman and mother, as the epitome of female beauty, dignity, and composure, was also portrayed through

1. portraits and busts presenting her with different hair-styles at different ages, to be copied by women;[9]

2. statues in which she is shown wearing a *stola* (toga-like dress) and *palla* (veil), the dress reserved for virtuous Roman women, the *matronae* and vestal virgins; and

3. monuments portraying her as serene mother and wife, such as in the *Ara Pacis Augustae* monument in Rome (see further).[10]

It is claimed that women copied Livia's hair and dress as a way of putting on her characteristics—beauty, fertility, fidelity—

characteristics that were praised in women in Roman societies, mainly because they predisposed to positive moral consequences.[11]

Roman citizens were constantly exposed to projections of Livia and other mothers/women/goddesses such that inevitably they were imbued with an understanding of "the ideal woman." Overall, through *numisma* (coinage), statues, busts, monuments, and portraits of Roman imperial mothers and goddesses, which littered Roman cities, at least two purposes were served: (1) the reinforcement of the idealized woman, and (2) the popularizing of the Augustan rule of peace.

This rule of peace was also known as the golden age or *aurea aetas*. It was "solemnly inaugurated by Augustus at the Secular Games (*Ludi Latini saeculares*), reestablished—and reinvented—in 17 BCE."[12] The rhetoric of the Augustan peace involved promoting fidelity and fecundity through the medium of marriage and through the Augustan laws involving marriage and procreation—the *Lex Julias* (18–17 BCE) and the *Lex Papia Poppaea* (9 BCE).

By upholding fidelity and fertility, the Roman Empire was assured of marital harmony (*concordia*), one of the highest of Roman values, and the peace of the gods (*pax deorum*), an ideal for the Roman state in which peace was secured because its gods were appeased. *Concordia* and *pax deorum* were especially portrayed on the famous *Ara Pacis Augustae* or Altar of Peace monument in Rome. The monument was built and dedicated to Augustus in Rome in 9 BCE, in celebration of his pacification of the Roman Empire and his safe return from "a long tour of the provinces."[13]

On its various wall panels, the altar depicts "the blessings of a peaceful reign using poetic and bucolic imagery."[14] The propaganda the altar sought to communicate was "peace and its consequences for Italy and the world, for the Roman aristocracy and high-ranking provincials."[15] Moreover, this message of peace implied growth and rebirth for the Roman Empire through its portrayal of flourishing plants, an abundance of fruits, and animals— all symbolizing a golden age. The fruits suspended from the garlands sculpted in the altar represent all four seasons of the year, "so magical that they all bloomed at once," reminding the viewer that "Augustus' peace spanned the entire course of the year"[16] (see fig. 3.4).

Figure 3.4: Garland on an internal panel of the *Ara Pacis Augustae* monument. *Ara Pacis* Museum, Rome. Photo © C. Lledo Gomez, October 2, 2015.

Of special interest on the *Ara Pacis* monument is a representation of a youthful and beautiful *matrona* "with two small children sitting on a kind of rock-hewn throne," found on an external panel of the altar[17] (see fig. 3.5); it gives a "programmatic message of peace and prosperity…enhanced by mythological and allegorical imagery."[18] Various theories exist regarding the identity of this *matrona*. One theory suggests an intended ambiguity. It is possible she was a culmination of "personifications and divinities."[19] But Barbara Spaeth has theorized that the figure is Livia, portrayed as Ceres.[20] This makes sense because "Livia, the emperor's female counterpart, was the foundation of the imperial family and the *concordia* of that family is one of the other significant themes of the *Ara Pacis*."[21] It is also fitting that Cornelia, mother of the Gracchi, would be the woman being portrayed on the *Ara Pacis* panel, just as much as she could be a representation of *Tellus* (Earth), or *Italiae* (Italy), *Pax* (Peace), or some Roman goddess. But given that the *Ara Pacis* is a monument centered on the Augustan peace and the Julio-Claudian clan, it is most likely that the woman alludes to Livia.

Figure 3.5: The matron with two infants on the *Ara Pacis Augustae* monument. *Ara Pacis* Museum, Rome. Photo © C. Lledo Gomez, October 2, 2015.

Appearing on the same side of the monument as the *matrona* with two infants is the goddess *Roma* (see fig. 3.6). Note that both Livia and *Roma* are seated rather than in their usual standing position. Regarding the women's uncommon, seated position Kleiner states,

Figure 3.6: The goddess *Roma* sitting on weapons symbolizing the subduing of war, on the *Ara Pacis Augustae* monument. *Ara Pacis* Museum, Rome. Photo © C. Lledo Gomez, October 2, 2015.

It serves to underscore the nurturing function of the women who were not the political movers and shakers but rather contributed to the Augustan peace through their marital fidelity and fecundity. The themes stressed in this side of the Ara Pacis are correct female behavior that included the inclination and ability to bear children through youthful fecundity, the joys of motherhood, the unbreakable bonds of family life, hereditary succession, and the general abundance brought to Rome and the empire by the Augustan peace.[22]

The city of Carthage, North Africa, would exhibit an adapted version of the *Ara Pacis* relief of the seated matron with the two infants (see fig. 3.7) and it would also build its own temple to the *gens Iulia*.[23] There are a few differences between the Roman and Carthaginian panels, but both contain three central figures—a seated matron with two infants—and fruit on the matron's lap (and a bull and pig at her feet), and a figure on each side of her.

Among various interpretations of the figures on the Carthaginian panel, one of which is that it was the matron Isis and her sons Hathos and Osiris on her lap, Spaeth argues that the matron is also Ceres, but a Carthaginian version, Tanit, the local primary goddess associated with the primary god of Carthage, Baal Hammon. To verify Tanit's identity, Spaeth points out that the child seated on her left offers the mother a lotus instead of fruit, as found in the original version. The lotus was known locally in Carthage as the symbol for Tanit.

Figure 3.7: Carthage's own version of the *Ara Pacis* mother with two infants panel. Picture of plaster cast of marble original stored in the Louvre Museum, Paris. *Ara Pacis* Museum, Rome. Photo © C. Lledo Gomez, October 2, 2015.

The panels from both the *Ara Pacis* of Rome and that of Carthage signify abundance, blessedness, and fruitfulness, which, in turn, communicated an assurance of peace for the Roman Empire and its inhabitants, something that was continually pursued by the empire through the *pax deorum* (peace of the gods). The inverse perception was also true: the peace signified by the entire *Ara Pacis* and its various panels would communicate abundance and blessings for the people of the Roman Empire, as well as fecundity and continuity for generations. It is in the Carthaginian context, of experiencing instability, disunity, and uncertainty both within and outside of Cyprian's Carthaginian community, that Livia, as symbol of assurances of peace and stability for the empire, would become relevant for Cyprian and his Christian community. However, before looking for cultural influences upon the portrayal of the church as woman and mother, we must ask about the extent of such influences and whether it is even plausible to suggest it.

CYPRIAN'S REJECTION AND APPROPRIATION OF ROMAN CULTURE

Several authors believe Cyprian's Roman pagan upbringing had a major influence on his role as a bishop.[24] Certainly, while he outwardly rejected his cultural surroundings, his view of the church was not left unaffected by it. Patristic scholar Allen Brent argues that, on the one hand, Cyprian adamantly detested his pagan past, but, on the other hand, he was inevitably influenced by it and expressed it in his ordering of church structure.[25] Brent states, for example, that Cyprian applied Roman jurisprudence to the church, which, Brent argues, ultimately destroyed the basis for the church of martyrs. This was so the bishop could gain control and a hoped-for unity in the church.[26] Similarly, Vincent Hunink sees Cyprian as a Christian and Roman gentleman who wished to leave the world, but who was also very much a "man of the world."[27]

In contrast, Peter Hinchliff claims that the Roman culture had no appeal to Cyprian and that he did not utilize any part of it in his rhetoric. However, Hinchliff also acknowledges that Cyprian had a pagan-Roman mindset.[28] He says, "Cyprian hankered after a dignified, moral Roman past and…he became a Christian, at least in part, in revulsion against the degradation of Roman society. He longed for the kind of world that there had once been."[29] It is possible that this "world that had once been" was the dignified moral and peaceful Roman past referred to as the golden age or *aurea aetas*. It was an age lauded and reinforced in literature, law, and art from the time of early Roman antiquity.

But Cyprian and his Carthaginian community lived over two centuries after the reestablishment and reinvention of *aurea aetas* in 17 BCE, the building of the *Ara Pacis* in 9 BCE, and the deaths of Augustus and Livia in 14 CE and 29 CE, respectively. Cyprian became a bishop in 248 CE. How is it possible that the Augustan program of peace would influence Cyprian and his community?

Zanker explains the effect of Roman art on the public:

> Through didactic arrangements and constant repetition and combination of the limited number of new symbols, along with the dramatic highlighting of facades, statues, and paintings, even the uneducated viewer was indoctrinated in the new visual program. The key messages were quite simple, and they were reiterated on every possible occasion, from festivals of the gods to the theatre, in both words and pictures. Even the rich decorative program of the Forum of Augustus was built around very few images.[30]

While Zanker comments here on the age of Augustus, the account is still very relevant for Cyprian's contemporaries, given that the symbols, facades, statues, and tools of engagement such as coins were still very much present during the third-century CE Roman Empire. Thus, even when Cyprian and his Carthaginian-Roman community avoided touching and viewing Roman statues,[31] since this was considered idolatry, their use of *numisma* in daily economic exchange alone would have constantly exposed them to the Roman idealized woman-goddess and the virtues she represented (such as *pax, pietas,* and *concordia*).

Reflecting on Cornelia, mother of the Gracchi, Suzanne Dixon observes that "Christian authors who, like their non-Christian forebears, valued selfless devotion in wives and mothers, tacked Cornelia and a few other traditional wifely models on to their exemplary lists."[32] She notes that ancient imagery had such longevity and impact, beyond their own lifetimes, that references to them appeared in texts of pagan and Christian writers alike.

But there is an indication that Cyprian himself accepted the image of the Roman virtuous woman as a mother or *matrona,* as he, himself, states:

65

In the theatres also you will behold what may well cause you grief and shame....Adultery is learnt while it is seen... the matron [*matrona*], who perhaps had gone to the play chaste [*pudica*], returns from the play unchaste.[33]

Cyprian does not name any Roman mothers like Cornelia or Livia in his writings. But, as we will note in the next section, the church as a mother, a place of unity and peace, has much in common with the revered virtuous and pure ancient Roman *matrona* who gathers her children on her lap. Just as this mother conveyed a sense of stability, peace, and continuity, so would Cyprian seek to present Mother Church. While the *lapsi* rushed toward emperor worship and threatened the peace and unity of the church, Cyprian would call upon an image similar to this revered *matrona* on the *Ara Pacis*.

Allen Brent theorizes that when the Christians undertook the necessary imperial cultic sacrifice to obtain their *libelli*, it was not just undertaken out of fear of Roman law, but also because it was inherent to Carthaginian culture to believe in the power of the Augustan augury.[34] He explains that the Carthaginian *Ara Pacis* "would have stood on the straight, major road that ran from the NW to the SE of the city," projecting the implications of peace brought about by Augustus, his divine father Julius, and his successors, through various images, including the *matrona*-goddess.[35] He further explains that, evidently, the Carthaginian *Ara Pacis* was in view near the altar at which Carthaginian Roman citizens were asked to make sacrifice to the gods and goddesses. Roman pagan formation would have instilled in the minds of these citizens the high value of *pax* and *concordia* (especially in a time of disunity and disintegration) and the achievement of this was by following the orders of the *pontifex maximus*, the Roman emperor, to make imperial sacrifice.

Why was there a need to make this sacrifice, and why was it in conflict with the church? In the next section, we explore the ecclesial and sociocultural circumstances in which Cyprian felt compelled to use the mother metaphor for the church.

CYPRIAN'S APPROPRIATION
OF THE *MATRONA*

Church Context

The church-related events that led Cyprian to write of the church as woman and mother were the following:[36]

- His assumption of the bishopric of Carthage in 248 CE. In that year he wrote his first treatise, *On the Dress of Virgins*, employing a mother-virgin metaphor to address ecclesial virgins.

- Decius's decree in December 250 CE requiring Roman citizens to participate in emperor worship or face persecution. This decree became the major cause of division within the Carthaginian church. The culprits were grouped as follows:

  sacrificati—those who engaged in the emperor sacrifice;

  certificati—those who appeared to have made the sacrifice without having done so and who simply obtained certificates as proof;

  libellatici—those who used a "legal subterfuge" or bribed "an official to obtain the certificate which attested to their having performed the rituals";[37] and

  thurificati—those who were "unwilling to participate in animal sacrifices but had simply been allowed to burn incense instead."[38]

Together, all were known as the lapsed or *lapsi*; they had participated or had appeared to have participated in the requirements of the decree. The *lapsi* later requested pardon and reentry into the Christian community, which became the primary issue for Cyprian in his uses of "Mother Church," as presented in ten letters and three books written between 250 and 251 CE:

- March 251 CE—Novatian (200–258 CE, antipope Mar. 251–58) is voted in as an opposing bishop to Cornelius (251–53) in Rome. Novatian took the "rigorist" position on the treatment of the *lapsi*. He argued that the *lapsi* may be offered forgiveness and be returned to the church only on their deathbeds. The followers of Novatian, the rigorists, stood in stark contrast to the "laxists." The laxists believed the *lapsi* should be forgiven immediately.

- Easter, March 23, 251 CE—the laxists become a formal schismatic group. There were then three bishops with different approaches to the lapsed:

  Novatian, who led the rigorists;

  Privatus, who led the laxists; and

  Cyprian, who called for restraint in making any decisions until the council of bishops met to decide on the fate of the *lapsi*.

At this time, the first Council of Carthage met and concluded that the fate of the sacrificers was to do penance before reentering the church, while the certified could be reconciled.

- June 251—Decius dies, and Gallus assumes rule as Roman Emperor from 251 CE. He remains in power for the rest of Cyprian's life. Cyprian dies in 253 CE.

The Church as Fecund *Matrona* with Her Infants

While Cyprian presented a "virgin-mother Church" in his address to virgins in 248 CE, the more dominant female church image presented was the fecund *matrona* gathering her infant children to her *sinus* or *gremium* (embrace/lap/bosom/hiding place/place of concealment).[39] Of nineteen textual references to "Mother Church" during 251 CE, Cyprian uses *sinus* five times and alludes to this image as a container or place of containment by juxtaposing the verbs "remain," "return," "receive," and "gather" alongside *sinus*. More specifically, he portrayed Mother Church as someone who could be forsaken/abandoned,[40] rejected/refused,[41] denied,[42] or separated from as children;[43] or as one to whom one returns to,[44] remains with,[45] cleaves to,[46] makes peace with,[47] or gathers around her bosom/lap.[48] The following is an example of Cyprian's use of the *sinus* (bosom/lap) to refer to Mother Church to gather the people:

> For my part I hope, dearest brothers and sisters, and I urge and press it upon you, that, if possible, not one of the brothers and sisters should perish, but that our Mother should have the happiness of clasping to her bosom [*gremio*] all our people in one like-minded body.[49]

The recurring references to "return" or "remain" within the bosom or lap (*sinus*) of Mother Church recalls the "persistent references to children being reared *in gremio matris* or *in sinu matris*"[50] in Roman literature. The references suggest "a typical intimacy and affection between the mother and the young child."[51] Such intimacy was highlighted in children's funerary reliefs by "the greater grief characteristically displayed by mothers" at the death of their child.[52] On this characteristic grief of mothers, it was assumed fathers and mothers had equal affection for their children, but mourning over one's child was the role belonging particularly to the mother. For "to mourn at all was *mulieribis* (womanly); to mourn with abandon was particularly the lot of the bereft mother."[53]

It seems even Cyprian made use of this grieving mother myth as he describes the great grief of "Mother the Church" when her children separate from her:

> I pray that as our Mother the Church bewails the downfall and the death of very many, by your joy you may dry her tears, and by the challenge of your example you may confirm the resolution of the rest who yet remain standing.[54]

This text is from a letter written at the beginning of 251 CE, just after Decius proclaimed his emperor worship decree. The alternative to remaining within the church, that is, a separation or dissociation from the mother, was unthinkable for Cyprian. He even argued that abandoning Mother Church was an act of *impietas*. As he himself said, "It is an act of impiety [*inpietatem*] to knowingly [*agnoscant*] desert [*deserere*] your mother."[55]

Such a call upon the value of *pietas* draws upon the very foundations of Roman citizenship. In Virgil's *Aeneid*, the pious Aeneas, who in legend is shown to be the national hero of the Roman race, is presented as exemplifying Rome's highest familial and civic value, *pietas*. It is said that Aeneas carried the household gods, the *Penates*, and his father Anchises on his back while holding his son Ascanius by the hand, saving them all from the city of Troy while it burned.[56] *Pietas* was that value that presented as both duty and affection for family members, and it placed a great weight upon the psyche of the citizens of ancient Rome. Further, if a Roman abused his mother or father with insults, the urban prefect was to treat it as a public offense.[57] Cyprian's clever implementation of *impietas* as a description for abandoning Mother Church not only provides connotations of having committed a Roman offense, but also indicates that such abandonment is in complete opposition to the heroism of Aeneas.

The image of the church as the fecund *matrona* while her members are like the infants of the *Ara Pacis* panel become especially evident in Cyprian's classic text *On the Unity of the Catholic Church*:

> The Church forms a unity, however far she spreads and multiplies by the progeny of her fecundity....So too the Church glowing with the Lord's light extends her rays over the whole world; but it is one and the same light which is spread everywhere, and the unity of her body suffers no division. She spreads her branches in generous growth over all the earth, she extends her abundant streams ever further; yet one is the head-spring, one the source, one the mother who is prolific in her offspring, generation after generation: of her womb are we born, of her milk are we fed, of her Spirit our souls draw their life-breath.[58]

Cyprian used this picture of Mother Church at a time when early Roman-African citizens perceived the world as unstable and insecure—at a critical time for the empire. Several factors contributed to this perception:

> the instability brought on by a constant change of Roman emperors,
>
> continual "natural disasters such as plagues or famines," and
>
> "a combination of wars, frontier threats...manpower shortages, a sense of moral decline."[59]

This is known as the third-century crisis of the Roman Empire, which, in the end, led to changes that would mark a new era in the Roman way of life, called late antiquity, or the early Middle Ages. Christians saw this crisis as a sign of Christ's second coming, and their initial response was to counter the disintegration by the sacrifice of the Eucharist and to trust in the order created by ecclesiastical structure. Brent suggests Cyprian's reaction to the crisis was one of anxiety, but Rankin believes Cyprian saw the decline as part of the natural order of things.[60] Such a mentality gave purpose to Christianity as a means of restoring an order that the Roman emperors failed to exercise.[61]

The contrasting non-Christian response to the crisis was to seek to appease the gods recognized by the Roman imperial state so that the *pax deorum* (peace of the gods) could be brought about. This was what undergirded Decius's decree. As *pontificus maximus* in charge of ensuring *pax deorum*, Decius issued an order by which Roman citizens were required to sacrifice to the gods at their altars in their central shrines, and subsequently to receive a certificate (a *libellus*) to show that the requirement had been fulfilled.[62] Such sacrifice did not need abandonment of one's current religious practice or allegiance, including Christian ritual and belief, but it did require each person "to appear before a locally established commission, to testify to having been always a worshipper of the gods protecting Rome and to demonstrate that piety in its presence by pouring a libation, offering incense and eating the sacrificial meats."[63]

While many Christians readily complied as soon as the imperial commission was established, there were some who did initially
refuse to participate in the decree's requirements. But under torture and persecution, many succumbed to its demands. There was
only a minority who refused to submit and consequently died as
martyrs. Those who initially sacrificed but saw their error sought
the help of confessors (those on their way to martyrdom) to intercede for them before Christ. It seems that confessors were on the
same level of power as the martyrs. The intercession of the confes-
sor/martyr was such that it overpowered anything on earth, including the authority of the church as exercised through the bishops. In
the tradition of the martyrs of the church, their sacrifice equaled
the power of eucharistic sacrifice (*ordinatio per confessionem*) exercised by those who received the imposition of hands by bishops and
presbyters. The *lapsi* asked for certificates of commendation from
the confessors, hoping to return to the church immediately and
with little or no penance imposed.

How did the martyrs/confessors reach such a status as to be
able to offer the same sacrifice (eucharistic sacrifice) usually held
exclusively by presbyters and bishops? First, we must understand
the religiopolitical world of sacrifice in which this tradition of martyrs in the Roman Empire flourished. We know that order and
peace in Rome, the *pax deorum*, was enforced by the commanding
of Roman citizens to participate in imperial sacrifice. This was not
only seen as appeasing the gods of Rome but also as giving recognition to the emperor's role and status as leader of the Roman state.
But Christians saw Jesus as the alternative leader and the sacrificial
victim (through his death) announcing an alternative *pax deorum*
with his *basileia tou Theou* (kingdom of God). As George Heyman
explains, "[Jesus's] death, reinterpreted by sacrificial language, was
constitutive of a new type of power made ritually available to his
followers through baptism and Eucharist."[64]

From this flowed the concept that the act of accepting the fate
of martyrdom (but not necessarily dying from it) was paralleling or
mimicking Jesus's sacrifice and the sacrifice of the Eucharist itself.
Furthermore, the martyr who refused to engage in imperial sacrifice became *the* sacrifice her- or himself, for the Christian faith and
its community, repeating Jesus's own sacrificial act, and mimicking

the sacrifice in baptism and the Eucharist. In fact, the martyrdom text *Passio Perpetua et Felicitas* (203 CE) presents the martyr as being able "to act *in persona Christi* in view of impending martyrdom."[65] The martyr's power was as such that "just as Jesus' sacrifice on the cross effected the redemption of humanity (Romans 5:15–18), the same atoning power was at least rhetorically available through the sacrificial act of the martyr."[66] Cyprian was thus in a predicament because both the formally ordained through the imposition of hands by the bishop, and the confessors who received *ordinatio per confessionem*, could offer "eucharistic sacrifice"—the first via ordination and the second because of martyrdom, respectively.

With such powers, the confessor could give absolution through the form of a *libellus pacis*, a certificate of peace or reconciliation with the church. This *libellus* acted as a counter to the *libellus* that the Christian Roman citizen had gained for undertaking the required imperial but idolatrous sacrifice. Cyprian acknowledged the tradition of the martyrs to be able to absolve.[67] His strategy was then to praise the sacrifice of the confessors but to downplay their power. The purpose was to give focus to order in the church, which was achieved by emphasis on the role of the bishop and on listening to his commands.[68]

It was the *lapsi* who sacrificed (the *sacrificati*) or who had appeared to sacrifice whom Cyprian predominantly addressed when utilizing the church as mother, as the mother of infants.[69] For as the *lapsi* apostatized in varying degrees, Cyprian determined that the ecclesial hierarchy needed to respond accordingly: the level of penance to be imposed needed to suit the seriousness of the offense. But this kind of penance, he believed, should be applied only after the council of bishops had gathered, an event that was likely to occur only after the persecutions had ended. The confessors Lucianus and Celerinus, contemporaries of Cyprian, readily provided forgiveness to the lapsed. This was the laxist position represented by the party of Felicissimus, but it was seen in the same light as Novatian's rigorist position, which was the offering of forgiveness only at one's deathbed. In Cyprian's view, it was these actions of the *lapsi* defying his commands as the bishop of his community, to wait until the end of the persecution to reenter the church and live a life of penance, that created disunity in the church. For Cyprian, Lucianus and his group did not make the necessary distinction between the "official Church Order constituted by ordained ministry whose source is the episcopal hands" and "that of the martyrs."[70] That is, they would "not admit the validity of the separation of ministries in terms of the martyr/confessor who absolves and the officially and formally ordained presbyter who offers the Eucharistic sacrifice."[71] This led Cyprian to write *On the Unity of the Catholic Church*, *On the Lapsed*, and many *Letters*, urging unity and requesting members to remain in the Mother Church or apostates to return to her.[72]

In presenting the church as one's *sinus* to whom one must return or remain, Cyprian presented a promise of peace and unity as similarly exemplified by the *matrona* in the *Ara Pacis*. For just as the figure of a woman communicated a picture of peace, unity, flourishing, and security for the Roman Empire, so Cyprian's Mother Church was similarly presented. This rhetoric of peace found in the Catholic Church competed with the rhetoric of the power of the martyrs/confessors to forgive and give peace to the *lapsi*, to allow them to return to the church. For the true church would recognize only the power of the bishops over the martyrs; and that true church was in the *sinus* of the church-*matrona*, not in the hands of or determined by confessors.

The importance to Cyprian of presenting this female church, a symbol of unity and peace, is particularly evident in his own revision of paragraph 4 of *On the Unity of the Catholic Church*. His initial version highly emphasizes the role of the bishop as a symbol of unity. The second version or the *textus receptus* version shows Cyprian still emphasizing the role of the bishop as a symbol of unity, but justifying the argument by presenting the female church, who is also a symbol of unity herself.[73]

The *textus receptus* version is described as a "toning down" of the Roman bishop's authority over the whole church, which was already taken as a given in Rome.[74] This involved the presentation of the church as a female and as a dove from the Song of Songs, as found in paragraph 4 of *On the Unity of the Catholic Church*. In the subsequent paragraphs, 5 and 6, there are parallels between the seated *matrona* with her infants on the *Ara Pacis* and Cyprian's Mother Church. That is, just as the *matrona* encapsulated fecundity, loyalty to the one spouse, moral uprightness, stability, and unity amid imperial and ecclesial disunity, so does Cyprian's Mother Church appear as

> the fecund mother, birthing children (para. 5);
>
> like the *univira*, who is morally upright through her chastity (para. 6); and
>
> stability and unity, which she provides (para. 5) by being the sole mediator to God the Father (para. 6).

Furthermore, just as Tertullian had tapped into the associations regarding family, that is, Roman citizenship (versus alien status), belonging, inheritance, and even adultery, so does Cyprian (para. 6).

One thesis proposes that the location of the motherhood of the church moved from the community to Cyprian as the bishop (who, as bishop, represented the wider church) to ultimately the college of bishops.[75] The power of decision making for the community initially belonged to the community. But when the apostasies and idolatrous sacrifices began to occur, Cyprian stepped in to be the final arbiter of decision making for the community. Yet, later, he realized that to truly be united as a church, all the bishops, as representatives of their churches, must be united in thought and decision making. In Cyprian's reign as bishop, a record number of councils were held because of this focus on unity, which is exemplified in paragraphs 4–6 of *On the Unity of the Catholic Church*.

In *Letter* 47.1.1, Cyprian as bishop and representative of Mother Church "pleads" with his audience to return to the Catholic Mother:

> My dearest brother, I have judged it to be an obligation upon me and my religious duty towards you all to write a brief letter to the confessors over there in Rome who have forsaken the Church, seduced through the viciousness and perversity of Novatian and Novatus. My purpose is to induce them out of fraternal affection to return to their own true mother, that is, to the Catholic Church.[76]

Letter 47 is addressed to Cornelius, informing him that Cyprian has written a letter to the confessors in Rome. Cornelius was to decide whether the letter was to be forwarded to the confessors. Clarke notes that Cyprian treads cautiously in this letter, given that he has already offended Cornelius by sending Caldonius and Fortunatus to Rome to heal the conflict arising from the factions created in the church there that not only resulted in the worsening of the situation but also was seen as breaking "established custom."[77] Interestingly, Cyprian contrasts the confessors with the Catholic Church as a whole by describing attachment to the confessors as loyalty through fraternal affection, compared to loyalty toward the "true" mother.

Later, in *Letter* 48.3.1, Cyprian employs *matricem* to associate "mother" with the very source of Catholic faith:

> To all who were sailing away we explained to them the situation individually so that they should not be scandalized on their travels, exhorting them to discern the womb and root [*matricem et radicem*] of the Catholic Church and to cleave to it.[78]

By *Letter* 48, Cyprian had written to Rome, acknowledging Cornelius as its rightful bishop. The purpose of the letter was to reassure Cornelius of Cyprian's support despite a period when "Cornelius' claims had not been fully recognized" by the council of bishops.[79]

THE HEALING MOTHER VERSUS STEPMOTHER IMAGES

By 252 CE, Cyprian no longer presented the female church as fecund mother with her two infants, the *radix et matrix*, the one to whom one should cleave,[80] or remain within, or the one to whose *sinus* or *gremium* one should return. Rather, after the waivers relating to the Decian persecution, Cyprian returned to his community and began to present the church as one who offers a healing embrace (*salutaris sinus matris*) to the *lapsi*, the fallen. To emphasize this, Cyprian contrasts the image of the healing embrace of his Mother Church with the *mater nouerca*, the "stepmother" who poses as the Mother Church, the churches under Novatian and Privatus, whom he describes as preventing Christian children from reaching their true mother:

> By their deception and lies they thus ruin any repentance which these poor wretches might do, and ensure that they do not appease the wrath of God....True reconciliation they destroy by their false and fallacious reconciliation; the stepmother impedes them from reaching their true mother's healing embrace, anxious to prevent her from hearing any sobbing and weeping coming from the hearts and lips of those who have fallen.[81]

The *mater nouerca* was, in fact, a notorious image in ancient Rome, notwithstanding the actual reality. Evil stepmothers pervaded Latin literature. For example, "Tacitus refers routinely to *novercalia odia* ('stepmotherly-hatred') as a self-explanatory term for Livia's alleged antipathy to Agrippa Postumus."[82] Even when the stepmother acted in a "motherly" way, the prejudice remained dominant. The negative attitude among ancient Romans toward stepmothers stemmed from the understanding that stepmothers would live in the same household as their stepchildren and have the same status as the biological but absent mother, yet they would advance the interests of only their own natural children. Cyprian thus integrated the dominant cultural image of the evil stepmother into his use of the Mother Church metaphor, and by providing this contrast he brought to the fore even more strongly the powerful cultural understanding of the imagined nurturing love of a mother for her natural children.

THE SISTER-BRIDE/MOTHER-BRIDE CHURCH

Relating to the question of rebaptisms for heretics and schismatics, in the period after the upheavals resulting from the Decian decree (253–56 CE), Cyprian applied the sister-bride (*soror-sponsa*) and mother-bride (*mater-sponsa*) metaphors, from Song of Songs 4:12 and 6:9, to Mother Church. In *Letter* 69, Cyprian says,

That the Church is one is declared by the Holy Spirit in the Song of Songs, speaking in the person of Christ: *My dove, my perfect one, is but one, she is the only one of her mother, the favourite of her who bore her.*[83] And the Spirit again says of her: *An enclosed garden is my sister, my bride, a sealed fountain, a well of living water.*[84]

This argument reinforces Cyprian's earlier one in *On the Unity of the Church, textus receptus* version, paragraph 4, regarding the church's unity under one episcopate and one baptism, where he also used Song of Songs 6:9 to present the mother-daughter image of the church.

After 256 CE, the use of the term *Mother Church* took this more forceful approach compared to previous approaches of pleading for the Christian to return to the church or to remain within her *sinus*. Considering the Novationist debate, this forcefulness was needed because the church's holiness seemed to be at stake. The first three councils of Carthage had addressed issues of entry and reentry into the church, leading to a focus on the rebaptism issue, in the following sequence:

The penance of sacrificers (first and second Councils of Carthage, 251 and 252 CE, respectively);

infant baptisms (second Council of Carthage); and

readmission of sacrificers to communion (third Council of Carthage, 253).[85]

Then the rebaptism controversy was revisited at the fourth Council of Carthage (255) and then again after Easter, March 256, at the fifth Council of Carthage.[86] With the urgency of pitting the Catholic Church against the Novationist stance, Cyprian thus presented a focused mother-bride image of the church, where the church is the *only* bride of Christ, the *only* pure church that can claim to have valid baptisms.

It is in both *Letter* 74 (256 CE) and *On the Unity of the Church* (251) where Cyprian aligns the church as one bride and mother inextricably with God the Father. In *Letter* 74, he highlights the singular location of true baptism. As the only bride of Christ, the

Catholic Church is the pure bride and mother, the only one who can validly give birth to children of God. In contrast, heresy is not a bride of Christ: it is impure, not sanctified by Christ, and produces invalid baptisms.[87] In *On the Unity of the Church*, the earlier of the two texts, the focus is more on remaining in that one true church. But in both texts, we find Cyprian's famous dictum, "If a man is to have God for Father, he must first have the Church for mother."

PARALLELS WITH ORIGEN'S FEMALE CHURCH

Cyprian's uses of the church as "perfect bride" in *On the Unity of the Church* and in *Letters* 69 and 74 show parallels with Origen's reading of the Song of Songs:

> In Cyprian's naming of Christ as "the voice" of Song of Songs 6:9 (*Letters* 69 and 74, and *On the Unity of the Church* 4);
>
> in naming the church the "perfect bride" (*Letter* 69.2.1);
>
> in Cyprian's insistence on the church as the "only one bride" of Christ (*Letters* 69.2.1; 74.6.2; 74.7.2; 74.11.2); and
>
> in aligning the "perfection" of the "church as bride" with "purity" or "holiness" ("The Bride of Christ cannot be defiled," *On Unity* 6; *Letter* 69.2.1).

For Origen, the Song texts are Christ's "marriage song" to his perfect bride, with whom he is about to engage allegorically in a nuptial act.[88] In Origen's view, the perfect bride is the church collectively but *also* the individual soul—not simply one or the other.[89] For Origen, the reader of the Song of Songs (the individual or the whole church) is spiritually transformed and undergoes a journey toward moral and intellectual perfection,[90] such that he/she is prepared to receive the kisses (the teachings)[91] of Christ through the Song texts. In this, the soul/church becomes the perfect bride and unites with Christ the Word.[92]

The purpose of the Song texts was to explain the Scripture readers' journey of spiritual transformation in an erotic sense. Prior to the reading of the Song of Songs, the soul would have been engaged with other scriptural texts such as the Prophets and the books of Wisdom, and reading these would have prepared the soul finally to be able to read the Song of Songs. At this level of reading, the texts of the Song of Songs are allegories.[93]

Can we say that Cyprian understood Origen's view of the reader and of the reading of Scriptures, more particularly, the Song of Songs, when Cyprian imaged the church as a woman, bride, sister, and mother? If Cyprian did, then we could imagine that he viewed members of the church, the faithful, as being at various levels of faith, and the bride as being the one who has reached the highest level, so that she is ready to receive Christ's "kisses" (teachings), as seen in the Song of Songs.

Certainly, we can say that Cyprian's female church resonates with Origen's ideas of the church and of the individual soul imaged as the bride. Cyprian's focus was on pinpointing the true church, who gave valid baptisms. Thus, the bride was anyone who remained in that church, regardless of his or her level of spiritual faith. To reinforce this visualization of the church as bride of Christ, Cyprian used Christ as the actual speaker of the Song texts himself where Cyprian quotes the Song of Songs, to give forcefulness to his argument.

Before we leave this exploration of Origen's imaging of the church as woman and mother and its possible influence upon Cyprian, it would be important to recall a theory by J. Christopher King that Origen's reading of the Song of Song texts did not negate bodies, sex, eroticism, or marriage.[94] This theory is important because, today, imagining the church as woman, mother, and virgin suggests to many that the church *does* negate bodies, sex, and eroticism. King argues that Origen affirmed these concepts—of bodies, sex, and eroticism—but that he wished to point the reader of the Song of Songs to higher levels of meaning for them. If this was what Origen intended, and if, indeed, Origen influenced Cyprian in this bridal imagery for the church, it is a shame that such nuanced reading of the Song of Songs does not seem to be expressed in Cyprian's imagination of the church as a bride. Nevertheless, it can be argued that Cyprian does provide a positive understanding of the embodied and fecund female church through reference to the mother with the two infants image and the call to the *sinus* of the church, and through the healing mother image versus the despised stepmother image, and through the church as a mother-bride image, the *mater-familias* of ancient Roman culture. The opposite can also be argued: in presenting the female church as the ideal Roman woman, equivalent to a goddess, Cyprian did anything but value women in their real embodied existence and in their diversity. Instead, he reinforces a Roman ideal where women become a homogenous group, valued only for either their fecundity or virginity.

RELEVANCE FOR THE TRADITION OF THE CHURCH AS BRIDE, HOLY, VIRGIN, AND MOTHER

What does Cyprian's imagination of the church as the fecund *matrona*, as the healing mother, as the true mother, and eventually as the sister-bride/mother-bride tell us? In the least we can say that Cyprian presents culturally resonant images of the female church by presenting her as being similar to the ideal Roman woman. Moreover, this "woman" is not a concept but embodied in real women such as Livia and Cornelia.

Livia and Cornelia were idealized, even elevated to the point of divinization, by their own people. They were used as models for other women to emulate and their images ultimately communicated an assurance of peace and unity for the Roman Empire. In one sense, this is a positive valuation of marriage, motherhood, and of woman, as it affirmed that woman could embody the very virtues of Rome, such as *concordia, iusititia,* and *pax.* In fact, because of her elevated image, Roman fears associated with the crisis of the third century were countered. But again, this portrayal limits the idea of being woman, since it suggests that a woman can be revered only in so far as she can be a mother or a virgin. Like Margaret Atwood's *The Handmaid's Tale,* women are seen not for themselves but for their fecundity. This is consequently utilized to alleviate societal fears regarding the future of an empire or nation. By assuring a

81

society that there are mothers dedicated to the creation of its next generation, a future for this society is also assured. Slave women of ancient Rome, by the work of their own hands, also contributed to the continuity and peace of the ancient Roman Empire. But it is not their virtuousness, through the work of their hands, that ancient Rome holds up. Rather, it is woman and her ability to mother the next generation that is held up. Even the virgin communicated to her ancient Roman society that the woman's ultimate role is as a mother. For as a virgin she presents to them as a contradiction. In this contradiction she reminds them of woman's true and ultimate purpose—that is, to be a mother for her society.

When Cyprian eventually utilizes the sister-bride/mother-bride images for the church, even though he uses the youthful bridal image from the Song of Songs, he still attaches a culturally resonant image of the ideal Roman woman onto the church. That is, instead of the fecund mother, Cyprian presents the church as an *univira*, the woman who was revered for being the singular, pure, and virtuous wife to the one husband, even after his death. Whatever arguments exist regarding the existence of ahistorical, asomatic, and eternal images of the church as a female, at least in the case of Cyprian, Irenaeus, and Tertullian—as we have seen so far—culturally resonant images have been utilized, even if they are idealized.

Amid these critiques regarding Cyprian's utilization of the Roman woman to convey the church's nature and position on beliefs such as on rebaptisms, we must be mindful that Cyprian's aim was neither to affirm nor disparage women, marriage, bodies, or sex. His priorities were to combat heresy and preserve unity for the church. This meant, for him, using every rhetorical device available. One such device was the imaginative use of woman as mother and bride for the church. This device could strongly convey such arguments as the indivisible connection between the Catholic Church and Christ or God the Father; that the only true baptisms were those within the Catholic Church; and that the church had strong associations with important ancient or Roman concepts, such as marriage, virginity, and purity. In particular, the use of the image of the church as the lap or bosom to which one remained or returned was a powerful rhetorical tool of reassurance for him and his third-century ancient Roman audience.

CONCLUSION

Cyprian imagined the church as woman and mother at a time of disunity and instability in the Roman Empire. The maternal image portrayed was initially the fecund mother whose infants gather at her *sinus*, resembling the seated mother with her two infants from a panel on the famous *Ara Pacis Augustae* monument. A similar panel existed in Carthage and was very much in view when Roman-Carthaginian citizens were asked to sacrifice under the Decian decree. This panel with the mother and two infants sought to communicate abundance, blessedness, and fruitfulness, which, in turn, communicated an assured peace (*pax deorum*), *concordia*, stability, and continuity for the Roman Empire and its inhabitants. Cyprian's call to unity and order, repeatedly requesting the faithful to remain with or to return to the mother, echoes this Roman imperial desire of the crisis-ridden third century for unity and order.

The seated *matrona* with her two infants, although created centuries before Cyprian, has been an image perpetuated over the centuries throughout the empire via the media of coinage, portraiture, dress and coiffure, literature, ceremonies, and funerary art. The Carthaginian Christian community would have been immersed in such imagery and the associations given to the fecund mother with her infants. Cyprian's later employment of the mother-bride and sister-bride images from the Song of Songs for the church appeared after the persecutions (or at least the fear of them) dissipated and the rebaptism controversy had become a focus for the Christian Carthaginian community. In this reimagining, the female church was still associated with a culturally resonant image of woman—the *univira*. Even though Cyprian utilized the youthful bride from the Song of Songs to present this female image of the church, the value of the singular, faithful, and therefore pure and upright wife would have still resonated with his audience.

Like Cyprian, Origen also in his reading of the Song of Songs saw the church as a bride in relationship with the bridegroom, Christ. There seemed to be parallels between Cyprian's and Origen's naming of Christ as "the voice" of Song of Songs, in naming the church as the "perfect" and "one and only bride," and in aligning the "perfection" of the "church as bride" with "purity" or

83

"holiness." A theory exists that Origen's reading of the Song of Songs affirmed bodies, sex, and eroticism, but there is no evidence that Cyprian applies these affirmations either in his use of the Song of Songs texts or in his appropriation of Origen's view of the church as bride and Christ as the bridegroom. This is unfortunate given that today the presentation of the church as woman, specifically as a virgin mother, can serve to reinforce the view that the church, or Christianity for that matter, has a negative approach to bodies, sex, and eroticism.

The figuring of the church as a woman, perceived today as removed from reality, was not intended as such by Cyprian. Rather, he used it as a rhetorical device to address ecclesial concerns. How such imaging could be implicitly communicating over the centuries either the negation or even the tolerance of bodies, sex, marriage, and women was not Cyprian's concern. Just as the image of a specific woman was used to communicate the assurance of peace, unity, and continuity for the empire, so Cyprian, as a product of his time, used the image of a particular kind of woman for the church to locate peace and unity inside what he considered to be the one and only true church. The important point here is that Cyprian utilized culturally resonant images in order to communicate effectively with his audience. Are these images of the church as female culturally appropriate in the postmodern context? Can they be appropriated to speak in a meaningful way today? Or is it time to find other metaphors to communicate the nature, purpose, beliefs, and roles of the church?

4

The Virgin-Mother-Bride Church

What bride has more children than holy Church,
who is a virgin in her sacraments
and a mother to her people?

—Ambrose, *On Virgins* 1.31

For Aurelius Ambrosius, or St. Ambrose (334–97 CE), it was a given that the church was a woman and a mother. It seemed his greater concern was convincing his audience that the church was necessarily a virgin if it was to be a mother. The research of some patristic scholars does not focus on Ambrose's combination of the two seemingly contradictory images into the one. Rather, their concern is about how this paradoxical image, the mother-virgin, previously attributed solely to the church, became transposed onto the order of ecclesial virgins.[1] As Hunter says, in Ambrose "the 'virgin bride,' traditionally used as a figure of the church, became the celibate Christian, particularly the virgin female, and ultimately the preeminent virgin, Mary."[2] This brings into question the idea of Mary, the Mother of Jesus, as always having been a type of the church right from its very beginnings. In this chapter, we observe that it was through Ambrose that Mary as virgin-mother became significant for the church's modeling of its maternal-virginal characteristics.

Ambrose was governor of Aemilia-Liguria, northern Italy, in 370 but his headquarters were in Milan. He also became bishop of Milan, in 374, the first to be attributed the distinction of having a high office in both the secular and ecclesiastical worlds. He was bishop for over twenty-three years (373–97), until his death on Easter Eve.

His writings show an obsession with virginity, which represented the seeking of purity from the bodily and sinful taint of sexual intercourse. This obsession is reflected in the church in Ambrose's assertion of the Catholic Church's possession of "an inviolably holy body, possessed of unchallengeable, because divine, authority" over Roman society.[3]

Ambrose's enthusiasm for virginity and consequent imagining of the church and of Mary as a virgin derives from the significance of virginity in the Roman Empire, particularly through the vestal virgins and the foundations of Rome based upon a virgin. Ambrose not only encouraged ecclesial virgins, whose power and significance was to align with the vestals, but he also went beyond this by making the ecclesial virgin a *matrona* as well. Just as the vestal virgin symbolized the *res publica* (republic) of Rome, so would the ecclesial virgin figured in the mother-virgin Mary symbolize the *res publica* (religious government) of the mother-virgin church.

VESTA, THE VESTAL VIRGIN, AND THE *RES PUBLICA* OF ROME

The power given to virginity and virgins in ancient Rome has significance for how we view Ambrose's rhetoric on the church as a woman, mother, and virgin. We begin this exploration of ancient Roman views on virginity with Vesta and the vestal virgin cult. Vesta is said to be the original divine virgin, the virgin par excellence.[4] She was the goddess of the hearth of Rome, the family, and domestic life. She was the only goddess in the ancient world who was not portrayed as a human-like figure, but was represented as a flame. Her absence or invisibility was equated with her virginity. Her priestesses, the vestal *virgines*, kept her flame alive and celebrated her feast from June 7 to 15. Her flame was renewed and relighted on March 1 each year until 391, when the Christian Emperor Theodosius I (r. 379–95) forbade all public pagan worship.[5]

The significance of the vestal virgins was not just in terms of Roman culture but also in terms of the very self-identity of Romans themselves.[6] For the very foundations of Rome itself were dependent upon a vestal virgin named Rhea Silva, who gave birth to the twins Romulus and Remus, the putative founders of Rome.

The vestals took on virginity as their defining characteristic. They kept Vesta's flame alive in the court of Vesta situated beside the Roman forum, which was the center of political life.

Inside Vesta's court, inscriptions of *purissima* (most pure) and *sanctissima* (most holy) reminded vestals of what they were to embody and judiciously keep intact through the symbol of their bodies. If they broke their virginity through *incestus*, that is, by engaging in sexual activity with anyone,[7] they were to be punished by the *pontifex maximus*, by being buried alive. For, as a representative of the *res publica*, a vestal virgin's desecration was also a desecration not just of the *ius sacrum*, the sacred duty to Vesta, but a desecration of Rome itself. Military success, the prospering of Rome, and the keeping of its *pax deorum* depended upon vestal virgins fulfilling their sacred duty and keeping their bodies chaste.

Vestal virgins did more than remain chaste and keep Vesta's flame alight, however. They also attended to other tasks associated with the "hearth" of Rome as a larger "household." Such tasks included preparing and storing ritual food; appearing in theaters, ceremonies, and various public events; and even participating in legal matters, presenting personal testimonies in court (no other women could do this), or keeping official records for the Roman state. Their life was far from being cloistered even if they were to keep chaste. As a symbol of the *res publica* of Rome, the vestal virgin was expected to be seen, and her appearances were quite orchestrated—from secular and religious festivals to magistrate and senate appearances—to remind the public constantly of her significance.

Thus, vestals were not just at the center of religious life but also of Rome's legal and political spheres. The virgins, however, did not have the same power as politicians per se. Rather, their *appearances* were very political. For example, in times of political crisis, one would ensure the vestals were on Rome's side. Vestals were sent on petitionary missions on behalf of Rome when Rome's very existence was at stake. Likewise, in civic jurisprudence, a vestal's power came from her religious significance. She had the power to overturn a civic decision to put a criminal to death, but only insofar as the criminal happened to cross her path. As a person who could move through the religious, political, and legal spheres, a vestal thus embodied the entire republic of Rome, and special rules applied to her, depending on which sphere she dwelt in. Ultimately, virginity, or at least its appearance, influenced all spheres of life in the ancient Roman world.

The power given to virginity and virgins in ancient Roman culture, but also the power given to motherhood and to being a wife, was such that it affected Ambrose's call for more virgins for the church. Even the way a girl or woman dedicated her virginity to the Roman state or the way she preserved it for her groom as a bride resonated with Ambrose's ritual for girls and women who became virgins for the church. The *captio*, the ritual that established the (pagan) vestal priestess, was reminiscent of the capturing of prisoners in war. Kroppenberg observes that this act was not only a violent one, wrenching a girl away from her family, but it also "symbolically reenacted the founding of the Roman Republic. It signified the transition from a state of tyranny before the law was introduced, to a new order that was regulated by the law. In other words, law began with the founding of the Roman Republic."[8]

Besides alluding to the founding of Rome, the *captio* also alluded to the events leading up to this founding. According to Roman legend as told by Roman historian Livy (59 BCE–17 CE), Rhea Silva, the mother of the founders of Rome, was initially the daughter of the King Numitor of Alba Longa, who was a descendant of the Trojan hero and first hero of Rome, Aeneas. Rhea was clutched from the hands of her father and forced to become a vestal virgin, then raped by the god Mars, and subsequently gave birth to Romulus and Remus.

The *captio* of the girl for virginity also seems to have paralleled the ritual of abduction of a bride for a Roman wedding.[9] Moreover, vestal virginity presented elements that were distinctively Roman matronal. For example, the dress that a vestal wore, the *stola* (long dress), and the *vittae* (bands around her head), were items of attire that were specific to the Roman *matrona*—"so specifically associated with that status as to be used as a catch-phrase for the legally married woman in the comedians and elegists."[10] Recall from the previous chapter the commonality regarding purity that only virgins and matrons could be seen as exemplifying in society. According to Mary Beard, there is evidence that virgins were given a matronal status because (1) they played a significant part in a festival that was specifically celebrated only by married women, the *Bona Dea*, and they were associated with *matronae* of the city in the secular games, *Ludes Saeculares*; and (2) in 9 CE, Augustus granted them the same rights as those granted to women who had given birth.[11]

Consequently, the concept of the virgin-mother may not have been too much of a stretch for the Roman imagination as it would be for that of society today. As ancient Roman mothers were imagined as pure and upright, so were virgins, and vice versa: the *virgo* held the status of a *matrona*, just as the *matrona* in her purity and uprightness held the status of the *virgo*. With the power given to virginity and the high esteem given to both virginity and motherhood, the use of the image of virgin-motherhood would be a potent tool for Ambrose to promote Mary as the ultimate virgin and mother. Let us now examine to what extent these highly significant cultural considerations regarding the vestal virgin affected Ambrose's portrayal of the church as woman, and more specifically as a mother-virgin.

AMBROSE'S REJECTION AND APPROPRIATION OF ROMAN CULTURE

While it is understood that Ambrose thought that being a Catholic Christian entailed no blurring of boundaries between opposites, such as soul and body, church and *saeculum* (or human history), "Bible truth and 'worldly' guesswork,"[12] he in fact had a less dichotomous and a more complex view of the world and of Christianity. Certainly, along with his contemporaries, Ambrose believed that a person's identity was located in his or her immortal soul and that the body was a prison from which one was released only at death;[13] nevertheless, he understood that there is an integral relationship between the soul and the body. Thus, the body could not be disregarded. Three significant strands of thought governed Ambrose's view:

1. his understanding of the proper harmonious relation of soul and body that God intended;

2. the present corruption of the soul and body that resulted from the fall; and

3. the challenges that sensual distractions pose for the soul trying to follow the will of God.[14]

Hence, Ambrose did not repudiate the body, but rather emphasized its significance:

> At best the body is like a musical instrument, which, when properly controlled by the sovereign rational soul, produces "music in euphonious accord with the life of virtue." At worst, if not properly directed and restrained by reason, the body is the source of the passions, and thus the source of distraction and deception.[15]

Therefore, in contrast to the dichotomous approach, which pits the body against the soul or the world against the church, it was philosophy combined with Scripture that influenced Ambrose and provided the content for his writings. This concurs with Marcia Colish's argument that Ambrose combined philosophy and Christianity in such a way as to generate an amalgam of the two that "bears a distinctive Ambrosian stamp."[16] She challenges the notion that Ambrose's exhortations to depart from physical pleasure were evidence of a "dualistic, Platonic conception of human nature."[17] While she admits the presence of Platonic motifs and ethics in his writings, she says, nevertheless, that "he appropriates them in light of non-Platonic philosophy and Christian thought."[18] More precisely, Colish argues that Ambrose's ethics, "including ethics for the celibate, is one of moderation," rather than one of extremism.[19] Therefore, despite the frequent depiction of Ambrose as an advocate for asceticism, leaning toward a dualism between the sacred and secular, he had in fact a rather integrative approach.

Regarding Ambrose's views on virginity and women's place and role in the world, and his adaptation and appropriation of these for Christianity, there is evidence that the vestal virgin cult influenced Ambrose's thought and writing—especially, as we will see, in his incorporation of a modified ceremony of *captio* of a young girl for vestal virginity, and of a bride for marriage, into the ritual for "capturing" virgins for the church, for life. Similarly, the views on women, marriage, and family were ingrained in the daily life and environment of a Roman citizen, especially Ambrose. As one who governed a Roman city, they must have influenced his thought and writing—especially since, as we will also note, he viewed himself as having a *paterfamilias*-like role over the virgins he "veiled" (*velatio*) for the church. Now, let us examine Ambrose's ideas on virginity and discuss, especially, his appropriation of the *matrona-virgo* image into the church as a woman and mother.

AMBROSE'S FEMALE CHURCH

The Birthing Virgin-Mother

Of the 129 or more extant literary works of Ambrose, including ninety-one epistles, at least twenty references from fourteen works are made to the church as a mother either implicitly (by reference to her children or her birthing) or explicitly. For the most part, Mother Church is presented as an implicit image: in the indication that she (*Ecclesia*) has children (*filios*), or in the imaging of fecundity (*fecunditas*) or parturition (*parturientes*). Ambrose took for granted that his audience already imagined the church as a mother. He often does not name the church as such. Rather, he names the church's maternal actions—which are birthing,[20] weeping,[21] exhorting,[22] healing,[23] offering her children for Christ,[24] bringing them up in her bosom,[25] and experiencing anxiety for their success[26]—or he simply assumes that she has children.[27] Many of these actions reflect the acts of the ancient Roman mother,[28] as they had for Tertullian and Cyprian. But, of all these acts, it is "birthing" the faithful that Ambrose primarily images when presenting the church as a woman and mother.[29] The birthing is not just about creating new members for the church through baptism,[30] for it is also applied to current members in the encouragement of their growth into spiritual adulthood. Ambrose understood that growing into such adulthood involves "birthing Christ" in the individual "mind," in the individual's hearing of teachings.[31]

The "labor" involved in "birthing Christ" is the demanding work of becoming virtuous. This arduous work is aligned with both virginity and martyrdom, as exemplified in St. Agnes (291–304 CE). In *On Virginity*, Ambrose refers to Agnes, who kept her virginity for Christ, as an example of a new kind of martyrdom.[32] As he says, "in one victim a twofold martyrdom, of modesty and of religion. She both remained a virgin and she obtained martyrdom."[33] With the end of the persecutions, when Roman Emperor Constantine (272–337) converted to Christianity (312) and made it the Roman state religion, Ambrose could not repeat the tactic of the other early church fathers, Irenaeus, Tertullian, and Cyprian, which was to equate the martyrdoms of church members with the birthing of the church. Instead, with his enthusiasm for virginity, Ambrose associated the "suffering" in "birthing" Christ with virginity and its reward of becoming virtuous.[34]

For Ambrose, it was possible for all to conceive and birth Christ. But there were conditions. First, to conceive Christ, one must have a "virginal" disposition. After receiving Christ the Word of God through the teachings of the church, it is then possible to carry Christ. Yet, carrying Christ does not necessarily mean being able to birth him. On this Ambrose explains:

> But not all bring forth children, not all are perfect; not all can say: *"We have brought forth the spirit of salvation on earth"* (Isa 26:18). Not all are Marys [*Mariae*], who conceived Christ by the Holy Spirit, and gave birth to the Word. There are those who abort the Word before its birth; there are those who carry Christ in their womb, but as yet He is not formed.[35]

The Spirit conceives Christ in the womb of the mind,[36] but it is the individual who gives birth to Christ.[37] Ambrose makes a distinction between the conception and birth of Christ by stating that conception is the planting of the Word of God within the chaste soul,[38] but birthing is dependent upon the individual's response to the "Father's will":

> Do the Father's will and you will be Christ's mother. Many have conceived Christ but have never brought Him into the light of day. She who brings forth justice, brings forth

Christ: she who brings forth wisdom, brings forth Christ.
She who bears the Word, carries Christ.[39]

It is the chaste soul, then, that gives the individual that "virginal" disposition. But the chaste church also, through "her" sacraments, allows the church to bear children:

> So the holy Church, ignorant of wedlock, but fertile in bearing, is in chastity a virgin, yet a mother in offspring. She, a virgin, bears us her children, not by a human father, but by the Spirit. She bears us not with pain, but with the rejoicings of the angels. She, a virgin, feeds us, not with the milk of the body, but with that of the Apostle, wherewith he fed the tender age of the people who were still children. For what bride has more children than holy Church, who is a virgin in her sacraments and a mother to her people.[40]

Hunter describes the inseparability of the church's maternity and its virginity as its "paradoxical quality of spiritual fertility."[41] The relationship between the two works conversely: as the church's virginity is necessary for its maternity, so spiritual maternity is a necessary consequence of the church's virginity. But what does it mean to have a chaste or virginal disposition, according to Ambrose?

Ambrose on Virginity, Chastity, and Virtuousness

On virginity, Ambrose speaks of Mary's holiness as a mother and states, "No human semen ever entered the sacred sanctuary of the Virgin's womb."[42] For Ambrose, virginity not only countered the human tendency to sexual immorality,[43] but it also avoided its consequence—"earthly corruption."[44] While this view seems to repudiate sex and the body, it needs to be seen within the larger context of Ambrose's views on chastity.

Ambrose believed chastity could be practiced equally within the three states of life: marriage, virginity, and widowhood. Ambrose says, "Every *stuprum* is *adulterium*; nor is it lawful for the man what is not lawful for the woman."[45] In ancient Roman law, whether a woman was guilty of adultery, *adulterium*, depended upon her marital status, and *stuprum*, which refers to sexual intercourse with an unmarried woman such as a widow or virgin, was not seen as adultery according to the marriage laws of Roman Emperor Augustus. But here, Ambrose states that both are crimes of adultery.[46] In all three states—marriage, virginity, and widowhood—chastity was not just about abstaining from sexual intercourse. Rather, for Ambrose, it concerned intentionality, moderation, and the cultivation of other virtues.[47]

Within marriage, following "almost verbatim" its Roman legal definition, Ambrose speaks of intentionality, saying, "Marriage is made not by physical consummation but by marital consent."[48] In terms of moderation, Ambrose criticizes the Roman cultural and legal norms, which allow "prostitution, concubinage, and a master's sexual use of his slave."[49] Under a new life in Christ, a baptized person could engage in sexual relations with her or his spouse only. This would produce children who are legitimate under Roman law and in the church. Chastity in marriage encouraged virtues such as mutual fidelity, mutual respect, and selflessness, which in turn affected other areas of a couple's lives. Thus, chastity in marriage would ultimately lead a couple to look beyond themselves in order to attend to the needs of others.

Similarly, Ambrose's views on chastity within virginity involved intentionality, moderation, and the cultivation of other virtues. In fact, he was unimpressed with mere abstention from physical intercourse without concurrent asceticism in behavior; this was his accusation against the vestal virgins. For, as we saw earlier, the vestal's role was to be seen, and many exclusive privileges came with the role. For Ambrose, then, vestal virgins were superficially chaste because they were not required to practice asceticism in other areas of their lives and they enjoyed many exemptions and privileges. Furthermore, their service lasted for only thirty years and to Ambrose this was a superficial example of virginity compared to permanent or lifelong virginity. Moreover, for Ambrose, the vestal virgin's life (as well as that of a priest of Pallas who also took up virginity[50]) did not produce evidence of the cultivation of other virtues such as moderation, temperance, and charity toward one's neighbor.[51]

Ambrose's views on virginity are found too in his praise of Judith from the Old Testament/Hebrew Scriptures and in his perceptions about Mary's perpetual virginity. Ambrose praises Judith for putting her virginity at risk to save her people, the Jewish nation. Meanwhile, Mary is praised for "her daily activities and interactions with people around her [which made] her a prime exemplar for his own consecrated virgins."[52] Both examples demonstrate that Ambrose was not simply promoting an ascetic agenda in a purist physicalist sense, in a time when asceticism itself was growing in popularity. Rather, as he says himself, "It is better to preserve a virgin mind than a virgin body. Both are good, if it is possible to have both. But if it is not possible, let us at least remain chaste, not in the eyes of men but in God's sight."[53]

As chastity may be practiced within motherhood, virginity, and widowhood, Ambrose claims the church may be imagined as a mother, virgin, and widow. He says, "Therefore, all have an example to imitate: virgins, married women, and widows. And for this reason, indeed the church is a virgin, a married woman, and a widow, for they are all one body in Christ."[54] For Ambrose, "spiritual fertility" results from the virginal disposition of Mother Church, Mother Mary, virgin, mother/wife, or widow. In the keeping of "virginity," the fruit is in the cultivation of virtues, or the doing of the "Father's will," or the bearing of justice, wisdom, and the Word, the creation of good Christians, and the "birthing of Christ." Just as the virgin was given the same status as the mother in the ancient Roman context, so it does not seem too unreasonable to imagine the church as at the same time being a mother, virgin, and even a widow (since it is assumed the widow was once a mother) in that context. While we have only scratched the surface of Ambrose's motivations for portraying the church as a woman, virgin, and mother, his portrayal of the church in these different yet similar ways allow us to see he addressed diverse groups in the church—virgins, mothers, and widows.

CONTEXTS DRIVING THE
MOTHER-VIRGIN RHETORIC

The Cultural-Religious Milieu

Ambrose's views on virginity and chastity were supported and fostered by a specific religious milieu built up from several contributing factors, including the following:

> growing interest in the monastic life, and its belief in the possibility of "immediate contact with God and the invisible world," in both the Eastern and Western cultural worlds, by the last quarter of the fourth century;

> the practice of virginity among women *and men* since the time of the apostles; and

> the presence of a cultural mystique surrounding poverty, and the expression of this in the religious conversions and consequent ascetic lives of wealthy men and women, from the second half of the fourth century to the beginning of the fifth.[55]

Together, all three phenomena created an atmosphere bent toward the divine or the eschatological over earthly or simply temporal matters.[56] In addition, the Christian emperor Constantine repealed the penalty laws for bachelors and childless persons in 320, leading to the growing popularity of asceticism in the fourth century.[57] These show that Ambrose was not unique in his great interest in virginity and was a product of his time and place. The difference with Ambrose, though, is that he tied virginity to something beyond physical purity, that is, to intentionality, moderation, and the cultivation of virtues, as we have already seen. Added to the factors just discussed, the centrality of virginity in Roman culture was a contributing factor, as was the fact that Ambrose's own sister, Marcellina, was dedicated to virginity herself from when he was a young boy. She lived a semisecluded life in her family home, alongside a companion, Candida, who was also a virgin. This points to the pious household in which Ambrose had been raised. Marcellina would later become the subject of the third volume of Ambrose's first book, *Concerning Virgins*. In all, Ambrose lived and breathed ideas regarding "virginity" all his life.

The Church Context

In 355, the Roman Emperor Constantius II (317–61) deposed the Nicene bishop of Milan, Dionysius (bishop ca. 349–55), and installed Auxentius (bishop ca. 355–73/4), the pro-Homoean, as Milan's bishop. The Homoeans were an Arian group that taught that God the Son was similar to God the Father but rejected the use of the categories of substance and essence employed by Nicea.[58] Many Milanese converted to Christianity under Auxentius and became pro-Homoean themselves. But many Christian Milanese also remained pro-Nicene, that is, *Homoousians*—in opposition to Homoeans, and inherited a reputation as a group of troublemakers, especially after the deposition of Dionysius.

When Auxentius died in 374, Ambrose entered the picture as provincial governor with a mediating role between the pro-Homoeans and pro-Nicenes, who were deadlocked in debate about the choice of Auxentius's successor. On the one hand, the pro-Homoeans thought Ambrose, as a representative of secular authority, would continue to uphold their rights as the established church of the city. On the other hand, when the pro-Nicenes burst into Auxentius's basilica to challenge the election of his pro-Homoean successor, they seemed confident "that the usual stern punishments for public disorder would not be imposed against them."[59] Their confidence proved to be "well founded" and the governor seemed to speak on their behalf in his intention to allow them to "regain their voice" within a church that had marginalized them for twenty years.[60] With this demonstration of support, the pro-Nicenes responded by insisting Ambrose become the next bishop of Milan.

After initial hesitancy, Ambrose finally relented and agreed to be enrolled in all the ecclesiastical offices from porter to lector, exorcist, acolyte, subdeacon, deacon, priest, to finally bishop, in just under a week. But it would take Ambrose two years to write his first book, *Concerning Virgins*. The choice to write about virginity may be a happy accident; it was something Ambrose "stumbled upon" that worked to his advantage.[61] Indeed, some theorize that Ambrose pursued virginity as a topic because he felt incompetent to speak on theological-doctrinal matters.[62]

Despite being voted into his ecclesiastical role, there still were no guarantees that Ambrose had the support of Auxentius's congregation or clergy. Moreover, there would be further challenges to Ambrose's authority, given the context of Homoean-Nicene tensions. One challenge arose because of the entry into Milan in 379 of boy emperor Valentinian II (b. 371; r. ca. 375–92) and his dominant mother, Justina (340–91), from the Arian (Homoean) sect. The tension was only temporarily eased when Gratian (r. 367–83), a pro-Nicene, moved from Trier to Milan in 383. But with his death in the same year, the challenges from Justina and Valentinian II increased with a request to Ambrose for a return (or loan— Liebeschuetz says this was not clear) of one of the Milanese basilicas to the pro-Homoeans.[63]

It was in this tension between the Homoeans and the Nicene followers that Ambrose wrote his *Commentary on the Gospel of Luke.* This commentary contains many references to the church imagined as a woman as part of Ambrose's argument, but it also presents a church that models itself on Mary, who is mother and virgin. Following the basilica controversy of 386, during which Ambrose prevented the Homoeans' use of any of the Milanese basilicas, he came into conflict with the emperor, Valentinian. Ambrose states in the *Commentary* that Mary's motherhood and perpetual and "unblemished" virginity models the church's own purity and ability to birth Christians through baptism. Further, by paralleling Mary's motherhood and virginity with the church's own motherhood and virginity, Ambrose distinguishes the church from heretics and the scriptural Jews. It seems that Ambrose referred to the Jews metaphorically for anything heretical in the *Commentary* to show that heresies, new, old, or forthcoming, were really old challenges to the church—"as old as the scriptures themselves."[64] For Ambrose, as he explains in the *Commentary,* while Jews and heretics live literally in luxury and faithlessness, producing no fruit even when they have the chance, Christians are known for their simplicity, fruitfulness, and Nicene faith. This hints at how Mary's motherhood and virginity becomes an essential figure in Ambrose's arguments concerning the mystery of salvation.[65] Moreover, the church as a woman and mother modeled after Mary as mother and virgin became a political argument, intended to resolve the Homoean-Nicene debate, an ecclesiological argument about the nature of the church as virgin and mother, and an argument about Christian belief itself (virginity of the mind as a prerequisite to spiritual motherhood or the birthing of personal virtues).

The Number of Ecclesial Virgins and Ecclesial Credibility

One advantage from enrolling more virgins for the church concerned the validation of Ambrose's ecclesial position. Ambrose is credited with the role of promoting the ceremony of formally consecrating virgins in the church, the *velatio*, or veiling of virgins.[66] This ritual paralleled the Roman wedding, with the virgin wedding Christ through the church. The ceremony also drew from the veiling of Roman vestal virgins.[67] As representative of Christ but also of the church, the bishop acted as the mediator of this relationship and presided over the ceremony. As presider, the bishop took on a quasi-*paterfamilias* role, as we see in Ambrose's own words: "She whom I offer in my role as priest, whom I commend [to Christ] with fatherly affection."[68]

The *paterfamilias* role continued after the ceremony, by which the bishop became responsible for ensuring that the virgin's spiritual and material needs were met. This did not mean the virgin lived under the roof of the bishop. Rather, she remained in her parents' home. But, if the parents subsequently died, the bishop had to find a new home for the virgin, one in which there lived a "good" Christian woman. This paralleled the situation by which the *paterfamilias* had authority over his family and those within his household, and the *pontifex maximus* had authority over vestal virgins who left their families and the care of their *paterfamilias*.

The ceremony for enrolling virgins in the church communicated an image of ecclesial authority that Ambrose cultivated, given that he had little clerical experience himself, as we have seen. Yet Neil McLynn says, "Ambrose hesitates to claim any authority over the virgins."[69] McLynn cites *Concerning Virgins*, where Ambrose "confesses himself to be 'too weak to teach, unequal to the task of learning.'"[70] McLynn says Ambrose "could offer them only affection, instead of the magisterial authority of Cyprian's classic treatise [*On the Dress of Women*]."[71] In other words, Ambrose felt self-conscious about his theological abilities,[72] and this is why he wished to win the virgins by affection rather than by teaching authority.

Ambrose's encouragement of ecclesial virgins impinged on family territory. After the formal and public ceremony of being veiled, with ecclesial virgins continuing to live in their parents' home, some parents of virgins believed they could still use their daughters as pawns for marriage. Bringing in women from outside Milan to be consecrated as virgins within Milan would help overcome this difficulty. At the same time, it would fulfill the theatrics of presenting Ambrose as successful in his role as bishop, to the point that outsiders would choose to come to be veiled in Milan under his authority.

In fourth-century Milan, while there were wealthy women and men who converted to Christianity and lived ascetic lives, there were many converts who remained "unchristianized" and highly pagan. Among them were upper-class Christians engaged in Roman public careers. They were continually exposed to pagan worship, which permeated the empire. Roman sons kept the pagan religions of their fathers in public even after their mothers and wives had converted to Christianity. Many noblemen were happy to remain catechumens, leaving baptism to their deathbeds because of the fear of failing to meet its requirements, which could entail loss of their ability to engage in public life and loss of property.

Enter Ambrose with his encouragement of consecrated ecclesial virginity. By encouraging virgins for the church, Ambrose was establishing the Catholic Church as a political power amid an unchristianized, highly pagan society. Young girls who wished to present themselves as virgins for the church were often daughters of widows, at a time when male control over women, including their possessions and finances, was diminishing. There was reluctance, especially among the rich but even among pious widows, to give up their daughters for Christ, for the encouragement of ecclesial virgins entailed the handing over of one's riches to the church. Consequently, this was also about establishing the church's wealth literally as well as symbolically. When Ambrose said, "A virgin is a royal palace hall, subject to no man, but to God alone,"[73] he expressed the virgin's potential as a source of wealth for the church as well as her symbolic value as a container, a "hall," free from the taint of the unsacred. (Yet the poor were also part of the church's wealth, according to Ambrose.) The wealth of the ecclesial consecrated virgins and widows was not only passed on to the church, but their celibacy also "brought into the Christian household and the Christian basilicas a breath of immortality."[74] In other words, increased numbers of ecclesial consecrated virgins promoted the church as an image of pure divine power and authority.

The Power of Roman Virginity and Motherhood Myths

The power of the Roman Empire depended on Roman *matronae* for growth through the birthing of sons and daughters and the dispensing of their wealth to society. If *matronae* provided sons and daughters for the empire, it continued to have an image of immortality. If women did not become mothers and wives, then there was prestige tied to becoming virgins for the empire. As much as the empire depended on mothers, it depended too upon vestal virgins. Ambrose's call to ecclesial virginity competed with this dual rhetoric calling women to roles of prestige and recognition as *matronae* or *virgines* and calling for Roma's *pax deorum* and continued growth.

One of the purposes for employing the image and metaphor of "mother" for the church was to associate it with the high values family and procreation were given in Roman-Milanese society. The pairing of motherhood and virginity encouraged Ambrose's audience to accept his version of ecclesial virgin-motherhood, in that a virgin, although a celibate for life, would herself be fruitful as a mother in the spiritual sense.

THE CHURCH AS SPOUSE

Reinforcing this profamily argument, Ambrose would employ the metaphor of the church as a spouse (*sponsa*). This would assist in arguing about the nature of the relationship between the church and Christ:

> [While] our mother the church does not have a human husband [*virum*]…she does have an eternal spouse [*sponsum*]; she is wedded to the eternal Word of God without loss of purity, both as the whole church and as the individual human soul.[75]

Hunter says, "The use of marital imagery is central to Ambrose's apologetic argument on behalf of asceticism. Early in the work [*Concerning Virgins*], he first appeals to the virginity of the Church who, as the bride of Christ, embodies the paradoxical quality of spiritual fertility."[76] After establishing the church's virginity as the basis for the value of asceticism, Ambrose applies the argument to the Christian virgin, who "function[s] as a bride of Christ in a manner that [is] simply not open to other Christians, not even to other celibate Christians."[77] Here, Ambrose uses Psalm 45 and Song of Songs 4:7–8 as justification. Although Psalm 45 names two distinct sets of characters—daughters of kings (*filiae regum*) and a queen (*regina*)—Ambrose blurs the distinction between the two to uphold the daughter-queen-virgin-bride figure. In addition, Ambrose uses Song of Songs 4:7–8 ("You are altogether beautiful, my love; / there is no flaw in you. / Come with me from Lebanon") to argue for "the perfect and faultless beauty of the virginal soul";[78] for, through the ascetic marriage between the church and Christ, the Christian virgin is made spiritually beautiful, pure, and royal, like a queen, as in Psalm 45. Hunter describes Ambrose's attribution of purity to the ecclesial virgin, saying,

> By characterizing the consecrated virgin as the "bride of Christ," Ambrose is able to ascribe to the individual Christian virgin all of the purity and spiritual stature that he had previously attributed to the church.[79]

Again, this taps into the ancient Roman concept of the virtuous *matrona/materfamilias,* who was regarded as equally virtuous to the vestal *virgo* by the behavior she displayed. To be the bride of Christ as a virgin would be to exemplify ultimate virtuousness, since the ecclesial virgin would be both a spouse and a virgin.

Ambrose's choice to espouse the mother-virgin church to Christ was based on cultural considerations. Clark says a virgin who rejected earthly nuptials to become no one's wife was too shocking for the ancient Roman mind and could have deterred a woman from choosing virginity over marriage.[80] But, as we have seen, the vestal virgins were just as much a part of the culture of the ancient Roman Empire as the *matronae*; both helped *res publica Roma* to flourish, each in its own way. To overcome the incomprehensibility of one who chooses ecclesial virginity over marriage, though, Clark argues that the image of Christ as the celibate bridegroom of Christian virgin brides was introduced.[81] Imaging Christ as a bridegroom for the ecclesial virgin bride demonstrates the influence of Origen's portrayal of the church and the individual soul as bride to Christ, and, setting aside any shock from choosing to be unmarried, it gave some divine approval for the choice to become an ecclesial virgin.

Clark argues too that the ecclesial virgin as bride could be respected by making Christ and the virgins wedded but celibate. Thus, any notions of eroticism between them in relation to their union could be dismissed.[82] However, this was not necessarily the case with Ambrose, for, as we noted earlier, his idea of virginity was about intentionality and the cultivation of virtue, not just about being antierotic or antisex. Nevertheless, as a then-new concept, it would take some effort to convince Roman-Milanese Christians to understand another way of respectable living for a woman beyond the already accepted views of womanhood, including virginity.

Ambrose's concept of permanent virginity would have also communicated a permanent rejection of what was seen to be the ultimate destiny of woman as mother and wife. For even the Roman vestal virginhood was pointing to motherhood: the very absence of her practice of mothering pointed to what she should really be doing as a woman—mothering—according to ancient Roman culture. That is why vestal virgin service began when a girl was six to ten years old and would last for only thirty years. The expectation was that most vestal virgins would move on to marriage after their service. The alternative—of not ceasing service, and the consequent loss of mothers for society—would have an impact on Rome's future. For "the noble woman still carried with her the pride of the fertile womb," whereby "the power of Rome grows."[83] In becoming a virgin of the church, families were denied that Roman pride. Espousing the mother-virgin church to Christ the bridegroom introduced to Ambrose's audience a new way of living for a woman and it needed to tap into culturally accepted notions regarding woman and families to become accepted in the Roman-Milanese Christian community.

INCORPORATING MARY
AS VIRGIN-MOTHER-WIFE

To push further for the validity of ecclesial virginity and the argument that it too exercises a type of motherhood, Mary's virginity and motherhood were paralleled with the church's motherhood and virginity:

> Every soul that believes conceives and brings forth the Word of God and recognizes His works. May Mary's soul reside in each one of us to rejoice in God. According to the flesh there is only one Mother of Christ, but by faith Christ becomes the fruit of each one. For every soul receives the Word of God—on condition that it keeps chastity and that free from vice it preserves its purity immaculate.[84]

Church members imitate Mary, the Mother of God, by birthing Christ in their minds through their believing. But they cannot imitate her in birthing Christ in the flesh.[85] By promoting the virgin Mother Church, the virgin mother Mary, the fecund ecclesial virgin, in her growth in virtues, the *matrona-sponsa* and *virgo* figures were replaced as primal images of fecundity, purity, and continuity for the Christian Roman-Milanese.

We have already seen that Ambrose drew on Mary's example during the Nicene-Homoean debates. Mary as model of virgin motherhood was also essential to his argument for the valid calling of women to become ecclesial virgins for the church. Building on this, aligning Mary as mother, virgin, and wife with the church as mother, virgin, and wife helped communicate the church's nature, function, and relationships: it put forward the necessity of a "virginal" disposition for the church to be a mother and to birth children who were members of the church, and even to suggest the bishop's role as earthly "spouse" to the church.[86]

Ambrose explains Mary's role as wife, virgin, and spouse in relation to the church as wife, virgin, and spouse as follows:

> She was a wife, and she was a virgin. Virgin means that she never had any sexual intercourse with man; while the status of wife preserves her from the stigma of being thought to have lost her virginity once her pregnancy became apparent. The Lord preferred that some should doubt His divine origins rather than that they should cast suspicion on the purity of His Mother. In this way the virginity of holy Mary was preserved without detriment to her purity and without loss of reputation, even with those outside the Church. Also it would never do to give virgins of somewhat doubtful conduct and shady reputation the excuse that even the Mother of the Lord seemed under a cloud.[87]
>
> A married lady gives Him [Christ] birth, but a Virgin conceived Him. A wife conceived but a Virgin brought Him forth.[88]

As a wife, Mary's pregnancy was made valid even though she "became fruitful by One who was not her husband."[89] As a virgin, her purity and uprightness were upheld. Ambrose was so intent on affirming Mary's unusual situation that he would even allow for the questioning of Christ's divine origins provided that Mary's virgin-motherhood was elevated, respected, and undoubted. This was in part the role of Mary's spousal status, to avoid doubt being cast on her virginity/purity.

Another reason for referring to Mary to argue for the mother-virgin nature of the church was to oppose popular opinions that were against the superiority of virginity over married life, or that were against the ascetic having a particular privilege in this life and the next. Jovinian, who was condemned as a heretic in the synods of Rome and Milan (ca. 390); Helvidius, a fourth-century author who believed the mention of Jesus's "sisters and brothers" in the Bible indicated Mary was not a virgin postpartum; and the bishop Bonosus (fl. 391–414)[90] all notably questioned the virginity of Mary and the specific role of virginity in the economy of Christian salvation.

The Jovinian controversy posed the greatest threat because of its popularity and longevity, even long after Jovinian was condemned. In 396, Ambrose wrote a long letter, *Letter* 14, to the Vercelli church, "urging them to resist the efforts of some followers of Jovinian."[91] In this letter, Ambrose referred to the church as a bride to argue for the superiority of virginity over marriage.

Jovinian had taught that

1. virgins, widows, and married women were of the same merit because of baptism;

2. those who had been born again in baptism with full faith could not be overthrown by the devil; and

3. there was no difference between abstinence from food and receiving it with thanksgiving.

Of Jovinian's three theses, the first was especially controversial as it questioned the choice of those who lived the celibate religious life, including St. Jerome (ca. 347–419/420), St. Ambrose, and later, St. Augustine (354–430). It also questioned Ambrose's push for ecclesial virginity, since, with it, virginity would be regarded as equal to marriage, and marriage was already the preference of Roman citizens. While Jovinian argued for the equality of marriage and virginity, Jerome put forward the superiority of virginity by disparaging marriage. Meanwhile, Ambrose focused his arguments on the church and Mary as virgin and mother. In particular, Ambrose focused on Mary having kept her virginity after Jesus's birth (*virginitas post partum*).

Interestingly, the idea of *virginitas* was first applied to the church before its virginal nature was said to be exemplified by Mary.[92] As already noted, Ambrose's *Concerning Virgins* 1.31 speaks of this mother-virginal status of the church in what Hunter names the paradoxical status of the church in her fruitfulness and virginity. By the time Ambrose responded to Jovinian, Hunter says that it is no longer about defending Ambrose's personal thoughts on Mary but about an ecclesiological statement on the church's "supernatural character."[93]

Adding all the arguments together, Ambrose's *perpetua virginitas* (perpetual virginity) teaching connected to Mary and the church was important and vigorously defended: it involved an intricately woven argument involving christological, ecclesiological, and soteriological statements.[94] The arguments would fall apart if the motherhood in virginity of the church as modeled in Mary was questioned.

Not all references to the church as wife, virgin, and mother, however, point to or equate with Mary the Mother of God. In fact, Mary is not the only biblical figure Ambrose used for the Mother Church. He also referred to Miriam the prophet, from Exodus 15:20, because of her example of virginity "with unstained spirit" (see *Concerning Virgins* 1.12). In this passage, Ambrose explains that while the female church is figured in a few people such as Miriam, the life of the church as "virgin" exists in much more than the types.

PARALLELS WITH ORIGEN'S READING OF THE SONG OF SONGS

To support the image of the church as the spouse, bride, or betrothed, Ambrose refers often to passages from the Song of Songs,[95] but he also refers to it to support the image of the church as sister,[96] daughter,[97] virgin,[98] and mother.[99] Ambrose's image of the church as widow[100] is the only female or feminized ecclesial image that does not draw upon the Song of Songs.

The Song of Songs references speak of a conjugal relationship, which Ambrose uses to present the intimate relationship between the church and Christ as bride and bridegroom— especially in his sermons on Psalm 118. The relationship is not just between the church collectively and Christ, but also between the individual soul and Christ.[101] In *On Faith*, the church as sister is represented as an individual in an intimate relationship with Christ.[102] There are allusions to the Roman *matrona* or *materfamilias*[103] in this Mother Church, in the weeping mother,[104] in the one who breastfeeds good teachings,[105] and in the one to whom one shows *pietas*.[106]

Like Cyprian's portrayal of the church as bride, and using of the Song of Songs to justify this imaging, Ambrose shows parallels with Origen's reading of the Song texts and the visualization of the church as bride:

> in naming Christ as "the voice" in the Song of Songs 5:2;[107]

> in naming the church as bride to the bridegroom, Christ;[108]

> in stating that Christ feeds the church with his teachings, called "kisses," as shown in the Song of Songs,[109] just as Christ also feeds the church with his sacraments;[110] and

> in arguing that the church is worthy to be the bride of Christ, because "she" is graced and pure or "without blemish."[111]

In the previous chapter, we noted that Cyprian's understanding of the church as a bride resonated with Origen's visualization of the church as bride in his reading of the Song of Songs. Like Cyprian, Ambrose uses the Song of Songs as support for imaging the church as a bride. The difference between Cyprian's and Ambrose's uses of the bride metaphor, though, are that, where Cyprian imagined the collective church as the bride of Christ, Ambrose imagines the bride as both the church collectively and the individual soul; but both are wedded to Christ. This gives Ambrose justification to push for the argument of the ecclesial virgin married to Christ, fruitful or fecund spiritually, modeling her motherhood and virginity after the mother-virgin-spouse church and the mother-virgin-spouse Mary.

RELEVANCE FOR THE TRADITION OF THE CHURCH AS BRIDE, HOLY, VIRGIN, AND MOTHER

The earlier patristic writers used the image of church as a woman and mother as part of their inside-outside rhetoric in the face of heresy and schism. While for Irenaeus, Tertullian, and Cyprian, the mother was their dominant ecclesial metaphor; for Ambrose, it comes second to the image of spouse/bride, alongside the image of the virgin. This rhetorical development signals a change in ecclesial contexts and concerns from a focus solely on the demarcation of Christian identity by determination of the true mother (the orthodox church who nurtures and births her children), to the apologetic defense of the virgin church (made fruitful by the Holy Spirit and thus free from heresy), and the church as the bride of Christ (through whom alone is found salvation). The concern was no longer a mere presentation of the "better mother" (in Irenaeus's case). Neither was it a simple alignment of the church as mother with the culturally familiar Roman *materfamilias* (as it was for Tertullian), nor with the *matrona* with whom one remains or to whom one returns (as it was for Cyprian). For Ambrose, this complex image of the church as a mother-virgin-bride is used fruitfully to address the controversies and ecclesial issues raised by the Arian and Jovinian movements, but also the cultural concerns regarding ideas on the family and women's roles for the Roman Empire. The images of *matrona* or the *materfamilias* alone could not adequately capture Ambrose's message of the power of virginity, as was instilled in him as a Roman citizen and governor amid his cultural religious milieu. For Ambrose, the church—feminine in nature—is every woman, mother, wife, queen, and virgin, as needed for particular rhetorical purposes.

A highly significant aspect regarding Ambrose's imaging of the church as female, and a richness that needs to be recovered, is his imagination of the church as organic, with its members expected to grow from spiritual infancy to adulthood, by bringing forth justice and wisdom.[112] They are not merely to conceive Christ by their "excellent intentions but produce nothing in the way of good works."[113]

Notable is the complexity of female metaphors for the church. On the one hand, mother, virgin, and bride as understood by Ambrose and his predecessors, in nuanced ways, provide rich metaphors to facilitate ecclesiological, christological, and soteriological understandings. On the other hand, we are left with a tradition that originally had rich meanings but that, today, would encounter resistance from contemporary cultures, especially in the visuals of Mary and the church as virgin-mother, and in the argument that Mary labored without pain. Some of those rich meanings include the intent on the cultivation of virtues; having an integrated view between body and soul such that the body is a fine-tuned instrument when virtues are cultivated; and chastity as being about moderation rather than extremism. We are faced again with the same question as I posed at the end of the last chapter: Is it possible to reimagine these ecclesial metaphors of virgin, mother, and bride in order that they might continue to communicate the church's nature and its relationships?

CONCLUSION

In presenting the various factors that contributed to Ambrose's imaging of the church as a virgin, mother, and spouse, and to his ultimate introduction of Mary as virgin, mother, and spouse to justify his portrayal of the female church, possibly the most influential of the cultural influences upon Ambrose were the ancient Roman senses of the significance of the *virgo*. These senses were exemplified in the vestal virgin cult that is found at the very foundations of Roman civilization itself, and permeated Roman living at least until 394—given that in 391, Emperor Theodosius I had closed the temple and by 394, the cult was no longer publicly approved, and the vestals had disbanded.

In contrast to theories that categorize Ambrose as being enthusiastic about virginity and asceticism, we have seen that rather than taking a dualistic approach regarding the sacred and secular, the bodily and divine, Ambrose took a more hylomorphic approach. Thus, in his appropriation of Roman culture into his ecclesiology, and his enthusiasm for virginity, his intent was on presenting moderation rather than extremism, and harmony, such as between the soul and body, and in using whatever tools were available to him to justify his arguments.

We have also seen that Ambrose's appropriation of the *matrona-virgo-sponsa* image for the church had various motivations, which were a result of his convictions amid a mix of political, ecclesial, personal, and religious contexts. His view of the church as necessarily virginal to be matronal tapped into the Roman senses of the equal status of the virtuous *virgo* and *matrona*. But it also introduced the new concept of the ecclesial virgin-mother into Roman society, another valid way of life for a woman, which was not becoming someone's wife, or a vestal virgin, or being under the tutelage of agnates (male kin).

Introducing Mary as a model of virgin-motherhood gave validity to that way of life too. Moreover, defending Mary's virginal motherhood involved defending christological, ecclesiological, and soteriological arguments that go beyond the idea that Ambrose simply promoted the mother-virgin image because of his enthusiasm for virginity.

Resonance with Origen's images of the church and the individual soul as the bride of Christ are apparent in Ambrose's own portrayal of the church as female, as in Cyprian's imaging of the female church. The difference between Cyprian's and Ambrose's imaging, however, is that in Ambrose, there is a clear call to grow from an individual's spiritual infancy to spiritual adulthood, to become a spiritual mother for others and to reflect the motherhood-virginity of the church and Mary.

While there are contemporary criticisms toward the early church fathers' views of women, Ambrose's contexts promoted the application of specific female images for the church—images that aligned with culturally accepted ones and that also responded to political and church issues. Moreover, it is with the significance of virginity and motherhood, which permeated his Roman culture, that he thus applies the culturally resonant metaphor "virgin-mother-spouse." In turning now to Augustine's imagination of the church as every female hitherto conceivable—daughter, mother, wife, virgin, sister, and queen—we will see that these are also applied in response to complex contexts.

5

The Formidable Mother against the Heretics

The whole Church, our mother,
which exists in the saints
...gives birth to each and every one.

—Augustine, *Letter* 98.5

By the time Augustine used female metaphors for the church, his predecessors had already set the stage. Every female recognized and respected in the surrounding Roman and pagan culture and in Scripture was prime picking for Augustine—the daughter, bride, virgin, queen, wife, mother, and widow. These figures had previously been used to present a specific church—whether as a stern authority, loving parent, protected entity, or an exalted and glorified version of herself. Further, the idea of the church as at the same time mother, spouse, and virgin, modeled after Mary as mother, spouse, and virgin had been made possible through Ambrose.

Augustine (b. 354, Thagaste; d. 430) became the bishop of Hippo Regius, North Africa. But before he was bishop, he had led a cosmopolitan lifestyle in Rome and Milan, where the Catholic Church was engaging with the surrounding culture to transform it. This contrasted with the North African experience of the church (i.e., in the experiences of Tertullian and Cyprian's Christian communities), where it saw itself in contrast with the world around it.

In this chapter, we explore Augustine's use of various female images for the church in response to multiple heresies, and whether the church must necessarily be called virgin, mother, bride, queen, or some other female figure to describe herself for all times and circumstances. We examine the utility of such descriptions, but also their limitations. Moreover, we see that in Augustine, the church is

113

not simply the virgin-mother reflected in Mary; rather, in terms of female figures, the church is any woman who would help to address the controversies, concerns, and needs of the church in Augustine's time.

AUGUSTINE'S RHETORICAL APPROACH

Like the Catholic Church of Rome and Milan, Augustine did not completely reject his surrounding milieu. In fact, he was "prepared to plunder pagan culture of everything that is of value, on the understanding it rightfully belongs to Christianity, and to reject anything that is alien to it."[1] Augustine's criterion for selection was the Scriptures. If it was of use, it might legitimately be adopted, studied, taught, and adapted by the Christian. At the same time, he believed "pagan" wisdom paled into insignificance when compared with the Bible itself, which contained all knowledge.[2]

In his *On Christian Teaching*, Augustine shows that signs have meaning not in themselves but because societies have come to an agreement on the meaning for them.[3] In the same way, whatever rhetorical tool or concept Augustine applies for his audience, they must have agreement on its meaning, including that of the church as a woman, mother, bride, or virgin. Augustine's desire was particularly to teach the faith at the level of his hearers, and he believed that "love" should be the motivating factor.[4]

To be heard, Augustine went to such lengths as to identify and journey with his audience. In her analysis of the audience for the *Confessions*, Annemaré Kotzé argues that, despite the tone of the text, which opposed the heretical group, the Manicheans, the text was addressed both to what she called the marginal Christian, one who was wavering toward Manicheanism and doubting his or her Christian stance, and to the marginal Manichean, one who was doubting the teachings of its founder, Mani, but needed good reason to switch allegiance to Christianity. In book 3 of his *Confessions*, Augustine presents himself as one who travels along the same journey as the doubter, experiencing Manicheanism and Christianity, struggling between the two choices, but finally making the hard decision of committing to Christianity, hoping in turn that both the marginal Manichean and the marginal Christian would be convinced to choose Christianity.[5]

On the use of rhetorical devices to connect with his audience, particularly as personified Mother Church, Augustine says,

> Wishing also to bring the issue of the Donatists to the attention of the very simplest people and, in general, of the ignorant and unlearned, and to do so in a way that would be as easy for them to remember as possible, I made up a psalm that went through the Latin alphabet and that could be sung by them, but it only got as far as the letter V….While it is true that I left out the final three [letters], in place of them I added something at the end to serve as a sort of epilogue, as though Mother Church were speaking to them….I did not want to do this in some other song-form lest the requirements of meter would force some words on me that were less well known to the general public. This psalm begins in this way: "All you who rejoice over peace, now judge the truth." This is also its refrain.[6]

This was a reference to Augustine's *A Psalm against the Party of Donatus* (written between end of 393 to start of 394), composed to convince the Donatists to return to unity with the Catholic Church. The Donatists had been a group against whom, from the moment of his ordination to priesthood, Augustine had spent the majority of his time refuting and requesting them to return to the "most true" church, the Catholic Mother.[7] Carl Springer, in fact, comments on Augustine's *A Psalm against the Party of Donatus* that, for the first time in patristic history, "Mother Church" spoke for herself, using the rhetorical tool *prosopopoeia*—giving voice to what otherwise would be a silent object.[8] After beginning the psalm with the refrain and then in the course of repeating it twenty-one times, Augustine issues a final impassioned closing speech where he has Mother Church say, "O my sons, what do you find wrong with your mother? I want to hear why you have deserted me."[9] After repeating that the choice to return to unity with the Catholic Church was in the hands of the Donatists, the use of the mother metaphor was a final plea to convince rather than to command the Donatists to return to unity. We see in the next section why Augustine applied such a powerful rhetorical tool for the church. But first, we investigate Augustine's idea of the church as based on the image of his own mother, Monica, in his engagement with the Donatists.

THE CHURCH AS MONICA THE ROMAN MOTHER, AGAINST THE DONATISTS

The description Augustine provides in the *Confessions* regarding his mother fits the description of the revered Roman *materfamilias, univira,* and Roman citizen:

> She had been married to one man only, had loyally repaid what she owed to her parents, had governed her household in the fear of God, and earned a reputation for good works. She had brought up her children, in labor anew with them each time she saw them straying away from you…she took care of us all as though all had been her children, and served us as though she had been the daughter of all.[10]

As wife to one man only, Monica was *univira.* In paying due respect to her parents and laboring over the faith of her household, particularly her children, she fulfilled her Roman (and Christian) duty of *pietas.* Bringing up her children and leading her household to practice *pietas,* she was *materfamilias* and a good Roman citizen. This Roman *matrona* was also like the Mother Church in the following ways:

> Monica was a mother who sought and corrected her child, as we see in the previously stated text from *Confessions.* In this way, she was like the Mother Church, with her own dealings with the heretical group, the Donatists, who strayed from the church and who Augustine tried to convince to return;[11]

As Monica comforted Augustine with her milk, so Mother Church feeds her children with the "food of faith";[12] and

The sorrowful Monica cried tears of intercession for her son and mourned his spiritual death,[13] just as Mother Church despairs in *A Psalm against the Party of Donatus*, where she asks what she has done to offend the Donatists.[14] Her final appeal to her wayward children is presented as a crucifying pain at their death or their leaving of her, the church.[15]

There is further evidence of parallels between Mother Church and Monica in Springer's exploration of Augustine's use of "mother" for Monica and the church. There are parallels between Augustine's depiction of Monica as a peacemaker in the *Confessions* and Mother Church's peacemaking with the Donatists in *A Psalm against the Party of Donatus*.[16] As Monica sought to win over her son to Catholicism through many tears, so did Mother Church in this psalm seek to win over the Donatists. Further, Augustine's resistance to conversion could be paralleling the Donatists' insistence on maintaining their version of Christianity and resistance to Catholic conversion.

The Donatist movement had its beginnings around 312, when Bishop Felix of Abtugni ordained Caecilian, successor to Mensurius. All three, Felix, Mensurius, and Caecilian, were considered *traditores* (traitors) to the Catholic Church. Caecilian's opponents, the Numidian bishops, elected a rival bishop, Maiorinus, who died shortly afterward. Donatus of Casae Nigrae became his successor and the "party of Maiorinus" became known simply as the "Donatists."

In 401 and 403, the sixth and eighth councils of Carthage, respectively, were called to invite the Donatists to return to Catholic unity. By 404, the ninth council of Carthage, after negative responses from the Donatists at previous councils, including violent responses from several members, "called for firm action against the Donatists."[17] In 405, the Eastern Roman emperor, Arcadius (r. 383–408), and the Western Roman emperor, Honorius (r. 393–423), concerned with the preservation of the Catholic Church in Africa, called for unity between the Catholics and Donatists, and produced the edict of ecclesiastical unity (as well as other edicts making

117

rebaptisms invalid). In this edict, the Donatists were identified as a schismatic group that had grown into a heresy and thus were subject to Roman antiheretical law. But Honorius then issued a law of religious tolerance. The 410 council of Carthage rejected Honorius's tolerance law. A council was held in Carthage in 411 where 285 Donatist bishops and 286 Catholic bishops met, resulting in antischismatic legislation against the Donatists, and where Augustine was proven to be "the champion of Catholics."[18]

Like the rigorists from Cyprian's time, the Donatists saw the administration of sacraments by *traditores* as invalid, but unlike the rigorists, and beyond the thought of the laxists, the Donatists allowed for the rebaptism of the *lapsi* (from the Diocletian persecution of 303). The Donatists were thus no arrogant Christian schismatic group wanting to set up their own version of Christianity. Rather, they wished to stay true to the North African ecclesial tradition set by Tertullian and Cyprian.[19]

Springer says that when Augustine appealed to the Donatists to return to the church for the first time, Mother Church was not merely spoken of but also spoke for herself. Augustine's initial approach was not to force the Donatists into unity with the church but rather to appeal to them through reason or argument. As the Mother Church of the Cyprianic-Tertullianic tradition was persecuted, so did this Catholic mother present herself persecuted by the Donatists—wounded or torn (*laceror*) and crucified or deeply suffering (*crucior*) by their desertion of her (*deseruistis*).[20]

But the appeal to the minds and hearts of the Donatists using *prosopopoeia* was of no avail as the Donatists remained in opposition to requests to return to Mother Church. In fact, the Donatists claimed that as the persecuted Mother Church themselves, they were the true "mother." Augustine responded by adjusting his version of the mother. Having failed to persuade them using the persecuted mother image, as one who pleads for her children's return in *A Psalm against the Party of Donatus*, Augustine portrays Mother Church as a disciplinarian to force the Donatists to return to the Catholic Church. This kind of mother disciplines her wayward children for the sake of their salvation:

Whatever, then, the true and lawful mother does, even if it is felt to be harsh and bitter, she does not repay with evil, but applies the good of discipline to expel the evil of iniquity, not out of harmful hatred, but out of healing love.[21]

Augustine further justifies the use of force by claiming that God enforces righteousness on both the good and the bad.[22]

Why were the Donatists so stubborn in their ecclesiological thinking? For them, in following the African ecclesial heritage, the purity of the church depended on the Tertullianic baptismal oaths and the Cyprianic sense of the unity of the church—the good pure church, contained as a sealed fountain or enclosed garden, against the hostile impure world. Anyone considered impure or a sinner was to be cast out.[23] But some ministers who thought of themselves as following the African tradition did not consider moral purity to be part of the Tertullianic-Cyprianic requirements.[24] Consequently, the presence of immoral ministers and *traditores* among those who stayed true and pure within the Catholic community led Donatists to question the guarantee of purity in the church. Naturally, the Donatists began to claim that only a church that rid itself of immoral and unworthy ministers and members could have the guarantee of the indwelling of the Holy Spirit, and of valid sacraments.

Augustine challenged the Donatists by stating that one could not really know and guarantee the holiness and worthiness of a church minister or recipient of the sacrament.[25] Indeed, church numbers had grown so large that the moral and spiritual maturity of ministers or of recipients of the sacraments could not be readily verified. The holiness of the church had to depend on something beyond the merits of individual church members. In addition, if sinners were to be cast out from the church of saints, Augustine feared their chance at salvation would be lost.

Augustine found his solution to the Donatist arguments through the theology of Tyconius, a great Donatist theologian himself, but one who was excommunicated by his own community for his rejection of their "pure" form of Catholicism. Tyconius recognized that the church contained a few saints among many sinners, so rebaptism was of no consequence. Tyconius also saw the church

119

as the "Body of Christ," with "two parts, or the one Body, which could be seen simultaneously as holy and as wicked."[26] Augustine (using Tyconius) thus proposed mixed membership for the church on earth, saints with sinners, and was adamant that only at the Last Judgment were they to be separated. In fact, it was already the church's practice to have sinners among its saints, including among the Donatists, and it was only the Donatist claims to purity of their ministry that jarred with orthodox Catholicism on this matter.[27]

Augustine also introduced the concept of Christ as head of the church, which, along with his body, made up the whole Christ (*totus Christus*), pointing to the true source of holiness—Christ, not the church member—as enabling the validity of the exercise of sacraments. The closeness in relationship between Christ the head and his Body the church through the *totus Christus* analogy also facilitated the analogy of nuptial unity between Christ and the church.[28] For Augustine, Christ is the bridegroom, king, and savior while the church is his bride, his redeemed people. As the head, Christ must have a body so he takes on flesh via "the bridal chamber which is the Virgin's womb."[29]

With the church on earth consisting of sinners and saints and Christ as its head, the sinful minister could administer the sacraments without diminishing the effect of the sacrament (*ex opere operato*) and the purity and truth of Mother Church could remain intact. The clear demarcation between the church and the world as promoted by the Cyprianic-Tertullianic tradition was ecclesiologically too narrow for Augustine, especially since the church was no longer a sect that pitted itself against the world. Rather, it had legal and social legitimacy within the empire and it was assimilating many of the elements of its surrounding culture. Furthermore, Augustine's cosmopolitan experience in Rome and Milan prevented him from adopting the Donatists' narrow thinking on church membership.[30]

Since the church entailed sinners mixed with saints, Augustine shifted the picture of the absolute purity of the church from completely existing in the temporal earthly realm (as per the North African tradition) to existing in its completeness in the eternal (eschatological) realm. The understanding of the early church thus changed from a pure church against the impure world (a world that had intermittently persecuted the church) to a church that was supported by this world through Roman imperial favor upon it (against schismatics and heretics).

However, it does not necessarily follow that the church on earth, inclusive of sinners, was not pure. In the Augustinian terminology of the "two cities," the city of God and the city of the temporal earthly realm, it is not as if Rome equates with the church on earth while Jerusalem equates with the church of heaven. Rather, while the visible church consists of both good and evil people, there is, within this church, saints who follow God's will and live by charity and love. Therefore the "city of God" exists in both the present and the future. That is, the church in the historical present (*ecclesia quae nunc est*) aims to image the church as it would one day be in the eschatological future (*ecclesia qualis futura est*) via its members who seek the will of God in faith and charity. It is even claimed that Augustine named the church on earth that "reconciled part" of the world.[31] Interestingly, Augustine pursues purity more vigorously than the Donatists, distinguishing between Christians who belong in the church and physically engage in the sacraments but who do not grow spiritually, and faithful people who grow together spiritually in faith and love as part of the community. Even with these two distinctions, there remains only the one church—an argument put forward against Donatist accusations that the Catholics had created two churches.[32]

Drawing on these distinctions, Augustine pictured the church of saints as "a lily in the midst of thorns" and as his "beloved in the midst of daughters" (Song 2:2): the lily represents the good people of the church while, surprisingly, the thorns and daughters represent the sinners within the church, not the world outside. Augustine's picture of the church as the sinful daughter notably contrasts with the city as a daughter motif of ancient Near Eastern societies where, in fact, the city as a daughter was to be protected from invading parties and kept a "virgin." With this mix of sinners and saints in the temporal earthly realm, Mother Church was no longer the monolithic holy figure presented by Cyprian and Tertullian. Rather she is the beloved bride who represents the good within the church but who is also a daughter representing sinners.

THE CHURCH AS DAUGHTER-QUEEN-BRIDE-VIRGIN OF PSALM 45

Augustine had no interest in using bridal ecclesial language until the Donatists and Manicheans used this language to claim to be the pure brides of Christ. He was also reluctant to adopt the Song of Songs[33] and preferred other texts to describe the union between the church and Christ (e.g., Ps 44 or Eph 5:23–32).[34] But in the end, Augustine used Psalm 45 and the Song of Songs to reclaim the image of the Catholic Church as the true and pure bride of Christ.

With the Donatists, Augustine read the Song of Songs in terms of Psalm 45, which contains a female figure who is a daughter, bride, virgin, and queen. As the Donatists used certain Song of Songs texts to claim the true Mother Church, describing her as a sealed fountain in the Cyprianic tradition, so Augustine applied the same texts to reclaim Mother Church for the Catholic tradition.[35] The sealed fountain did not refer to the entire church, as argued by the Donatists, but only to those called by God, the just, and those who exercised charity, among the sinners and saints. Augustine even made the distinction between sinners and saints by taking the images of a garden and a fountain from the Song of Songs and stating that the garden signified those outwardly baptized while the fountain represented holy citizens of the angelic city/society.[36]

With the Manicheans, Augustine utilized the female figure of Psalm 45 as prefiguring the church in the Old Testament. This, in turn, proved the Manicheans erroneous, for they rejected the Old Testament altogether. Manicheanism originated in the latter half of the third century, with Mani (216–76 CE), a Persian, who was from a Jewish-Christian background. Manicheanism was a rival to Christianity in replacement of classical paganism. Manicheanism's central figure was Christ and it imitated many Christian elements. Its main attraction was its syncretism of various religions and philosophies, combined with reason and asceticism. Manicheanism provided answers to existential questions like evil, creation, and the order of the world. Its answers were dualistic, pitting light against dark, God against earthly matter, the Old Testament against the New. In fact, Manicheans not only rejected the Old Testament but also parts of the New that did not agree with their theology. Salvation depended on the separation of good from evil, which in creation existed as a mix of the two. Salvation was acquired through gaining special knowledge (*gnosis*) and undertaking ascetical practices like fasting and refraining from sex because of a hatred of the body.

Manicheanism mimicked Christianity in other ways too, such as in its hierarchical structure[37] and practices.[38] Augustine spent nine years early in his life within this sect until his disillusionment with it after meeting their most "learned" bishop, Faustus. After many dialogues with Faustus, Augustine lost confidence in Manicheanism and became a sceptic. Moreover, Augustine came to see Manicheanism as a Christian heresy of a dangerous type.[39]

In *Against Faustus,* Augustine sought to reclaim the "virgin-bride" title from the Manicheans.[40] In this text, the Mother Church has "full-grown children" and a "son" in Augustine, and is named virgin and bride to reclaim the "virgin-bride" title. Augustine does this, on the one hand, by saying that the truth is found only in the "milk" (teaching) and "bread" (Eucharist) of the church. On the other hand, Augustine says the Manicheans with their "impious vanity" and "astonishing shamelessness" are "sacrilegious" and "impure." Therefore, for Augustine, the true Mother Church's children need to keep their minds uncorrupted by the heretics' impurity. Furthermore, he says Mother Church's full-grown children are in no danger of taking in their errors. But the babes or spiritual infants need Augustine's "food" and his counsel against the Manicheans.[41] Note that in this feeding, Augustine as bishop acts like Mother Church, but remains distinct from her, just as Cyprian represented Mother Church but also remained distinct from her.[42]

THE CHURCH AS THE "NEW EVE"

For Augustine, the church imagined as a woman is also the "new Eve," a contrast from the original Eve, who births children only to die in the end. The life into which the children of Eve are born is one in which it is the human condition to sin, that is, to follow in the footsteps of Adam and Eve, the couple representative of the human race who disobeyed God and were thrown out of the

Garden of Eden to live a life of suffering and death. The inheritance that Adam and Eve passed on to their children is a life characterized by suffering, sin, and death.

On this understanding, Augustine presents the church as the new Eve, a contrast to the original Eve, and a bride to Christ. This church, together with Christ, rebirths and parents the children of Adam and Eve from a life marked by sin and death, to a life that gives new hope and calls people out of sin into eternal living through the spiritual life. Baptism is that key ritual performed within Mother Church that rebirths the children of Adam and Eve into a new life, a new hope of salvation, into eternal living. This is what it means for Augustine to call the church the "new Eve." For him, while Eve is the "Mother of the Living," the church as the new Eve is the "Mother of the Spiritually Living," as he says,

> Because two parents got us unto death, two parents have gotten us unto life. The parents who got us unto death are Adam and Eve. The parents who have gotten us unto life are Christ and the Church. My own father who begot me was Adam for me, and my own mother was Eve for me...brothers, in what way were we born? Certainly, to die....But father God and mother Church do not engender for this end. They engender for eternal life, because they themselves are eternal. And we have eternal life as the inheritance promised us by Christ...we are members of Christ, we must be hoping for the inheritance.[43]

Augustine's use of Mother Church as the new Eve was especially helpful in his refutation of the Manicheans, who wished to disregard the Old Testament in favor of the New and to regard Adam and Eve as simply products of a war between the kingdoms of light and darkness. For Manicheans, Adam and Eve were not created out of goodness, as both Genesis 1 and 2 attest. Rather, they originated from demonic parents and their purpose was to confine particles of light by sexual reproduction. However, by calling the church the new Eve, Augustine affirmed the Old Testament version of the Adam and Eve narrative, and affirmed the condition of concupiscence in humanity. Evil in the world is explained not in the way the Manicheans describe but rather by the choices of and tendencies toward disobedience and self-will that counter goodness. For Augustine, this is called *concupiscence*, and Adam and Eve's actions, which led to their exile from the Garden of Eden, exemplify this.

Augustine did not only call people to a new life by baptism into Mother Church as the new Eve. He also presented the church as the new Eve to call church members to spiritual growth. He says that they can choose to emulate Mother Church by growing spiritually and bringing others to baptism, or they can emulate the old Eve, be led astray in their minds, become unchaste, and consequently stunt their own spiritual growth:

> Preserve that virginity in your minds; virginity of the mind is the integrity of Catholic faith. In the same way as Eve was corrupted by the serpent's talk, so must the Church remain a virgin by the gift of the Almighty. And so, just as Mary gave birth in her womb as a virgin to Christ, so let the members of Christ give birth in their minds, and in this way you will be the mothers of Christ. It isn't something out of your reach, not something beyond your powers, not something incompatible with what you are. You became children, become mothers too. You were the mother's children when you were baptized, then you were born as members of Christ. Bring whomever you can along to the bath of baptism, so that just as you became children when you were born, you may likewise be able, by bringing others along to be born, to become mothers of Christ as well.[44]

Here, we see that Mary as virgin mother plays an important part in Augustine's rhetoric against the Manicheans. But Mary as virgin mother would become more important for Augustine in the refutation of the Jovinianists, who, as we have seen, argued for the equal value of marriage and virginity as paths to spiritual salvation. The virginity of Mary in her mind and body gives way to the birthing of Christ, modeling in an ultimate and unique way for members of the church (especially for ecclesial virgins) how virginity leads to spiritual fecundity.

THE CHURCH AS
"MOTHER-VIRGIN" MARY

In Augustine's imagination of the church as a mother, he presents a few matriarchs from the Old Testament (Sarah,[45] Rebecca, and Tamar[46]) in addition to the new Eve as models for the church. But it is the church as mother-virgin, modeled through Mary, that becomes the dominant female church metaphor for him as he fights the Jovinianists, in the last part of his life. In fact, the church as mother-virgin becomes one of two dominating church metaphors for him. The other is the church as the whole Body of Christ, *totus Christus*, where Christ is the head and the church is made of various parts of the body with their different talents, as seen in the Pauline text 1 Corinthians 12:12–14.

The use of *mother-virgin*, as we know from the previous chapter, comes out of the context of opposing Jovinian. While Jerome responded by valuing virginity at the expense of disparaging marriage, Augustine takes the middle road and upholds the goodness of both marriage and virginity, while nevertheless preferring virginity over marriage. In *On Holy Virginity*, Augustine upholds both by explaining that married women and female virgins are both able to spiritually birth Christ if they follow the "will" of God:

> Both married women of faith and virgins consecrated to God are Christ's mothers spiritually, because with holy practices and with love they do the will of the Father, *with a pure heart and good conscience and sincere faith* (1 Tim 1:5). Those, however, who give birth physically in the married state do not give birth to Christ but to Adam, and therefore, because they know what they have given birth to, they hasten to have their children made members of Christ by being bathed in the sacraments.[47]

Augustine thus prefers virginity over marriage because marriage produces children who are born into a tendency to sin, which leads ultimately to death, exemplified in Adam and Eve, but virginity leads to virtuousness and thus leads away from sin and toward eternal life.

Augustine's preference for virginity is likely to have been due to an influence from Ambrose, who also spoke of virginity in terms of the mind, as we saw in the previous chapter. But Ambrose was not so concerned with keeping a virgin body and in fact saw no point in bodily virginity if virginity in the mind was neglected. It is possible, too, that Augustine's preference derived from an internalizing of the Roman mythic meaning of vestal virginity. The most interesting possibility, though, points to Augustine's relationship with the mother of his son, Adeodatus, as leading to Augustine's preference for virginity not just in the mind but also in the body. Augustine had hoped to marry the mother of Adeodatus, but because she was of a lower class, Monica would not allow the marriage. Instead, Augustine's mother chose another bride for him to set him on the right path of good Roman citizenship. Brokenhearted, the mother of Adeodatus then chose celibacy for life. As Adeodatus's mother took up the secular celibate life, so did Augustine, but in the Christian sense, taking up the life he had postponed for so long.[48] The argument proposed by Asiedu is that Augustine had equated conversion to Christianity with taking up a life of continence, and therefore marriage for Augustine would have been a personally self-indulgent choice. However, in reading the *Confessions*, it becomes evident that Augustine's choice to be Christian and celibate was more complex than this argument suggests, even if his thought about conversion and continence was a contributing factor. But as Augustine's conflict with the Jovinianists show, the defense of virginity is a defense of the nature of the church and of the nature of salvation, in Augustine's perspective. In addition, his defense of virginity is made regarding his idea that virginity assists in the pursuit of virtuousness, while sex is about attending to the individual self and its carnal needs.

With his preference for virginity, even as he upholds marriage, Augustine challenges the Roman values of marriage and motherhood over virginity:

> No one should think, therefore, that actual motherhood can make up for the loss of virginity even for women who look for nothing in marriage other than to have children to dedicate to the service of Christ.[49]

Even if marriage and motherhood lead to the birthing of virgins for the church, Augustine says this is not a good about marriage but has more to do with nature.[50]

This need to give higher regard to virginity than to marriage so as to avoid sex is especially evident in Augustine's *Sermons* 191 and 192. The main addressees of these texts were the female virgins of the church who needed reassurance that even as they were virgins, they were married, but to someone who would not take away their virginity. Furthermore, Augustine argues that somehow the virgins were mothering, in the more fruitful way—the spiritual rather than the fleshly way. *Sermon* 191 demonstrates this:

> So the Church imitates the Lord's mother—not in the bodily sense, which it could not do—but in mind it is both mother and virgin....She, therefore, in whose footsteps you are following, not only conceived without staying with a man, but also gave birth while still staying a virgin. Imitate her as far as you can; not in her fruitfulness, because you cannot do this and preserve your virginity. She alone was able to have both gifts, of which you chose to have one; because you would lose this one, if you wished to have both....It does not follow, however, that Christ is nothing for you, just because he is the offspring of one single virgin. You have not, indeed, been able to bear him as a son in the flesh, but you have found him as a husband in your hearts; and such a husband that your fidelity can cling to him as redeemer, while your virginity need not fear him as ravisher....Nor should you count yourselves barren because you remain virgins; since this very integrity of the flesh, chosen for love, contributes to the fruitfulness of the mind. Do what the apostle says: since you are not thinking of the affairs of the world, how to please husbands, think of the affairs of God, how to please him in all things, so that instead of wombs fruitful with offspring, you may have minds fruitful with all the virtues.[51]

Why the need for such reassurances? We recall here the Roman prioritizing of the woman who married and mothered children. Even when a woman chose temporary vestal virginity, the very absence of husband and children in this way of living pointed even more to the woman's imperative contribution to the Roman Empire as wife and mother. Here, Augustine ensures the virgin understands she is no longer mother to "flesh," almost as if to say she is no longer a woman and mother existing for the Roman Empire. She forfeited motherhood for Rome by choosing permanent virginity in the church. At the same time, by presenting virginity in the church as then somehow fulfilling those Roman values, the virgin is presented as not only married but as having the better husband (Christ), and as mothering the more important child or children (the virtues). Thus, Augustine presents the best possible outcome, whereby virginity is upheld but fulfills ideals regarding the woman, and the virgin gets to keep her physical body intact even as she becomes a mother to virtues and is married to Christ—in colloquial terms, Augustine (with his preference for virginity and Roman mindset) and the ecclesial virgin (with her Roman mindset) have their cake and eat it too!

VIRGINITY OF BOTH MIND AND BODY THROUGH MARY AND ECCLESIAL VIRGINS

While Ambrose's focus on virginity was more about the mind than the body, Augustine calls for his audience to seek virginity in both mind *and* body. He particularly praises ecclesial virgins above other church members, such as mothers and widows (the latter having once been mothers or having engaged in sexual intercourse as married persons), because of their ability to reflect virginity not just in their minds but also in their bodies. Augustine describes the virgins as imitating Mary's virginity in mind and body, and this in turn reflects the church's own motherhood and virginity:

> Since, therefore, as the apostle says, the whole Church is *a virgin betrothed to the one man Christ* (2 Cor 11:2), what great honor is due to those of its members who preserve even in

their bodies what the whole Church preserves by faith, in imitation of the mother of its spouse and Lord! For the Church too is both virgin and mother. If she is not a virgin, why are we concerned for her integrity? If she is not a mother, why do we address ourselves to her children? Mary gave birth physically to the head of this body; the Church gives birth spiritually to that head's members. In both, virginity is no obstacle to fertility; in both, fertility does not extinguish virginity. The Church as a whole is holy both physically and spiritually, but she is not physically a virgin as a whole, though she is spiritually. How much greater is her holiness, therefore, in those of her members in whom she is a virgin both physically and spiritually?[52]

Given that one of Augustine's dominant metaphors for the church was mother-virgin and that Mary and the ecclesial virgins exemplified this—but especially Mary in her unique claim to both virginity and motherhood in mind and body—Mary would be the ultimate role model for both men and women in the church. We find, too, that Mary is presented as a model for the church in Augustine's *Sermons* 192, 196, and 370.

At the same time, Augustine puts Mary forward specifically as a model for the virgins, while he puts forward Anna as a model for widows, and Elizabeth for married women.[53] This challenges the idea that Mary is the singular model for being a Christian, and specifically as a model for women in her virgin-motherhood. Just as Augustine asked separate groups of women to turn to Anna or Elizabeth (from the New Testament) and used other scriptural women (Rebecca, Tamar, and Sarah from the Old Testament) as models for the Christian church, so it is possible to imagine various scriptural figures in the Old and New Testaments as models of faith beyond Mary as the singular model of the church and faithful discipleship.

IS MARY A BRIDE/SPOUSE AS THE CHURCH IS BRIDE/SPOUSE?

The church is not only a mother and virgin but also a spouse. If Augustine presented Mary as model for the church, whom he describes also as mother, virgin, and spouse, as the church is married to Christ, does that give us the awkward situation in which Mary is married to her own son, Jesus? Certainly, this incestuous relationship is suggested in *Sermon* 191.2: "So then, if faith can believe that God was born in the flesh, it does not doubt that each of these things was possible for God...for the infant bridegroom to come forth from his chamber, that is from the virgin's womb, without damage to his mother's virginity."[54] But the text reveals that the role of "spouse" to Christ is explicitly only for the church. Meanwhile, motherhood and virginity are the shared roles for Mary and the church, as Augustine says: "The Church imitates the Lord's mother—not in the bodily sense, which it could not do—but in mind it is both mother and virgin."[55]

In *Sermons* 187, 188, and 192, where the church is called to imitate Mary, the bridal chamber image appears. But this is an image that is undeveloped and no associations with this bridal image are made with Mary. As Geoffrey Dunn says of these sermons, the emphasis is on the marriage of the divine Word with human flesh, rather than on Mary as bride or bridal chamber.[56] In *Sermon* 195, the call is for the church to imitate Mary's fecundity and virginity while seeking to be Christ's spouse. Dunn says there is no attempt in this sermon to parallel the church's spousal role with Mary.[57] This clearly indicates that the identification of Mary with the church is not all-inclusive. Augustine recognizes the limits of his use of this image and deliberately excludes the unacceptable incestual paralleling of Mary as bride with the church as bride of Christ.

A DIFFICULT ANALOGY

While Mary as virgin mother and model of the church as virgin mother formed a large part of Augustine's argument with the Jovinianists, he saw the limitations of this modeling of the church on Mary. One of the greatest limitations was that Mary was unique in being able to birth Jesus both in her "mind" and through her body. If Mary had birthed Christ, and from Christ the church was birthed, that would mean that Mary would be above the church and not simply one of its exemplary members. Augustine could not accept that Mary was above the church, so he argued she was a member of it. *Sermon* 72A demonstrates Augustine's difficulty and his attempt to reconcile the difficulty:

> It means more for Mary to have been a disciple of Christ than to have been the mother of Christ. It means more for her, an altogether greater blessing, to have been Christ's disciple than to have been Christ's mother. That's why Mary was blessed, because even before she gave him birth, she bore her teacher in her womb….Christ is truth, Christ is flesh; Christ as truth was in Mary's mind, Christ as flesh in Mary's womb; that which is in the mind is greater than what is carried in the womb.
>
> Mary is holy, Mary is blessed, but the Church is something better than the Virgin Mary. Why? Because Mary is part of the Church, a holy member, a quite exceptional member, the supremely wonderful member, but still a member of the whole body. That being so, it follows that the body is something greater than the member. The Lord is the head, and the whole Christ is head and body. How shall I put it? We have a divine head, we have God as our head.[58]

Augustine emphasizes that the greater maternal act of Mary was her obedience to the will of God rather than her birthing of Jesus. This relegates her to being a member within the church instead of being above the church. At best, she is made exemplar of faithful membership, among other members of the church. But the difficulty remains: while the greater maternal role of Mary was birthing Christ spiritually, it is undeniable that she too had birthed Christ physically. The tension thus remains unresolved.

Moreover, this tension creates another one—this time in terms of ecclesial metaphors for the church. As noted, for Augustine, there were two metaphors for the church that became dominant for him. They are the church as virgin mother and the church as *totus Christus/corpus Christi* or the whole Body of Christ. When we consider the unresolved concept of Mary as mother to Christ and as not above Christ or the church but as within the church itself, the two metaphors appear to be competing rather than complementing each other. On the one hand, we have the church as fecund in her virginity; one who births, gathers, and teaches Christians; a singular figure. On the other hand, we have the church as the Body with its members and Christ at its head, a corporate image. The use of Mary as figure for the virgin Mother Church challenged the church's detractors, the Jovinianists and Manicheans, since Mary exemplifies the roles of mother and virgin in both the spiritual and physical senses. At the same time, these very same qualities of Mary prevent her from being just a part of the *totus Christus* who births Christ spiritually, since she has also birthed Christ physically. As both physical and spiritual mother of Christ, Mary also becomes mother of the Body of Christ, the church. However, Augustine did not accept the idea that Mary is the mother of the church, as this would elevate her over it. Rather, Augustine preferred to locate Mary as a member of the Body of Christ, the first disciple of her son. It can be seen, here, how Mary as model and type for the church presents an unresolved tension within Augustine's ecclesiology or understanding of the church.

MOTHER CHURCH AS JERUSALEM, THE COMMUNION OF SAINTS, MOTHER OF US ALL

In defense of infant baptism against another heretical group, the Pelagians,[59] Augustine also employed the image of a female church, the church as a mother. Augustine describes this Mother Church as "Mother of them all," an allusion to Mother Jerusalem, as he points to holy members of the Catholic Church and refutes his opponent, Julian of Eclanum.[60]

Julian of Eclanum (386–454) was a Pelagian bishop who accused Augustine of Manicheanism because his doctrine of original sin, where sin is passed on through parents (specifically, through the "seed") and their uncontrollable sexual lust (known as "concupiscence"), seemed quite close to the Manichean teaching that sin is passed on through the sinful body. But God's nature is to be all-loving and all-good (omnibenevolence) and God creates all human beings out of goodness (see Gen 1) rather than as sinful beings from the very beginning or as a result of evil, which was believed by the Manicheans. While Julian argued that concupiscence/sexual lust/desire is not a sin since it existed before the fall from God's grace by Adam and Eve in the Garden of Eden,[61] Augustine believed concupiscence to be an evil, that it does not exist when humans are created, but that it is then sowed by the devil and consequently put to good use by parents in their creation of offspring.[62] Julian asked how baptized parents pass on sin. This comes from the Pelagian understanding that baptism completely purified a person. Augustine responded, using the analogy of the olive tree, where even with proper attention and cultivation, the tree can still grow wild. In a similar vein, Augustine believed persons who are baptized are still able to sin.[63]

While Augustine proposed that grace alone (*sola gratia*) saves the individual soul, the Pelagians were afraid that this would lead to moral laxity and argued that a person's will and actions play a part in his or her own salvation. Therefore, for Julian, it is not concupiscence that is sinful but its excessive use. Meanwhile, Augustine insisted that, because of the fall of Adam and Eve, humanity inherits loss of control of the will, and sexual lust.

With such views on sex and desire, we see why Augustine preferred virginity and presented the good of marriage in pragmatic terms, without reference to passion or desire. This has implications for us today as we inherit these perspectives in which sex and desire can be seen with suspicion and even as deterrents to the way of faith and salvation. I agree with Augustine that grace alone saves, and as the medieval Christian theologian Thomas Aquinas highlights, that humans need to respond to the gift of grace. However, I disagree with Augustine that it is the inner tendency to sexual lust that is the evil we must resist as human beings, passed on from generation to generation. Instead, I believe it is the tendency to violence in the human being, which the French philosopher René Girard (1923–2015) called "mimetic contagion" or "mimetic violence." This is the evil passed on from generation to generation that humans need to resist. Girard theorized that Jesus was the willing scapegoat for this tendency to violence. That is, what saves creation and leads persons away from this tendency to violence is participation in the weekly sacrifice of Jesus in the Christian ritual of the Eucharist.[64]

With the emphasis on personal will and action as determinants for salvation, Pelagians challenged the idea of infant baptism, given that infants cannot fully consent to faith at the time of baptism. To this challenge, Augustine replies using the Mother Church image:

> There is no human being in this whole mass of mortals that comes down from Adam, not a single human being who hasn't been sick, not a single one who has been cured without the grace of Christ. What about the little ones, you ask; are they infected with the sickness from Adam? Well they too are carried along to the Church; even if they can't trot along on their own feet, they do so on other people's, in order to be cured. Mother Church lends them other people's feet to come by, other people's hearts to believe with, other people's tongues to confess with; thus since they are burdened with their sickness through another person sinning, it is right that when they recover health here they should be saved by another person confessing on their behalf.[65]

According to this text, all human beings, including infants, inherit Adam and Eve's original sin, which for Augustine comprises carnal lust, self-will, and disobedience. It is a "sickness" for which only Christ is the cure, through baptism. Augustine argues that just as infants inherit the sin of others (through original sin), so it is through others they are cured, through baptism and the confession of faith made on infants' behalf. But only "original sin" is cured through baptism. The ability to commit mortal or venial sin remains,[66] even with the baptized person, and this was what the Pelagians could not understand.

In his dispute with Julian of Eclanum, Augustine calls the church "Mother of them all,"[67] an allusion to Mother Jerusalem, who is described in Galatians 4:26 also as "mother of us all," as he says himself:

> By Jerusalem here we should understand not the Jerusalem which is in servitude with her children but rather the

Jerusalem which is, according to the Apostle, the free woman, our mother, eternal in heaven. There, after the toils of the anxieties and cares of this mortal existence, we shall be comforted like her little children carried on her shoulders and on her knees.[68]

Augustine also explicitly calls the church the "mother of us all" in the *Confessions*.[69] This Mother Church that points to the Mother Jerusalem of Trito-Isaiah, the unbreakable eternally existing temple, aligns with the idea of the church of the saints that exists in heaven and is reflected on earth in those who do God's will on earth. In fact, Augustine believed also that the Mother Church was the Communion of Saints:

Little ones are, of course, presented to receive spiritual grace, not so much from those in whose hands they are carried, though they do also receive it from them if they are good believing people....For they are correctly understood to be presented by all who are pleased that they are presented and by whose holy and undivided love they are helped to come into the communion of the Holy Spirit. The whole Church, our mother, which exists in the saints, does this, because the whole Church gives birth to each and every one.[70]

While Augustine refers, here, to the whole church as a mother, as the Communion of Saints, this does not mean Augustine was referring to the whole church, which he saw as composed of sinners and saints. Rather the Mother Church, who exists as the Communion of Saints, is that part of the church who does the will of God, births Christ "in the mind," grows spiritually, and calls others to baptism and spiritual growth. She can never be destroyed like the Mother Jerusalem of Trito-Isaiah. Rather, she exists from generation to generation to pass on faith in Christ and to give hope, healing, and reconciliation in the world.

RELEVANCE FOR THE TRADITION
OF THE CHURCH AS BRIDE, HOLY,
VIRGIN, AND MOTHER

All metaphors have their strengths and their limitations. There was no one who knew this more than Augustine, who was a master of rhetoric. As we noted earlier, he went to great lengths to empathize with his audience, to present himself as one of them. We recall here, too, Augustine understood signs as not having meaning in and of themselves but only insofar as a community assigned a specific meaning to them. Therefore, in terms of using female metaphors for the Church such as mother, bride, and virgin, Augustine would challenge using them simply out of tradition or in a way that did not resonate meaningfully with audiences.

Augustine used the mother metaphor in order to persuade rather than coerce the Donatists. He rightly saw the value in employing the metaphor, given that ancient Roman culture highly valued motherhood. While Augustine used his experience of his own mother, Monica, to describe the church as a mother, he was not just universalizing his personal experience. Instead, he was tapping into a culturally resonant image—the *materfamilias-univira*, which, in Augustine's view, was exemplified in Monica.

Augustine's introduction of Christ, the divine male, as the head of the female church, to make up the whole Christ, *totus Christus*, was again in line with his surrounding culture. That is, the cultural understanding was that the *paterfamilias* was the head of the *familia*, which included having power over the *materfamilias* and *filiusfamilias*. This female church was not one dimensional, but as Augustine described, contained "lilies" among its "thorns" and "daughters." As we have noted, Augustine employed these metaphors from the Song of Songs to refute the Donatists and expand the nature of the Church to include unholy members. The lilies were the saints, while the thorns and daughters were the sinners.

The metaphors of lilies, thorns, and daughters did have cultural resonance with their ancient Roman audiences: Lilies were a symbol of such things as purity, innocence, virtue, and chastity. Meanwhile, thorns were viewed as a curse, so much so that there was a Roman god, Spiniensis (from Latin, *spina*, meaning thorn), to whom one prayed to remove thorny plants from one's field and to not be injured by them. As well, daughters were not mothers but were in training to become so one day. Therefore, daughters were not virtuous like mothers but did hold promise into the future. When Augustine called Monica "daughter of all," he alluded to, but also distinguished her, from Jerusalem, the "mother of us all," which is a reference to the saints within the church. This also signified that Monica—and her motherhood—was to be placed in the category of sinners, who were exposed to the corruption of death, while Mother Jerusalem was the eternal mother who could never be corrupted or destroyed. Similarly, Augustine's use of "new Eve" for the church, as a contrast to the original Eve, demonstrated the nature of the church as birthing persons into eternal life rather than into eventual death, as in the case of the original Eve. This was no random use of metaphor but rather was especially helpful in refuting the Manicheans, in their rejection of the Old Testament.

Augustine's uses of the bride and virgin metaphors were for specific ecclesiological purposes and not simply because he had an enthusiasm for them, particularly virginity, or out of the need to use them to reinforce cultural traditions. We have noted already the complexities, strengths, and limitations of the uses of female metaphors in general for the church. Hopefully, this has encouraged thinking around the idea that female ecclesial metaphors are not necessarily part of the essence or nature of the church but rather were employed to communicate this essence or nature considering the Roman cultural milieu. Here again, we are led to question our uses of symbol and language, in general, inside today's churches. More specifically, if the mother, bride, and virgin metaphors are to be used in churches today, can they be appropriated for audiences of cultures different from the Roman culture? Or does using them entail imposing Roman culture, thus devaluing other cultures?

CONCLUSION

Augustine's use of the images of woman and mother for the church was based on certain principles that aimed to engage his audience, communicate ecclesiological truths, and refute his opponents. The female church Augustine presented appears as his mother Monica, but also as the Roman mother, virgin, and wife, as Mother Jerusalem, as the female figures of Psalm 45, as the new Eve, and as Mary as virgin and mother. Contrary to the idea that the female church is necessarily virgin, mother, and wife, for all time, we have seen that such analogies were applied to the church in response to various controversies in Augustine's time.

With the Donatists, Augustine presented a mother like his own, Monica, herself embodying the revered *matrona* of the Roman Empire. With the Donatists and Manicheans, Augustine presented a bride-virgin church, which he was initially reluctant to describe until heretical groups claimed for themselves the title of true "Brides of Christ." Augustine also presented the church as the "new Eve," one who brings new life in contrast to the life of mortal sin brought about by the "Old Eve." Moreover, this image of the female church came to be useful in countering the Manicheans, with their disregard of the Old Testament.

But it is the church as virgin-mother as exemplified in Mary (but also through the ecclesial virgins) that is Augustine's legacy to the church. Augustine used this female figure to counter the Jovinianists and to uphold marriage, motherhood, and virginity, while giving preference to virginity. This image for the church would remain for centuries, appearing in Vatican II documents as part of the tradition, although without its original context. The image participates in a tension between two dominating metaphors within the Council's document reflecting on the nature of the church, *Lumen Gentium*: a tension that, from its beginnings, was unresolved for Augustine.

Finally, against the Pelagians, Augustine employed the church as a mother who is the Communion of Saints, with allusions to the heavenly Mother Jerusalem, whom he describes as "mother of us all." This mother is the one that holds the true faith, is responsible for birthing, teaching, and nurturing, and yet encourages its children, the church members composed of both sinners and saints, to grow and become Mother Church themselves.

Augustine's creativity and diversity in the presentation of the church as female in a multifaceted network of associations (the church as mother, midwife, spouse, bride, daughter, queen, infant,

Jerusalem, the new Eve, and Mary) demonstrates the creative power of this metaphor, and ensures that this image would act as a living metaphor for his audiences, effectively resonating with his own and his audience's personal frames of reference. That Augustine admitted to the difficulties of some parallels between Mother Church and Mary ensures that the maternal image remains a metaphor rather than a one-on-one exclusive analogy between the church and Mary. In addition, any insistence on the uses of female metaphors for the church invites the question of their appropriation for today's audiences. Moreover, it invites reflection on the imposition of Roman culture, which had a singular image of the mother, bride, and virgin, onto other cultures. This has implications including the devaluing of other cultures, which can take a toll on those cultures.

6

Pope Francis's *La Chiesa*

*Woman has a particular sensitivity to the "things of God,"
above all in helping us understand the mercy, tenderness
and love that God has for us.*
   *I also like to think of the Church not as an "it" but as
a "she." The Church is woman, she is mother, and this is
beautiful. You must consider and go deeper into this.*

—Pope Francis, October 12, 2013[1]

Jorge Bergoglio (Pope Francis) was born on December 17, 1936, in
Buenos Aires, Argentina, to Italian immigrants. He graduated as a
chemical technician, but chose priesthood after a passing interest
in medicine. On March 11, 1958, he became a Jesuit novice; eleven
years later, he was ordained a priest; and another four years later,
he professed his final vows. Since then, some of his roles have
included the following: teacher of literature, philosophy, and theology; grand chancellor of the Catholic University of Argentina;
author; spiritual director and confessor; novice master; rector; par-
ish priest; provincial of the Jesuits in Argentina; cardinal; and now
supreme pontiff, or pope, since March 13, 2013.

   In this chapter, we explore factors that have contributed to
Pope Francis's vision of the church as a woman and mother. For
Pope Francis, "woman," in one sense, is not an abstract concept but
a real person with whom one can form a deep loving relationship,
as he had done himself, inside and outside of his home. However,
Pope Francis also idealizes "woman," and that idealization derives
in part from how woman is imagined at Vatican II. This chapter
then explores this "ideal" woman, which was the "Good Mother," as
envisaged in the 1930s to 1950s, in response to several cultural
issues of the time. After exploring such factors, we examine some of
Pope Francis's uses of the church as a woman and mother and the
purposes for these uses. Finally, the chapter presents an example of

Pope Francis's abandonment of female church rhetoric for pastoral reasons. This opens the possibility that the Catholic Church can engage with contemporary audiences, by reinvestigating and revising its uses of metaphor and symbol. It also suggests that the highest value that can be given to women is not determined by their biology but by the various virtuous lives they lead in order to give a lasting positive contribution to human history.

"WOMAN" EXPERIENCED

Women within the Domestic Sphere: Regina and Rosa Bergoglio

Bergoglio grew up in a family environment comprising a mother, father, two younger brothers, two younger sisters, and a grandmother and grandfather. His parents and grandparents were immigrants from Italy and had made a new life for themselves in Argentina. The Bergoglios were not rich but lived comfortably. They were luckier than many other immigrant families who came with nothing and had no home: the Bergoglios had secure housing, albeit in the poor neighborhood of Flores. Pope Francis recalls, "Though we had nothing to spare, no car, and didn't go away for the summer, we still never wanted for anything."[2]

In this family, the future pope learned to pray, play, and get along with family members. Before dinner, his father, Mario, would ask the family to pray the Rosary. His mother, Regina, is remembered for her selflessness in focusing her attention on her children. This picture of self-giving was heightened when she became an invalid after the birth of her fifth child. But Regina also had her passions, one of which was the opera. Pope Francis recalls fondly, "The truth is that two o'clock on Saturday afternoons with my mother and my siblings, enjoying music, was a wonderful time."[3]

On Sundays, the whole family would go to San Lorenzo stadium, instilling a lifelong love for football for the future pope. Pope Francis also recalls being taught risqué songs in the Italian-Genoan dialect by a great uncle; it was a childhood that included interactions too with characters who were not pious. Maria Elena, Jorge's sister, recalls this period of their life as quite formative: "It was Mother and Father who taught us the value of love between family members."[4] She also describes her brother as teaching her a life lesson: "Jorge taught me to be generous even if it required sacrifice."[5]

When asked about his earlier influences, the figure that stands out for Pope Francis is his grandmother Rosa. He says of her, "I feel a special devotion to my grandmother, for all that she gave me in the first years of my life."[6] She was kind, down-to-earth, and resourceful. He spent much of his time with his grandmother since his mother had her hands full with the younger siblings. Rosa taught him Piedmontese, another Italian dialect. She taught him to love Italian literature. Most of all, she taught him to pray and love the saints, including especially Mary. She also told him tales of her youth, when she was a Catholic activist siding with the church against the government, when it challenged the church's moral teachings and exercised greed. Later, when Jorge announced his desire to enter the priesthood, his mother tried to discourage him. Meanwhile, Rosa was encouraging. At the same time, she told Jorge that, whatever he decided, there was a place for him in her home. This taught the future pope a real lesson in how to accompany persons lovingly during grim times.

The various experiences of family life, marked by rich relationships within this Italian extended family, were where Jorge formed the picture of the ideal setting of the family. It was a contrast to the violence and dysfunction of the surrounding society, where, in Argentina from 1930, the year of the first military coup, to 1982, the year of the Falklands war, there were twenty-four successive presidents, naturally creating instability for the country. On a wider scale, in Europe, the fascist rules of Mussolini and Hitler were creating their own forms of dysfunction. Pope Francis's references to family life as a place where people learn to love, forgive, sacrifice, and live with differences, in texts such as *Amoris Laetitia* and in speeches such as those he gave at the Festival of Families in Philadelphia in the United States in 2015, surely derive from this rich background of seemingly harmonious family living.

It is also from within this setting that the future pope formed his ideas of the indispensable role of the woman as mother and nurturer of faith, and as instiller of values and a sense of security and love within families, even when there is turmoil outside the home. The woman, in this setting, is a person of deep faith, self-sacrificing, attentive to both the physical and spiritual needs of children, but she also has her own passions. In one sense, this was the idealized woman of Western societies from the 1930s to the 1950s, the period before the revolution of the 1960s and the great pastoral council, the Second Vatican Council, which saw the Catholic Church pursuing dialogue with and openness to the surrounding culture and its peoples, rather than treating it with suspicion.

The future pope would also encounter influential female figures outside of the domestic setting. There would be some who would become close friends, showing him that by their great skills and wisdom, they make an invaluable contribution to the good of society. These encounters surely form part of Pope Francis's idea of the "incisive female presence" that he acknowledges the Catholic Church greatly needs. In contrast, though, there would be at least one woman who would show Jorge the kind of woman who, in her position of power, does nothing to make society better.

Women in the Public Domain

Sisters Dolores and Rosa

At twenty years of age, Jorge contracted a severe case of pneumonia, causing him extreme pain and leaving him with a pulmonary deficiency for the rest of his life. No one could give him a satisfactory answer to his desperate question, "What is happening to me?" Only Sister Dolores, his catechist since the days of preparation for first communion, gave him an answer that would not only satisfy him but would also help integrate the earlier lessons on the cross, death, and resurrection of Jesus. Jorge recalls Sister Dolores's approach: "She said something that truly stuck with me and made me feel at peace: 'You are imitating Christ.'" For Francis, this was not about a glorification of the cross; rather, it was about facing the reality of life—that it contains pain on the way to happiness and fulfillment.[7] The Second Vatican Council theologian and Jesuit Karl Rahner described this awareness of pain in life as "Christian realism": it is an acceptance of the reality of death at one's door but also of the reality that there is more than the despair and immense pain, however extreme. In Jorge's experience of integrating the faith instilled in childhood, he experienced "woman" again as someone of deep faith, saving him from his despair. It is said that both sisters, Rosa and Dolores, taught Jorge the faith before he received his first holy communion, but it was from Sister Dolores that Jorge received a compelling and lasting answer.

Esther Ballestrino de Careaga

Jorge connected not only with women of deep Christian faith, he also became good friends with women in the secular world, even those whose political ideas ran counter to his own. One such woman was his boss, Esther Ballestrino de Careaga, with whom he worked in the foods section of the Hickethier-Bachmann laboratory. Esther had a doctorate in biochemistry. She was also politically active as a member of a socialist party. She later became one of the founding members of *Unión Democrática de Mujeres* (Democratic Union of Women) in Paraguay in 1946. Even with his great distaste for Marxism and communism, and with his own sympathies toward Peronism, Jorge still held Esther in great esteem, as he describes:

> I had an extraordinary boss…Esther Balestrino de Careaga….I loved her very much. I remember that when I handed her an analysis, she'd say, "Wow, you did that so fast." And then she'd ask, "But did you do the test or not?" I would answer, "What for?" If I'd done all the previous tests, it would surely be more or less the same. "No, you have to do things properly," she would chide me. In short, she taught me the seriousness of hard work. Truly, I owe a huge amount to that great woman.[8]

Esther's daughter and son-in-law would be kidnapped under the Argentinean military dictatorship called the Process of National Reorganization, in force from 1976 to 1982. The couple disappeared, and were most probably tortured,[9] but they would be just two people out of the 8,960 disappearances recorded by the National Commission on the Disappearance of Persons.[10] In the quest to find them, Esther, along with other Paraguayan mothers of disappeared children, marched at Plaza de Mayo, Buenos Aires, in March 1977, to protest a government that seemed to be undisturbed by the numbers who had disappeared. In a 2013 interview, when Rush Limbaugh called Pope Francis a Marxist, the pope had Esther in mind when he replied, "I have met many Marxists in my life who are good people."[11] When Esther herself disappeared in 1977 and her remains were discovered three decades later, Pope Francis approved her burial in the garden of Santa Cruz Church, Buenos Aires, even with full knowledge that she was not a Catholic. Esther's daughter made this burial request because "it was the last place they [Esther and other women] had been as free people."[12]

Other Women Friends

According to the respected journalist John Allen, Jorge Bergoglio has had numerous female friends, each with her own set of skills and experience and way of making a mark in society. Not all of them have necessarily aligned themselves with Jorge regarding political and religious thought, but nonetheless they have gained his respect and esteem.[13] There was Alicia Oliveira, the lawyer, judge, single mother of three, and left-wing Peronist. Francis protected her during Videla's dictatorship, and Alicia, in turn, would defend his reputation when asked about his past before his papacy. Several female journalists have been close to Francis, including Francesca Ambrogetti, who would coauthor his official biography, *Pope Francis: His Life in His Own Words*.[14] Then there was Clelia Luro, mother to six children, who separated from her husband, and who fell in love with Jerónimo Podestá, a bishop later stripped of his ecclesiastical authority. Clelia and Jerónimo had radically different views from Jorge Bergoglio regarding Catholic social activism, and Clelia, as a feminist, campaigned for women's ordination. But when Jerónimo became terminally ill and was hospitalized, Jorge was at the hospital anointing him, in my view, with the oil for the sick. Later, when Jerónimo died, Jorge and Clelia remained close friends for twelve years, until Clelia died eight months into Jorge's appointment to the papacy. It is said she sent the new pope a memoir of her forty years of married life with Jerónimo, "bound by love and the moral, social and political conviction that celibacy in the Catholic Church should be optional."[15]

These friendships evidence Pope Francis's credibility as someone who can speak of women in their realities—because he has had firsthand experiences of deeply loving relationships with them. His image of the good woman would most probably include a picture of his mother, grandmother Rosa, Sisters Rosa and Dolores, Alicia, Esther, and Mary as the Virgin of Lujan (seen as protectress of the Argentineans, especially when they entered the Falklands war) or as the Untier of Knots (a favorite of Pope Francis's). It may even include the ideal woman in the Argentinean mythology, Eva (or Evita) Peron, who was an advocate for labor rights and for the poor, but who also affirmed the place of woman by the side of her husband and not at the helm as president of a nation.

Further, the nineteenth-century Russian author Fyodor Dostoyevsky was a favorite of Pope Francis. In *The Brothers Karamazov*, the good woman, Grushenka, was the one who was not necessarily perfect and virtuous throughout the story but had personal integrity. Grushenka, in fact, was viewed as the town harlot. Those who really knew her had mixed opinions of her. But what gave her integrity was that she was always true to herself and tried to do the right thing, such as standing by the man who gave her food and shelter even when that invited social criticism or disgrace. Grushenka is contrasted with the selfish, beautiful, and inconsistent Katerina, who, in one moment, is declaring her love for Dmitry to acquire money from him to help her father, and in the next, turning on him out of fear for her future lover by incriminating him with a letter that he had written to save her future lover, Ivan. Unlike Grushenka, Katerina shows no gratitude to the man who had once rescued her. Like the early church fathers, Dostoyevsky elevates the status of the woman who cultivates virtue—in this case, by her personal integrity or inner beauty; he also lowers the status of the woman who does not cultivate such virtue or inner beauty.

We find this was the case with Cristina Fernández, wife of Néstor Kirchner, president of Argentina from 2003 to 2007, and president herself from 2007 to 2015. She was a beautiful and powerful woman, but one whom Jorge could not befriend. From the very beginning, the Kirchners distrusted the Catholic Church and clashed with Bergoglio on many issues. For example, under Cristina's first term as president, "gay marriage" law was passed. While the pope is known for his noncondemnation of gays, he took a hard-line stance against Argentina becoming one of the first nations to allow gay marriage. Moreover, it seemed that Bergoglio's popularity overtook that of the Kirchners, and Argentinean society sided with him on many issues. It was only when Néstor suddenly died that the people showed sympathy toward Cristina. In Jimmy Burns's biography of Pope Francis, Cristina is presented as lapping up this new attention, playing up the widow role, and using the situation to her full political advantage. Cristina's superficiality is seen, too, in her expression of womanhood, where she unabashedly layers on makeup and wears high-end couture. It is said she once confided to a close aide, "I like to seduce. I don't want people to just obey me. I want to convince them."[16] These presentations of superficiality have clashed with Bergoglio's own distaste for "ostentation in gesture and word."[17] Even Argentineans and diplomats decided that the key to understanding Cristina could be found in the chapter of her biography dedicated solely to her appearance.[18] This reminds us specifically of Tertullian's condemnation of the superficial woman, who, in his eyes, focused her efforts on putting on makeup, clothing, and jewelry, instead of beautifying herself with virtues. While there are women to be found all over the world who put on makeup and jewelry but who also do good in the world, in this case, Cristina is no credit to her own sex. She fulfills that caricature condemned even from the days of Tertullian. Moreover, Cristina contrasts with grandmother Rosa, Sister Dolores, the Virgin Mary, Esther Ballestrino de Careaga, and Alicia Oliveira— women who evidence virtues rather than superficiality, and who do good in the world without having to be in the highest seat of power. When Pope Francis is asked about women in leadership in the church, he possibly considers these good women and their contribution to society and contrasts them with Cristina, who in her highest seat of power adds nothing for the good of society.

THE IDEAL WOMAN OF THE 1930S
TO THE 1950S IN THE WEST

A history of political, economic, and social unrest contributed to the creation of the idealized picture of "woman" from the 1930s to the 1950s, the period immediately before Vatican II.[19] While Pope Francis has many encounters and deep friendships with different women that help to counter an idealization of woman, everyone is a product of her or his time and surroundings, and Pope Francis is no different. Thus, we explore here the cultural idealization of woman during the 1930s to 1950s. There are many biographies on Pope Francis that provide his Argentinean cultural and political context. We do not do this here but rather explore the larger context of the West, its picture of the ideal woman, a context in which Vatican II was envisaged, and that forms the background for which Pope Francis imagines the church as woman and mother.

In the period of unrest from 1914 to the mid-1940s, the creation of the image of the ideal woman was just one way of addressing the experience of postwar instability and insecurity. In order of occurrence, some of the noteworthy events include World War I (1914–18); Russia's fall to communist rule led by Lenin in 1917; Mussolini's march into Rome by invitation from the Italian king Victor Emmanuel III in 1922 and his consequent fascist rule of Italy; the Great Depression (from 1930 to the late-1930s or mid-1940s in most countries), creating worldwide economic and social unrest; Hitler's rise to fascist power in Germany from 1930; and World War II (1939–45).

One way the Western World sought to create stability was to turn to the domestic sphere to reemphasize the role of woman as mother and wife, for during wartime, women were called out of their domestic lives into the public sphere to help advance their country's war efforts. Reemphasis on the woman as dedicated wife and mother postwar created some sense of peace, stability, and security, at least on the home front. Moreover, postwar women were encouraged to bear and raise children, to be good wives, and to leave full-time jobs to war veterans.[20] The concern was for family, and yet many women post–World War II showed dissatisfaction with domestic work being the sole focus of their lives. Social scientists as well as the media at the time also observed the growing "seeds of discontent" in the postwar era.[21]

Jessamyn Neuhaus has observed this discontent from the perspective of cookbooks published in the 1950s. Those cookbooks sought to create an ideology of cooking as a completely fulfilling activity for the woman. They communicated that ultimately the home was the woman's place. Added to this, domestic life gained such attention that it forced the woman to make the home her center of existence, as Neuhaus explains: "Increasingly high standards operated for both housework and cookery, turning them into full-time occupations, despite all the labor-saving gadgets which filled the postwar home."[22]

Furthermore, Neuhaus points out the implications of the assumptions made within the cookbooks about women's ultimate vocation as being in the home:

> By stating assumptions about women's lives, cookbooks left room for those "assumptions" to be questioned. Cookbooks in their efforts to seal up the growing cracks in gender ideology, actually left traces and clues about just where the cracks had begun to show. The dominant discourse that positioned cooking and food preparation as a natural deeply fulfilling activity for all women spoke to the possibility that perhaps it was not. These texts articulated what must *not* be articulated but assumed, in order to maintain "traditional" gender roles. These books were instruction manuals in attitudes and desires that should have been "natural" to men and women, thus they actually denaturalized those attitudes and desires.[23]

The Christian world also engaged in this rhetoric of the woman and her ultimate vocation within the home. During the 1940s and 1950s, "mainline Christian editors remained reluctant to support women's working outside the home" for fear of women taking over jobs that were meant for ethnic minorities in America, and because "women outside the home would likely have an adverse effect upon the family life of America."[24] Betty Friedan's 1963 book,

The Feminine Mystique, gave a reason for this reluctance to support women working outside the home. She says that in the post–World War II era, there existed a "feminine mystique" that saw a woman's ultimate role and fulfillment as through being a mother and a wife.[25]

On the Catholic front, the encyclical of Pope Pius XI on Christian marriage, *Casti Connubii,* was published in late 1930. The document reaffirmed the teachings of *Arcanum Divinae Sapientiae,* the encyclical of Pope Leo XIII on Christian marriage, promulgated in 1880. *Arcanum*'s purpose was to address errors that had arisen due to developments in society. "Divorce, polygamy and the treatment of women in marriage" were the main errors *Arcanum* addressed.[26] Ivy Helman observes that "before much is even said in [*Casti Connubii*], Pope Pius XI takes the time to confirm *Arcanum divinae sapientiae* to be as true and valid in 1930 as it was when Pope Leo XIII promulgated it."[27]

Casti Connubii's view of women was that they were created for marriage, motherhood and domesticity (no. 11). This not only includes birthing and educating children, but also subjection to their husbands (nos. 26–29, 74, 75). These roles for women as mothers, wives, and companions to their husbands are, in fact, described as part of the "noble office" of the woman (no. 27). The order of the world presented in *Casti Connubii* is that "husband is the head of the wife" just as "Christ is head of the Church" (no. 26). A man is the "head" while the woman is the "heart" (no. 27). An "honorable and trusting obedience" is what "the woman owes to the man" (no. 74). The suggestion of men and women as equals is unthinkable (no. 74). Further, the emancipation of women, whereby "the woman is to be freed at her own good pleasure from the burdensome duties properly belonging to a wife as companion and mother" and "to devote herself to business and even public affairs" are argued as neither "the true emancipation of woman" nor belonging to her "noble office" (nos. 74 and 75).

In anticipation of protests toward this patriarchal view where man is normative and has rule over others, *Castii Connubii* argues that woman retains her full "liberty" and "dignity as a human person" (no. 27) and she could even disobey her husband if he is unreasonable or disregards her dignity as his wife (no. 27). Even in the social circumstance where the woman is forced to work outside the home, the document laments that this comes at a "great harm" to the family (no. 120). Even worse, *Casti Connubii* then complains that more help is given to the single and illegitimate mother than the legitimate mother and wife and her children (no. 122).

On so many levels, what is presented in *Casti Connubii* as an order of the world, so-called mandated by God, is highly problematic. There is no room to discuss all the issues, but we highlight the obvious two. First, we would be hard-pressed to find in contemporary Western society the validity of this patriarchal view, creating its own justifications that woman retains her full and equal dignity while insisting the primacy of one sex over another (the document anticipates this kind of argument would be put forward and criticizes it in no. 74). Second, despite any qualifications added to the view of order in the world whereby the one in power (man) must love the person subject to him (woman), this does not prevent the abuse of power. In fact, it can and has been used to justify abuse. In Australia, for example, most of the violence that occurs within people's private homes is often men toward women, and at least once a week a woman is killed by a partner or former partner.[28] It is the assumption that man has power and rights over woman that lends to the current epidemic of domestic violence against women, but this violence is also played out in public in many ways all over the world.

When feminist theology (the umbrella term in which all feminist theologies are often put under) is accused of fighting for the emancipation of women, there remain elements of this worldview—that the emancipation of women is at a cost to families, that the ideal is a woman at home as mother and wife, and that an emancipated woman seeks primarily her own pleasure than the good of society. On the contrary, engagement in feminist theologies is about uplifting the circumstances of women where societies retain patriarchal assumptions at a cost to women, in physically violent ways, as well as through unjust structures such as unequal pay and an imbalance in work load within both the private and public domains.

An interesting part of *Casti Connubii* is when the Christian woman is called to prove "herself superior to all the pains and cares and solicitudes of her maternal office with a more just and holy joy than that of the Roman matron, the mother of the Gracchi" (no. 15). What relevance or even understanding of this Roman woman would contemporary audiences have today? Nearly two thousand years after the Catholic Church adopted the ideal Roman woman for its arguments, *Casti Connubii* evidences the church's clinging on to its Roman characteristic, continuing to argue and communicate using ancient Roman metaphors and associations. Consequently, there is either an assumption that audiences still resonate with these metaphors or a disregard of current audiences with an insistence upon the use of language regardless of their connection with them.

Fortunately, the Catholic Church evidenced some changes in its view of women in the 1960s, in Pope John XXIII's encyclicals *Mater et Magistra* (1961) and *Pacem in Terris* (1963).[29] At the same time, remnants of the church's patriarchal view remained. In *Mater et Magistra*, women are considered part of the working class, but also part of the weaker members of society who must be protected (no. 20). In *Pacem in Terris*, women are given support in their choice to work outside the home (no. 15) and acknowledgment is given to the feminist movement (nos. 41–43),[30] but women's roles as mothers and wives are upheld (no. 19). The document does recognize women's natural dignity and increasing role in the public sphere (no. 41). This is quite a contrast from the condemnation of such concepts found in *Casti Connubii* and *Arcanum Divinae Sapientiae*. In *Amoris Laetitia*, Pope Francis also supports women working outside of the home, highlights their equal dignity, and going one step further than *Pacem in Terris*, affirms women's movements, saying they too have something worthy to say (no. 54). At the same time, he also reaffirms the maternal role of "woman," which we will explore later. While the Catholic Church has slowly improved elements on its views of women, it carries this perception, and it still has a long way to go. Pope Francis senses this and asserts that it is not enough to have a few token women on a Vatican commission, but a "more incisive presence" and a "theology of woman" is needed (limited in its use of the umbrella term *feminist theology*, but the intention is there). Let's now discuss these perspectives on the church as a woman alongside those of Vatican II, because a large part of Francis's Mother Church has a lot to do with Vatican II's vision of the church as a mother, underpinned by its own visions of the ideal or good woman.

VATICAN II AND POPE FRANCIS ON MOTHER CHURCH

Several documents considered formative for the mindset of Vatican II point to its assumed maternal imaging for the church. First, Pope John XXIII's opening speech for the Council, *Gaudet Mater Ecclesia* (October 11, 1962), evidently points to this assumption. In its article 17, the maternal church "raises the torch of religious truth in this Ecumenical Council" and "wishes to show herself to be the most loving mother of all, kind, patient, and moved by mercy and goodness towards her separated children."[31] Article 17 presents Mother Church as holder and teacher of religious truth, but one who desires to reach out and teach beyond her own members. This maternal church even acknowledges faith in those who are not her members. But she depends upon her members to represent her to the world, to correct error, and to promote unity and peace. This work toward unity is her "duty to work actively to fulfil this mystery of that unity for which Christ Jesus ardently prayed the heavenly Father on the eve of his sacrifice" (no. 19).[32] Interestingly, in his continual expression of a desire for peace and unity under Christ, John XXIII quotes Cyprian's *The Unity of the Catholic Church*, article 5. In John XXIII's translation, there is no sign of any reference to Cyprian's dictum "Outside of the Church there is no salvation" (*extra ecclesiam nulla salus*). Yet Cyprian wrote *The Unity of the Catholic Church* with this exclusionary idea in mind.[33] What seems to be more apparent in John XXIII's use of the Cyprianic quote is his image of Mother Church as desiring the unity and harmony of peoples under her guidance, correcting and teaching, rather than as desiring a return of all peoples to the Catholic Church as mother, which was Cyprian's purpose in writing his text.

John XXIII's maternal church is consistent with the kind of church Pope Francis has promoted from the very beginning of his pontificate—a church that opens its doors to all, rather than one that is insular, exclusionary, divisive, or caught up in its own structures and rules, as he said in a reflection in the early months of his papacy:

> Christians who ask to be let in should never find doors closed. Churches are not offices where documents and letters are presented when someone is hoping to enter God's grace....Let us think of all Christians of good will who err and shut the door instead of opening it. Let us ask the Lord to grant that all who approach the Church find doors open to encounter Jesus' love.[34]

Reflecting on God's mercy later, Pope Francis explains the significance of the door. He uses the metaphor to explain the need for the church to open herself to those who turn to her for help but also to all peoples, that they may experience God's mercy and forgiveness. He also speaks characteristically of opening the door to "allow the entrance of the Lord—or often the exit of the Lord—who is a prisoner of our structures, of our selfishness and of so many things."[35] This is also true of Pope Francis personally, who prioritizes attending to the person in front of him, rather than getting caught up in concepts, rules, and politics: "If you try to educate using only theoretical principles, without remembering that the most important thing is the person in front of you, then you fall into a kind of fundamentalism."[36] In *Amoris Laetitia*, he is more explicit about what it means to attend to the person in front of us:

> Develop the habit of giving real importance to the other person. This means appreciating them and recognizing their right to exist, to think as they do and to be happy. Never downplay what they say or think, even if you need to express your own point of view. Everyone has something to contribute, because they have their life experiences, they look at things from a different standpoint and they have their own concerns, abilities and insights. We ought to be able to acknowledge the other person's truth, the value of his or her deepest concerns, and what it is that they are trying to communicate, however aggressively. We have to put ourselves in their shoes and try to

peer into their hearts, to perceive their deepest concerns and to take them as a point of departure for further dialogue.[37]

This echoes Vatican II's concern for all peoples and the realities of their daily lives, in all areas of human living; it is summed up as the maternal concern of the church. The earliest expression of this at the Council is found in John XXIII's opening speech:

> Although she has no directly earthly ends, she cannot in her journey be disinterested in the problems and worries of here below. She knows how beneficial to the good of the soul are those means which render more human the life of those individual men who are to be saved. She knows that by giving life to the temporal order by the light of Christ, she is also revealing men and women to themselves, leading them, that is, to discover in themselves their own nature, their own dignity, their own purpose. This is why the living presence of the Church today extends by right and by fact to international organizations; this is why she elaborates her social teaching on the family, the school, work, civil society, and all the related problems, so that her teaching office has been raised to the highest level as the most authoritative voice, the interpreter and champion of the moral order, the defender of the rights and duties of all human beings and of all political communities.[38]

In comparison of these two texts, unlike John XXIII, Francis highlights the need for the valuing of persons as a good in itself and not so that the church may have credibility or authority as a teacher and defender of moral order. Nevertheless, from Francis's perspective, the church gains *greater* credibility as a teacher when she values persons in their realities.

The second and third influential documents pointing to the church's maternity that influenced the cardinals, bishops, and *periti* at Vatican II were Pope John XXIII's encyclical *Mater et Magistra* and his apostolic constitution *Humanae Salutis* (1962). In *Mater et*

Magistra's first paragraph, the church is imaged as mother and teacher, not just to its members, but "to all nations."[39] Like John XXIII's *Gaudet Mater Ecclesia*, his *Mater et Magistra*'s Mother Church presents herself as a custodian of the truth, as a teacher, and as a mother to all, desiring to reach out beyond her own members and to embrace them in love. Moreover, she expresses a hope that people may find completeness and salvation in her.

Consistent with this, *Humanae Salutis*, the document that convoked Vatican II, also called the church *Mater et Magistra*.[40] While drawing upon tradition, *Humanae Salutis* emphasizes the need to bring the church into dialogue with the contemporary world, and in so doing it sets a trajectory for the Council's aims. This image of "mother and teacher" is a link to the past but it also indicates what the church has to offer in the present.

It is unsurprising then that we find in Vatican II's Pastoral Constitution on the Church in the Modern World, *Gaudium et Spes* (*GS*), the church presented as a mother—primarily as one who teaches her children in the way of salvation, through Christ, so that they may be equipped for life. The ecclesial mother is represented in this Vatican II document not only by the clergy but also by the people (students, lay ministers, teachers in non-Catholic schools[41]), who witness in Christian lives and who engage in the apostolic work of the church. This parallels with the liturgical thinking of Vatican II, that the promotion of the "full, conscious and active participation" of the church's members in the liturgy was one of the Council's priorities.[42] The (mother) church as teacher, encouraging her children, both clerical and lay, to grow in faith by active participation, is the image communicated not just in *Gaudium et Spes* but also in many of the Council's documents.[43]

Similarly, Pope Francis also describes the church as a mother who teaches her children the ways of God's mercy and as a path to salvation, as he says in *The Joy of Discipleship* (2016):

> Can there be a Christian who isn't merciful? No. A Christian must necessarily be merciful, because this is the center of the Gospel. And faithful to this teaching, the Church can only repeat the same thing to her children: "Be merciful," as the Father is, and as Jesus was. The

Church is Mother, by teaching her children works of mercy. She learned this manner from Jesus; she learned that this is what's essential for salvation.[44]

In previous years, Francis also referred to the church as the mother who teaches God's mercy. While John XXIII's *Mater et Magistra* provides the concept of the church as a mother and teacher, giving life to individuals, it does not provide specific examples for the practical expression of this. In his general audience address on September 10, 2014, Pope Francis does provide specific ways, calling the church, as at Vatican II, to actively participate in works of mercy.[45] In this address, Pope Francis's Mother Church appears to be more than a teacher by word by being also a teacher by action and example through the saints, both those officially recognized in the church and those who remain anonymous.

Francis's description of Mother Church in this address also reads as a manifesto, a reassertion of Matthew 25:31–46, where God makes a final judgment upon all nations at the end of time. At this judgment, the children of God will be those who have fed the hungry, attended the sick, visited those in prison, and invited the stranger. They will be thus invited into eternal living or salvation with God. Meanwhile, those who called upon God as "Lord" but did not perform these "works of mercy" will be condemned to eternal pain and distance from God.

In calling the church a mother, Pope Francis surely recalls his own learning of the faith by word and example from maternal figures, particularly his grandmother. As well, he acknowledges that his audience comprises many mothers. In a parallel way, *Gaudium et Spes* sees the family as a mother instilling this type of education:

The family is, as it were, the primary mother and nurse of this education. There, the children, in an atmosphere of love, more easily learn the correct order of things, while proper forms of human culture impress themselves in an almost unconscious manner upon the mind of the developing adolescent.[46]

By using the metaphor of the church as a mother, Pope Francis not only calls on tradition but taps into both his own and some of his audience's experiences of parenting by example, to communicate ideas on the nature of the church. Though he acknowledges the mothers during the audience only once, it is as if he leaves this role of parenting primarily to them, rather than as a role to be shared with the father or with the elders and other members of the family.

Francis's use of the imagery of motherhood stirred up controversy when addressing a group of leaders of religious institutes when he likened unfruitful religious to a "spinster," in contrast to his call for religious sisters to be "fruitful" spiritual mothers:

> The consecrated woman is a mother, she must be a mother, not a "spinster"! Excuse me for speaking like this, but motherhood in the consecrated life is important, this fruitfulness! May this joy of spiritual fecundity motivate your life; be mothers, as a figure of Mary, Mother, and of Mother Church.[47]

For many this was received as insulting—toward religious sisters, who have given up physical motherhood to be available to more people, and toward the many single women ("spinsters") and widows who have contributed much to the church and upon whose work the very existence of local churches around the world depends. Moreover, Francis's comment tied the woman's primary value to her biology and communicated that when she is unable to exercise motherhood, she is somehow faulty or less valuable.

A danger in using more colorful and engaging metaphorical language is that nonintended meanings can be read into them. Of course, it would be the last thing on Pope Francis's mind to be deliberately insulting, especially when his mentality is against division, and is toward honoring the dignity of every human person and toward promoting unity in diversity.[48] At that specific audience, his intention was to inspire the religious to look at the fruits of their vocation as a presence of God's mercy in the world. It was unfortunate that the metaphor he used was poorly thought through in terms of its contemporary audience—though, for Francis, the backlash his comment unleashed would not be of too great a concern.

He would see this as an instance where, just as in families, words may unintentionally hurt, he might be excused, given the love underpinning the message.

A fourth document using the metaphor of the church as a mother that contributed to the mindset of Vatican II was Pope Pius XI's encyclical on Christian marriage, *Casti Connubii* (1930), which viewed woman's ultimate vocation as mother and wife. For Ivy Helman, the encyclical is the best source on the view of women by the Catholic Church before the 1960s.[49] She also states that a change in the view of women by the church in the 1960s is evidenced in Pope John XXIII's encyclicals *Mater et Magistra* and *Pacem in Terris*, where support is given for women who undertake work outside the domestic sphere, as we saw earlier.

The affirmation of women's valuable contribution outside the domestic sphere is also made explicit, though briefly, in Vatican II's *Gaudium et Spes* and *Apostolicam Actuositatem* (The Apostolate of the Laity).[50] But again, this contribution is qualified "in accordance with [woman's] nature" (*GS* 60), referring to personal characteristics belonging specifically to women in contrast to characteristics belonging primarily to men as part of their "nature," though these natures are not explained in *Gaudium et Spes*. Similarly, the closing message at Vatican II presented women with a vocation specific to their sex:

> The hour is coming, in fact has come, when the voca-
> tion of women is being acknowledged in its fullness, the
> hour in which women acquire in the world an influence,
> an effect and a power never hitherto achieved. That is
> why, at this moment when the human race is undergo-
> ing so deep a transformation, women imbued with a
> spirit of the Gospel can do so much to aid humanity in
> not falling.[51]

Where *Arcanum Divinae Sapientiae* saw women as unequal to men and considered the emancipation of women a crime toward women, God, and families,[52] the above address presents a stark contrast. Yet, even in this more recent support for women, it also seemed to retain the mindset of the 1930s to 1950s, what Betty

Friedan names the "feminine mystique." This is seen further in the later parts of Paul VI's speech at the close of the Council:

> You women have always had as your lot the protection of the home, the love of beginnings and an understanding of cradles. You are present in the mystery of a life beginning. You offer consolation in the departure of death. Our technology runs the risk of becoming inhuman. Reconcile men with life and above all, we beseech you, watch carefully over the future of our race. Hold back the hand of man who, in a moment of folly, might attempt to destroy human civilization….Women, you do know how to make truth sweet, tender and accessible, make it your task to bring the spirit of this council into institutions, schools, homes and daily life. Women of the entire universe, whether Christian or non-believing, you to whom life is entrusted at this grave moment in history, it is for you to save the peace of the world.

Thus, while there was a change in perception of the woman by the church from *Casti Connubii* in 1930 to *Mater et Magistra* and *Pacem in Terris* in the 1960s, there remained the imaging of the mother as teacher, primary carer, and source of life for her children. *Humanae Salutis* affirmed this image by calling upon *Mater et Magistra* and added to the maternal image a church desiring to reach out to all peoples and to embrace them. The primary pastoral intent of the Council thus found one form of expression by presenting this maternal image throughout its documents.

On August 15, 1988, more than twenty years after the conclusion of the Council, Pope John Paul II released his apostolic letter, *Mulieris Dignitatem* (*MD*), "On the Dignity and Vocation of Women on the Occasion of the Marian Year." To begin his letter, John Paul called upon Paul VI's closing speech at the Council, where he acknowledged the coming hour of women's unique participation in the transformation of the world. John Paul says of this quoted text,

> This Message sums up what had already been expressed in the Council's teaching, specifically in the Pastoral

161

Constitution *Gaudium et spes* and in the Decree on the Apostolate of the Laity *Apostolicam actuositatem.*

John Paul's references for this point to *Gaudium et Spes* (*GS*) 8, 9, 60 and *Apostolicam Actuositatem* (*AA*) 9, but only *GS* 60 and *AA* 9 speak explicitly of the need to affirm women's roles outside of the home. Yet *GS* 8 speaks of discord in the family that results from new social relationships between men and women, and *GS* 9 highlights the need "to establish a political, social and economic order which will growingly serve man [*sic*] and help individuals as well as groups to affirm and develop the dignity proper to them." This dignity, described as proper to everyone, was for John Paul the understanding of humanity as either man or woman only, and that woman's proper nature is feminine. For John Paul, this meant woman is ordered to physical motherhood or virginity. It also meant woman has and provides to others a moral and spiritual strength (*MD* 30). In John Paul's view, woman has a sensitivity to the things of God, in contrast to "a gradual loss of sensitivity for man" because of scientific and technological progress, which, however, leads to the attainment of material well-being (no. 30). In fact, John Paul even described the perfect woman:

> The "perfect woman" (cf. *Prov* 31:10) becomes an irreplaceable support and source of spiritual strength for other people, who perceive the great energies of her spirit. These "perfect women" are owed much by their families, and sometimes by whole nations.

The message here is that it is up to women to save the world from itself or, more pointedly, to save men from themselves, because women have certain beneficial characteristics that belong to their nature. John Paul points to Mary as the epitome of womanhood, unique in being both virgin (being celibate but also being completely consecrated to God, *MD* 20) and mother to Christ, but also a partner with Christ in the economy of salvation. To affirm women's important and specific role, *Mulieris Dignitatem* points to women as being at the center of salvation, for the Savior is born of a woman (no. 3), the women of the Gospels were the guardians of the gospel message (no. 15), and they were the first witnesses to Jesus's resurrection (no. 16). This highlights their essential but different role from the Twelve, which, for the Catholic Church, is reserved solely for men (no. 26) because Christ is the bridegroom, a man, while the church, which is intimately tied to Christ, is his bride, a woman (no. 26). Here, the 1976 "Declaration on the Question of Admission of Women to the Ministerial Priesthood," *Inter Insigniores,*[53] is referenced. This document was prepared by the Sacred Congregation for the Doctrine of the Faith (SCDF; now called the Congregation for the Doctrine of the Faith, and previously known in short as the Inquisition), a body within the church to "promote and safeguard the doctrine on the faith and morals throughout the Catholic world."[54]

Mulieris Dignitatem strongly defends gender binarism, or a distinctive womanhood and manhood, and the view that these are the only valid genders in the economy of creation and salvation. The document is explicit in its assertion of this belief, repeating fifty-one times that being human, or in the document's own words, being "man," is being man and woman. Thus, the insistence on the presentation of the church as a woman is largely about a defense of the two genders and their distinctiveness in relation to each other. There is a teasing out throughout the document of the exact meaning of the "genius" belonging to women. *Mulieris Dignitatem* seeks to affirm women and their equality in being made in the image and likeness of God (Gen 1:27) but it also asserts gender binarism, which in the document presents men in not such a good light. For example, it says men need women's "genius" to save them, and suggests men are less sensitive to the ways of God. These underpinning thoughts within *Mulieris Dignitatem* of gender binarism, the distinctiveness between man and woman, and the role of complementarity are found in John Paul II's "Theology of the Body."[55]

Mulieris Dignitatem also uses a quote from Pope Paul VI, who says,

> Within Christianity, more than in any other religion, and since its very beginning, women have had a special dignity, of which the New Testament shows us many important aspects; it is evident that women are meant to form

part of the living and working structure of Christianity in so prominent a manner that perhaps not all their potentialities have yet been made clear.[56]

This rhetoric, like Paul VI's closing speech at Vatican II, echoes Pope Francis's own words, when he was asked about the possibility of women priests in the future of the Catholic Church:

> On woman priests, this cannot be done. Pope Saint John Paul II, when the question was being raised, after very lengthy reflection, stated this clearly. Not because women aren't capable, but...look, in the Church, women are more important than men, because the Church is a woman. We speak of the Church as "she"; she is the Bride of Christ, and Our Lady is more important than Popes, bishops and priests. I must acknowledge that we are somewhat behind in developing a theology of women. We have to progress in that area. That is certainly true.[57]

In its original Italian, Francis, in fact, reasons that the church is a woman because she is "*la* Chiesa," not "*il* Chiesa": "*perché la chiesa è donna; è* la *Chiesa, non* il *Chiesa; la Chiesa è la sposa di Cristo.*" Argument based on grammatical gender is, as we know, weak. We know there is more to the matter than this and that it is merely following the mindset of the Catholic tradition back from John Paul II, to Paul VI, Vatican II, and even documents prior to Vatican II. The difference between asserting that the church is a woman, mother, virgin, and bride by the recent magisterium and by the early fathers such as Cyprian, Ambrose, and Augustine is that recent popes are responding to a different question, and may even be described as responding to a "threat" to the moral order in society. This moral order entails the preservation of two distinct genders, man and woman, which work complementarily and are the only two that participate in the order of marriage and procreation. With the revolution of the 1960s and the change of roles for men and women such that women no longer belong specifically to the domestic sphere, and with scientific discoveries and technological advancements, there is a constant questioning and expanding of boundaries. Holding onto family as composed of a man, a woman, and children offers some certainty amid change, but it also sustains other "orders." For example, it supports the idea that the church as the bride of Christ is intimately tied to Christ the bridegroom, and that ordained priesthood belongs to men, while women are called to imitate Mary the disciple rather than Christ as female ordained priests.

On the twenty-fifth anniversary of the promulgation of *Mulieris Dignitatem* (2013), Pope Francis affirmed the distinction between man and woman and reaffirmed the idea of woman, who is entrusted with a special task:

> What does this "special entrusting", this special entrusting of the human being to woman mean? It seems evident to me that my Predecessor [St John Paul II] is referring to motherhood. Many things can change and have changed in cultural and social evolution, but the fact remains that it is woman who conceives, carries and delivers the children of men. And this is not merely a biological fact; it entails a wealth of implications both for woman herself, her way of being, and for her relationships, her relation to human life and to life in general. In calling woman to motherhood, God entrusted the human being to her in an entirely special way.[58]

Then Francis warned of two dangers, somewhat echoing the view of woman in *Gaudium et Spes* in his first point, but also in *Casti Connubii* in his second point:

> The first is to reduce motherhood to a social role, to a task which, though regarded as noble, in fact, sets the woman and her potential aside and does not fully esteem her value in the structure of the community. This may happen both in civil and ecclesial circles. And, as a reaction to this, there is another danger in the opposite direction, that of promoting a kind of emancipation that, in order to fill areas that have been taken away from the

male, deserts the feminine attributes with all its precious characteristics.[59]

Francis does recognize that to esteem woman's motherhood should not be for the purpose of devaluing a woman and her full potentiality; this is probably a reference to the social convenience she creates in society in being an unpaid stay-at-home mother, and it calls his audience to value woman beyond her domestic abilities and skills. In this, he parts with his papal predecessors who see woman's role as primarily mother and teacher, even as they recognized that women have contributed, and do contribute, beyond the domestic setting, for the good of the world. Francis, however, acknowledges an undeniable reality that only woman "conceives, carries and delivers the children of men," but in this he does not narrow her primary value to motherhood. In fact, by calling his audience to esteem her potential and value in the community, he opens her role as being more than the traditional maternal-domestic figure.

However, Francis reiterates John Paul's and the SCDF's teaching in emphasizing "that woman has a particular sensitivity to the 'things of God,' above all in helping us understand the mercy, tenderness and love that God has for us." He then calls upon his favorite image of the church, which is that of a mother. He says, "I also like to think of the Church not as an 'it' but as a 'she.' The Church is woman, she is mother, and this is beautiful. You must consider and go deeper into this." This call to go deeper is a call to develop that "theology of women," which he referred to during his interview on the return flight from the twenty-eighth World Youth Day in Rio de Janeiro, 2013. Here, Pope Francis is wrestling with his view of women and their place in the church, a wrestling, too, regarding the language with which to speak about them. Most likely, with his encounters with different women, he is concerned with the limited images of woman presented to him in the magisterium, but he has shown resistance to images of women connected to political activism and aggression, which is associated with female emancipation. The dilemma is to show continuity with the tradition of the church without also disregarding the person in front of him, the various women he has encountered and continues to encounter.

WHEN FRANCIS ABANDONS
THE FEMALE CHURCH RHETORIC

There are times when Pope Francis abandons the female church rhetoric in gauging that it is not an appropriate response to his audience. An example of this was when he abandoned his prepared speech at the Festival of Families in Philadelphia on September 26, 2015. His prepared speech had contained ideas on the witness of other families, God's choice to be born into a family, the dignity of work, and the impact on families of a lack of access to basic needs such as housing and healthcare. Francis, in his desire to reach his audience, also planned on acknowledging the nature of families as being complex and imperfect, even though sound values and love may be learned through them. As well, he planned to present Jesus as married(!), using the metaphor of the church as a bride. As Ambrose used Mary as bride, virgin, and mother to encourage Roman Christian women to become virgins for the church, so Francis wanted to use an image of Jesus as married to encourage hesitant single persons to wed.[60]

It is highly likely that the pope thought to emphasize Jesus as married in response to the growing number of individuals who postpone marriage or having children, preferring the single life or being less encumbered financially and socially. This issue appeared even when he was archbishop of Buenos Aires (1998–2013) in his 2008 reflection on family coming out of the *Aparecida* document, which was prepared at the general conference of bishops of Latin America and the Caribbean in May 2007. Francis's reflection highlighted the need for proper preparation for marriage as a "fundamental challenge" for the church, in recognition of "a noticeable drop in Church marriages" and the preference of young people "simply to live together and not take on a lifelong commitment."[61]

The issue of hesitating or of postponing marriage would appear again nearly a decade later, in the pope's apostolic exhortation *Amoris Laetitia*, or the Joy of Love, a document prepared after consultation with churches all over the world and after two episcopal synods on the family, in 2014 and 2015. Many of the ideas on the family in *Amoris Laetitia* are based on the *Aparecida* document, which the pope himself calls the *Evangelii Nuntiandi* of Latin

America. In *Amoris Laetitia*, the pope also affirms marriage over the bachelor life.[62]

To present Jesus as choosing family life over singleness, the pope presents Jesus as a bridegroom and the church as his bride. This affirms Jesus's connection with the church, and that Jesus makes sense only if one does not disregard the church—again a response most likely toward people who claim to have faith in Jesus but not in the church. But, at the Festival of Families, after hearing speeches from six different families from all over the world, Francis abandoned his prepared address. Instead, he gave an address focusing mainly on love within families.

Of all the six families who revealed their lives, thoughts, reflections, desires, and hopes as a family, it was the story of a Ukrainian migrant woman, Lesya Boris, and her two sons (one of whom, Bogdan, has cerebral palsy) that seems to have captured most of the attention of Pope Francis. Lesya spoke of the joys she received from God through her sons, especially from Bogdan. She said, while others might see him as a burden, he is in fact a blessing and an inspiration to her as he chooses joy and faith to face his challenges. Lesya spoke further of Bogdan as an inspiration to her: people ask him to pray for them, and he hopes to create programs for children with disabilities, so they too can have fun, be challenged, and not feel limited. She also spoke of the struggles of living in Ukraine, of her migration to the United States, and then of single parenting after her husband had left her. With the help of Lesya's own mother, who inspires her to have faith, and Lesya's children, and her own practice of her faith, she told the pope she had survived her trials and continues with hope, while giving a message of hope to other families with children with disabilities.[63]

Pope Francis chose to respond to the issues raised by the six families rather than his prepared points on convincing young people among the audience of reasons to marry. Therefore, there was no need to counter the idea of a bachelor Jesus. However, it was not all seriousness for the pope at the prayer vigil of the festival. He showed his characteristic humor:

> Some of you may say to me: "Father, you speak like that because you are not married!" Certainly, in the family

there are difficulties. In families we quarrel. In families sometimes plates can fly [*hand movement showing the throwing of plates*]. In families children bring headaches. I'm not going to say anything about mothers-in-law! [*The pope laughs in jest.*]

The phrases are funnier in Italian, with the pope's well-timed pauses after each sentence, and with each laugh by the crowd. After entertaining the crowds, the pope showed he understood their hard lives, speaking of his experiences with workers with young families who had not had any sleep after attending to babies who had cried all night. His subsequent challenge to choose love over division and hatred was thus readily received:

> In families, always, always there are crosses. Always. Because the love of God, the Son of God, also asked us to follow him along this way. But in families also, the cross is followed by resurrection, because there too the Son of God leads us. So the family is—if you excuse the word—a workshop of hope, of the hope of life and resurrection, since God was the one who opened this path....In families, there are difficulties, but those difficulties are resolved by love. Hatred doesn't resolve any difficulty. Divided hearts do not resolve difficulties. Only love is capable of resolving difficulty. Love is a celebration, love is joy, love is perseverance.

The crowd was prepared to receive the message because the pope had shown he was with them, he had seen their realities, and he had desired their happiness. There was no empty theory involved. The theological cross was no abstract concept but was articulated in the daily struggles shared by the six families. Similarly, the resurrection was not an unconnected theological concept for the audience to accept—the stories of families witnessing hope amid darkness was a concretization of this Christian teaching.

In contrast, had the pope used the analogy of the church as a woman and bride to Christ, it would not have responded to the struggles of the six families. Similarly, warning against the use of "far too abstract" theological ideals for marriage, the pope, in *Amoris Laetitia*, instructs fellow bishops to attend to the realities of peoples:

> At times we have also proposed a far too abstract and almost artificial theological ideal of marriage, far removed from the concrete situations and practical possibilities of real families. This excessive idealization, especially when we have failed to inspire trust in God's grace, has not helped to make marriage more desirable and attractive, but quite the opposite.[64]

From this, we can hope that the desire to promote a "feminine genius" or a "theology of woman" with her "incisive presence in the church" would transform instead into a desire to meet women in their various and concrete realities. If Francis can encourage everyone in the entire church to attend to the person in front of them; to allow themselves to be exposed to the realities of all people; and to bring those experiences into dialogue with the teachings and practices of the church, then maybe it would truly be possible to create more authentic theologies of being men, women, and the entire of God's creation, that would be, in the Ignatian mindset, the most life-giving for all.

CONCLUSION

We have explored a range of factors contributing to Pope Francis's imagination of the church as a woman and mother. Through his encounters with female figures within the domestic and public spheres, his basis for creating an image of the good woman is founded on real women with whom he formed long and lasting loving relationships. At the same time, Pope Francis's vision of the woman is surely informed by idealizations of woman, largely through his devotion to the figure of the Virgin Mary, and possibly to a lesser extent through the mythologized Argentinean woman, Eva Peron, and portrayals of the woman of personal integrity by his favorite Russian author, Dostoyevsky. There were idealizations occurring at the level of Western culture from the 1930s to 1950s, and these were evidenced in Vatican II's own imagination of the female church, specifically as mother and teacher. Several papal documents from the nineteenth and twentieth centuries reinforced these idealizations.

Further, the Catholic Church would evidence progress (in very incremental ways) on its views on women and their place in the world. We saw the contrast in views between documents only a few decades apart, such as between *Casti Connubii* and *Pacem in Terris*, where in the former, the suggestion of woman going to work was a crime, while in the latter, the contribution of women in public life was being acknowledged. But the church still has a long way to go and the pope himself senses this. He would find further evidence if he made a comparison between portrayals of women in the magisterium and the realities of the lives of women he has deeply loved.

We saw also that a range of papal documents, from *Arcanum Castii Connubi* to *Amoris Laetitia*, have consistently clung onto a binarism in which woman and man are the distinctive genders that participate in the church's version of order in the world, and woman is viewed as having a distinctive "nature." These, too, have informed Pope Francis's imagination of the church as woman and mother. According to this vision, man and woman are the only valid genders to participate in the economy of creation and salvation. The two genders complement each other and, moreover, the church suggests that woman by her nature saves man and the entire humanity from themselves. We noted that, while the early church fathers' use of the church as a woman was in response to various heresies, the more recent papal use of this imagery was not only due to a desire to project a church that was more pastoral (informed by cultural idealizations of the good woman), but also a response to a threat to the moral order whereby the understanding of traditional marriage is questioned.

Since Pope Francis called for more study into a "theology of woman" and places it as a priority for a church that is more open to dialogue, even with those who differ significantly from it, there are real possibilities for the formation of more authentic theologies of women, men, and the church as truly a witness to the good news of

Jesus Christ. Pope Francis has a duty to honor the ongoing tradition of the Catholic Church. At the same time, he will not sacrifice his pastoral duty of attending to a living person before him for the sake of clinging onto teaching applied without context. In this there are hopes for the future of the church, and more specifically in its picturing of "women" in more concrete senses.

Conclusion

We began our exploration with two questions: Why is the church a woman? Why is it called a mother? In chapter 1, we noted that long before the Christian Church was portrayed as a woman and mother, ancient societies imagined their cities and countries as women. As a woman, the city could be imagined as a bride to the city's patron deity. As a mother, she could be seen as protecting its inhabitants. These images then provided the context in which Jerusalem/Zion was portrayed as a woman and as a mother in the Hebrew Scriptures.

In the Scriptures, various female roles were given to Jerusalem/Zion, which represented more than just a location but a people and their faith. As a daughter, Zion/Jerusalem was regarded as a city to be protected from invading forces. As a whore, she was seen to be breaking the covenant relationship with God. As lamenting mother, (Mother) Zion mourned the destruction and exile of her people. These female roles reflected ancient societies' views of women, but they also reflected the journey of a people from the destruction of their first temple, and their exile and return, to the destruction of their second temple.

It is the image of Mother Jerusalem/Zion, the eternal mother, existing beyond the second temple destruction, that informs Paul's vision of the mother of Galatians 4:26 and John's vision in Revelation 12:17. These texts have often been used to claim the Catholic Church was the Mother Church. But I have argued that Mother Zion, as mother-city, is bigger than the Catholic Church. Rather, it is a vision of the kingdom of God, where Jews, Christians, and all persons of good will live in a different world order, God's order, where love, forgiveness, and mercy reign, and care of the poor and marginalized is the priority.

When early patristic authors such as Irenaeus began to imagine the Christian Church as a woman and mother, she was eventually pictured as a mother giving birth to new members through martyrdom. As a bride and virgin, she was imagined as a true partner of God, in opposition to competing religious ideas. As breastfeeding mother, she was the source of orthodox truth. While Irenaeus employed the bride and virgin metaphors for the church to affirm embodied existence and the intimate relationship between God and God's people, these very same metaphors would later become problematic when they are used out of context, in fact communicating the opposite: a church that has issues with the body and sex, and the reinforcement of a patriarchal relationship between men and women.

These beginnings show that the development of the church as a mother was quite distinct from the development of Mary as mother for the church. The importance of this distinction became evident to us in Tertullian's and Cyprian's uses of the church as a woman, when we saw that the metaphor of "mother" was being applied to the community in response to certain needs, while the use of Mary as a mother was in response to separate issues.

In chapter 2, we saw this in Tertullian's understanding of the church as the *materfamilias-univira* to the one spouse Father-God, who was the *paterfamilias*. This metaphor was used at a time when the question of baptisms into the true or orthodox church was the concern of the Christian community. In addition, Tertullian emphasized the necessity of the *regula fidei* and a shared ritual discipline to belong to this orthodox church. By arguing that being a Christian in the ancient Roman world meant to have a mother and therefore to have the singular means to *Father-God*, Tertullian attached to the church highly regarded Roman values associated with family and belonging.

Furthermore, by rejecting the superficially decorated *matrona* and contrasting her with the virtuous *materfamilias*, we noted that Tertullian, in fact, did not have a general hatred for women. Rather, his condemnation was for those who concerned themselves with superficial beauty instead of with the beauty that comes by putting on the virtues. In this, Tertullian showed the *materfamilias* was like the *virgo* in the common pursuit and exemplification of the virtues and virtuousness. Meanwhile, Mary as a mother and virgin as a model to the church is nowhere to be found in Tertullian's writings.

In chapter 3, we outlined Cyprian's appropriation of the mother as symbol of unity and stability during the third-century crisis. We saw that Cyprian presented an image of the Catholic Church as a mother that aligned with the picture of the fecund mother with her two infants as portrayed on a panel of the *Ara Pacis Augustae* monument in Rome, and in Carthage. This panel, we noted, was in view when the Roman-Carthaginian Christians were called to sacrifice to the gods of Rome under Roman Emperor Decius's decree. By presenting the Mother Church as this fecund mother, Cyprian appropriated the ideas of blessedness, stability, security, and abundance, which were associated with this image of the ideal Roman woman. Although the monument was built centuries before Cyprian's time, the Carthaginian-Roman Christian community would have been immersed in the messages of this monument, particularly the messages of peace, assurance, unity, and order through the image of the woman, alongside other sculptures, coinage, and art that portrayed her as such and that pervaded the ancient Roman Empire.

It is only later, when the persecutions from the Decian decree ceased, that Cyprian applied the mother-bride and sister-bride images from the Song of Songs to address the controversy of rebaptisms. It is interesting to note that Tertullian and Cyprian applied the female metaphor for the church to address issues surrounding the area of baptisms—more particularly, the need to distinguish between true and false baptisms. The basis of the image of "woman," we noted, was no longer the fecund mother as exemplified by Livia, Emperor Augustus's beloved wife. Rather, she was portrayed as the bridegroom to Christ as Origen also imagined the church as the bride of Jesus the bridegroom, in his reading of the Song of Songs. Again, Origen's intent to affirm embodied existence is lost in Cyprian's application of the church as bride and Christ as the bridegroom, opening the possibility of later interpretations of the bride of Christ as an eternal, perfect, and disembodied figure, a contrast to the bodily existence of women, marriages, and the bodily act of sex. However, it was not necessarily Cyprian's intent to create this possibility. Instead, he was simply applying contemporary cultural understandings of "woman" in order to better communicate with his audiences. As in Tertullian, the tradition of Mary as a model to the Catholic Church as a mother does not appear in Cyprian's writings—because there was no need to do so at the time.

It is in Ambrose that we begin to see Mary portrayed as a model to the virgin mother church. In chapter 4, we saw the numerous factors that contributed toward Ambrose's visualization of the church as a virgin, mother, and spouse. This common imagery between the church and Mary was used to convince women to become permanent virgins for the church. Furthermore, by presenting the ecclesial virgin as fulfilling the roles of both (spiritual) motherhood and virginity for the church, the Roman ecclesial virgin was doubly fulfilling her role as a woman according to ancient Roman dictates or understanding. In one sense, Ambrose presented another way of respectable living for a woman in that ancient society, by providing the option of becoming permanent virgins for the church.

Though chapter 4 was not about reinforcing the common idea that Ambrose was simply enthusiastic about virginity, in terms of being enthusiastic about avoiding sex, we also noted that Ambrose's enthusiasm for it was because of its conduciveness to the cultivation of virtues, in the same way that Tertullian also was enthusiastic about the Roman *materfamilias* who exemplified the virtues of the *virgo*— when she was more concerned with lasting beauty (the virtues) rather than with superficial beauty (makeup, jewelry, and clothing). In fact, Ambrose preferred a person to be virginal in the "mind" than in the body. This was a criticism of the vestal virgins, who did not seem to embody virtuousness by their public appearances and shows, even though at the end of their careers they could publicly profess to having lived celibate lives for at least thirty years.

Why was Ambrose so keen to have ecclesial virgins for the church? There were various motivations, ranging from the political and social to the personal and religious. We saw that the significance of virginity permeated ancient Roman culture such that the mother-virgin figure became, in fact, a culturally resonant metaphor. More pointedly, in terms of the church, the mother-virgin model communicated something about the nature of salvation, the church itself, and about Jesus Christ. Considering this, therefore, it is not easy to discard the mother-virgin image without unraveling all the associated doctrines deeply enmeshed in that image.

In Ambrose, too, Origen's bridal church, married to the bride-groom Christ, makes its appearance, as in Cyprian. The difference in the portrayal of the bridal church between the two early church fathers is that, for Ambrose, it is expected that the individual soul would grow from spiritual infancy to spiritual adulthood, in order that the individual may mother others and, in turn, reflect the virgin-motherhood of the church and Mary.

Augustine would call upon not just the individual but the entire community to grow from spiritual infancy to spiritual adult-hood, as we noted in chapter 5, through his various portrayals of the church as a woman, and particularly as a mother. For Augustine, Mary as a model of the church's virgin-motherhood was just one way of communicating something about the nature of the church through various images of "woman." For example, in dialogue with the Donatists, he initially presented a pleading mother who paral-leled his own mother pleading with him to be baptized into the Christian faith. Monica also exemplified the Roman *materfamilias-univira* in the same way the church was presented as the *materfamilias-univira*. As Monica was the one, true, and faithful spouse to her husband, so was the church Christ's one and true virgin-bride. We also saw in chapter 5 that Augustine was, in fact, reluctant to use the virgin-bride image, but was forced to do so only to reclaim it from the Donatists and Manicheans. In addition, Augustine uses the image of the church as the "new Eve" in order to counter the Manicheans. In dialogue with the Pelagians, Augustine employed the church as a mother in the Communion of the Saints, with allu-sions to the heavenly Mother Jerusalem, whom Augustine described as the "mother of us all." As the mother of us all, she calls all nations into a church composed of sinners and saints, to grow in faith and become "mothers" to others ourselves.

Thus, Augustine presented a female church in many ways: as his mother Monica, the Roman mother, virgin, and wife, Mother Jerusalem, the female figures of Psalm 45, the female ecclesial vir-gins, and the new Eve. But it is the church as virgin-mother exem-plified in Mary that has become Augustine's lasting contribution to the church. Through his image of Mary, Augustine counters the Jovinianists, and upholds marriage, motherhood, and virginity, while giving preference to virginity. But these details were to be lost and the perception of Mary as virgin and mother collapsed in the tradition of the church as a virgin and mother. Moreover, Mary has become the dominant representation of these church characteristics.

While, for Augustine, the tension between his two favorite metaphors—the church as *totus Christus* and the church as virgin-mother—remained, this tension is not explicit in the reading of Vatican II's constitution on the church, *Lumen Gentium*. Thus, when the church is called a mother from Vatican II onward, we imagine Mary as our mother, placing ourselves under her care (see *Lumen Gentium* 62), rather than imagine the community itself as a mother, consisting of the baptized, continually called to adult faith and to minister to others. Understandably, this is largely due to the incorporation of Mary into the document on the church, such that Marian devotion only has validity relating to the faith of the church rather than as a separate act of faith. This was the right action for the church at the time of Vatican II, but it has also left us with the same unresolved tension as for Augustine: the Council's new emphasis, the church as the entire people of God and not just the religious and ordained, seems to compete with the church as virgin and mother imaged in Mary as mother and virgin.[1]

Where we have seen the origins of the imagination of the church as a woman, specifically as mother, virgin, queen, bride, and daughter, we have learned that the applications of these images were in response to specific circumstances. In addition, the images of "woman" used and portrayed were in line with a common cultural understanding of the epitome of feminine comportment in the formidable ancient Roman mother. Even though the Roman Empire encompassed various nations, which entailed a rich mix of cultures and religions, an environment far from homogeneous, the nations were united under the rule of Rome. Under this rule, the governing powers sent continual messages over many centuries to their people regarding such things as the power of Rome, the right forms of behavior and interaction, and the role of women, through art (e.g., sculpture, monuments, and the coiffure and dress of Livia), numisma, laws (e.g., the *leges Juliae*), mythology (e.g., Romulus and Remus), and religious institutions (e.g., the vestal virgins) and observances (emperor worship and sacrifices to local gods).

Around two thousand years later, we find ourselves asking why Pope Francis is calling the church a woman. Does it necessarily have to be a woman? Can we just name the church a sister, or some other more contemporary metaphor? Just as the early patristic writers used the female church, even if reluctantly, to respond to specific circumstances, can we say that Pope Francis is similarly responding to specific, albeit different, circumstances? The early patristic writers, however, were not simply reinforcing the tradition of the church as a woman. Rather, it was often because their opponents or detractors were using the same female imagery. Or, the use of the church as female proved to be the most useful rhetorical tool, where author and audience had a common understanding of "woman." While these understandings were the idealized and conceptualized female, there was a united way of thinking such that, for example, "virgin bride" did not appear incongruous but made perfect sense. If the virgin-bride church was discarded today in favor of some other more relevant metaphor, we would be left without a metaphor to convey the intimate relationship between the church and Christ. At the same time, we would also be left with a metaphor that reinforces patriarchy. It is the dilemma of conveying the nature of the church mined from its rich tradition, but not at the cost of women. The church must wrestle with this dilemma if it is to take seriously the epidemic of violence against women in many parts of the world. It is, too, a call for those who speak of an inclusive church to walk the talk and not just be happy we are doing the talk.

The concluding chapter was an exploration of Pope Francis's uses of the church as a female and specifically as a mother, which he says himself is his favorite metaphor. The least we can say about Pope Francis is that he should have some credibility when he speaks about women and uses female imagery as representative of an idea, because he has not only had brief encounters with women, but he has had deep loving relationships with them. And these women are not only those who align themselves with him regarding their political, religious, and social views; some of them even hold completely opposite views in these areas. In short, he has respect for many different women inside and outside of the home.

Nevertheless, when Pope Francis has spoken in ways that have been offensive, such as by referring to female theologians as "strawberries on the cake," or religious women as being called to be spiritual mothers rather than "spinsters," we should then question whether he really means to include women in his Vatican II–inspired push for a more inclusive church, a church that "welcomes," "opens its doors," and "dialogues with the other." Or is it a selective inclusion, where the poor do not necessarily include those who suffer from the ongoing presence of patriarchy in the church?

There is a real possibility the pope has a difficult struggle with how to speak about women and their roles within and for the church because, while he must uphold the richness of the teachings within the church, including those regarding women, his encounters with real women surely tell him there is more than what is presented in the magisterium. With his attentiveness to and priority for the person in front of him, and a great dislike for abstraction, there is a real hope that slowly, but surely, the thinking on women, the writings and teachings about them, and the task of relating with them within the church can develop and expand over time—even if this takes longer than we would wish.

Even with the papal and conciliar documents before, during, and after Vatican II, there have been steps—few, but revolutionary—on the thinking about women just within decades of each other. An overview of the context in which the church was imagined as a mother at Vatican II has been provided because this was not only the heritage of the church, which the pope carries, but it is also a tradition that he favors and promotes. We have also seen that the Vatican II documents were created at a time of instability and uncertainty. Hence, outside of the church there was a programmatic message about women and their roles to curb some of the anxieties created from surviving an era of war and depression. The Catholic Church participates in this program of communication, in its own way, through mixed messaging: women's dignity is to be highlighted, but also women are to remain the weaker sex; or women have much to contribute to the world, but their essential role is as mothers, whether by physical or spiritual motherhood. The insistence on presenting the female church is in response to a constantly changing world where boundaries are continually being challenged. Moreover, by arguing for a female church, the pope is also arguing for a certain order of the world to be maintained: that is, that there are only two genders that participate in the economy of creation and salvation; that the church is the bride to Christ the bridegroom; and women, with their "distinctive nature" from men, are called to be more like Mary the disciple than Jesus the priest because women have certain "capacities" that will ultimately "save" men and the rest of creation.

In the end, we the church need to ask ourselves this: What are we concerned about in the traditions we retain and the traditions we promote? That is, are we concerned about the order of the kingdom of God—nations, peoples, genders, ages, cultures, living in an order where the poor are a priority and our automatic response is reconciliation and healing? Or is the kingdom about a different world order, the order of the Roman Empire or of patriarchy, self-interest, fear, self-preservation, and selective inclusion? The church has its work cut out in this area—about how it views, interacts with, writes about, and uses women to convey its messages. But we live in hope because the Christian people are an Easter people, defiant against the cross and death as having the last words. Pope Francis has revived the Vatican II concept of a church opening its doors to dialogue and to its being transformed by it. Now that the dialogue has begun, that Pope Francis has reinforced Jesus's approach of attending to the "person in front of you," and that many women continue to do excellent work despite their hiddenness and invisibility, the entire church at some point will need to walk its talk—to not just speak of beautiful ideas about the good news and God's kingdom but to live it and witness to it. It is often recounted that Francis of Assisi, the person from whom Jorge Bergoglio took his papal name, once said, "Preach the Gospel and use words if necessary," but in truth he said,

> Let none of the brothers preach contrary to the form and institution of the holy Roman Church, and unless this has been conceded to him by his minister….Nevertheless, let all the brothers preach by their works.[2]

Dear Church, pray and preach the good news to and with women with your deeds and your works.

Appendix 1

Cyprian's *On the Unity of the Catholic Church*, Paragraph 4[*]

[First Edition]	[Second Edition]
And He says to him again after the resurrection: "Feed my sheep." It is on him that He builds the Church, and to him that He entrusts the sheep to feed. And although He assigns a like power to all the Apostles, yet He founded a single Chair, thus establishing by His own authority the source and hallmark of the [Church's] oneness. No doubt the others were all that Peter was, but a primacy is given to Peter, and it is [thus] made clear that there is but one Church and one Chair. So too, even if they are all shepherds, we are shown but one flock which is to be fed by all the Apostles in common accord. If a man does not hold fast to this oneness of Peter, does he imagine that he still holds the faith? If he deserts the Chair of Peter upon whom the Church was built, has he still confidence that he is in the Church?	It is on one man that He builds the Church, and although He assigns a like power to all the Apostles after His resurrection, saying: "*As the Father hath sent me, I also send you... Receive ye the Holy Spirit: if you forgive any man his sins, they shall be forgiven him; if you retain any man's, they shall be retained,*" yet, in order that the oneness might be unmistakable, He established by His own authority a source for that oneness having its origin in one man alone. No doubt the other Apostles were all that Peter was, endowed with equal dignity and power, but the start comes from him alone, in order to show that the Church of Christ is unique. Indeed this oneness of the Church is figured in the Canticle of Canticles when the Holy Spirit, speaking in the Lord's name, says: "*One is my dove, my perfect one: to her mother she is the only one, the darling of her womb.*" If a man does not hold fast to this oneness of the Church, does he imagine that he still holds the faith? If he resists and withstands the Church, has he still confidence that he is in the Church, when the blessed Apostle Paul gives us this very teaching and points to the mystery of Oneness saying: "*One body and one Spirit, one hope of your calling, one Lord, one Faith, one Baptism, one God*"?

---

[*] From Cyprian, *De Ecclesiae Catholicae Unitate*, text and trans. Maurice Bévenot, in Oxford Early Christian Texts, general ed. Henry Chadwick (Oxford: Clarendon Press, 1971), 61, 63.

183

Appendix 2

Sources for Ancient Works

Ancient Author	Ancient Works Cited, by English Title	Latin/ Greek Edition	English Translation/s
Ambrose	*Commentary on Psalm 118, Sermons*	PL 15	Ambrose, *Commentary of Saint Ambrose on Twelve Psalms*, trans. I. Ní Riain (Dublin: Halcyon, 2000)
	Commentary on the Gospel of Luke 2	CCSL 14	Ambrose, *Commentary of Saint Ambrose on the Gospel according to Saint Luke*, trans. I. Ní Riain (Dublin: Halcyon, 2001)
	Commentary on the Twelve Psalms— Psalm 47	PL 14	Ambrose, *Commentary of Saint Ambrose on Twelve Psalms*, trans. I. Ní Riain (Dublin: Halcyon, 2000)
	Concerning Virginity	PL 16	A. Christie (1843)
	Concerning Virgins	PL 16	*NPNF2* 10 (trans. H. De Romestin, 1979)
	Concerning Widows	PL 16	*NPNF2* 10 (trans. H. De Romestin, 1979)
	Instruction for a Virgin	PL 16	M. Colish (2008), P. Brown (2008), D. Hunter (2000)
	Isaac; or, The Soul	PL 14	J. Smith (2011)
	Letters	PL 16	*NPNF2* 10 (trans. H. De Romestin, 1979)
	On Abraham	PL 14	M. Colish (2008)
	On Faith	PL 17	NPNF2 10 (trans. H. De Romestin, 1979)
	On Repentance	PL 16	*NPNF2* 10 (trans. H. De Romestin, 1979)
	On the Death of His Brother Satyrus	PL 16	*NPNF2* 10 (trans. H. De Romestin, 1979)

Sources for Ancient Works *(continued)*

Ancient Author	Ancient Works Cited, by English Title	Latin/ Greek Edition	English Translation/s
	On the Good Death	PL 14	J. Smith (2011)
	On the Incarnation of Our Lord	PL 16	FC 44 (trans. R. Deferrari, 1963)
	On the Mysteries	PL 16	*NPNF2* 10 (trans. H. De Romestin, 1979)
Augustine	*Against Faustus, a Manichee*	PL 42	WSA I/20 (trans. R. Teske, 2007)
	Against Julian	PL 44	WSA I/24 (trans. R. Teske, reprint 2013)
	Against Julian, an Unfinished Book	PL 45	WSA I/25 (trans. R. Teske, reprint 2013)
	City of God	CCSL 47—48	WSA I/7 (trans. W. Babcock, 2013)
	Confessions	CCSL 27	WSA I/1 (trans. M. Boulding, reprint 2014)
	Expositions of the Psalms	PL 36—*Ps* 1–79	WSA III/17 (trans. M. Boulding, 2001)—*Ps* 51–72
		PL 37—*Ps* 80–144	WSA III/20 (trans. M. Boulding, 2004)—*Ps* 121–50
	Letters	PL 33	WSA II/1 (trans. R. Teske, 2001)
	On Baptism	PL 43	*NPNF1* 4 (trans J. R. King, 1887)
	On Christian Teaching	CCSL 80	OECT (trans. R. Green, reprint 2004)
	On Holy Virginity	PL 40	WSA I/9 (trans. R. Kearney, 1999)
	A Psalm against the Party of Donatus	PL 43	mine, Springer (1987)
	Reconsiderations	CCSL 57	WSA I/2 (trans. B. Ramsay, 2010)
	Sermons 22, 72A, 187, 188, 191, 192	CCSL 41	WSAIII/2, 3, 5, 6 (trans. E. Hill, 1990)
	To Cresconius, a Donatist Grammarian	PL 43	mine

Ancient Author	Ancient Works Cited, by English Title	Latin/ Greek Edition	English Translation/s
Cyprian	*Letters*	CCSL 3B, 3C	ACW 43/I (trans. G. Clarke, 1983)—*Letter* 10
			ACW 44/II (trans. G. Clarke, 1983)—*Letters* 44, 47, 48
			ACW 46/III (trans. G. Clarke, 1986)—*Letter* 59
			ACW 57/IV (trans. G. Clarke, 1989)—*Letters* 69, 74
	On the Dress of Virgins	PL	*ANF* 5 (trans. R. E. Wallis, 1978)
	On the Lapsed	CCSL 3	trans. M. Bévenot (1971)
	On the Unity of the Catholic Church	CCSL 3	trans. M. Bévenot (1971)
	To Donatus	CCSL 3a	*ANF* 5 (trans. R. E. Wallis, 1978)
Eusebius	*Ecclesiastical History*	LCL 153	J. Stevenson and William H. C. Frend, *A New Eusebius: Documents Illustrating the History of the Church to AD 337* (London: SPCK, 1987)
Irenaeus	*Against Heresies: Refutation and Overthrow of Knowledge Falsely So-Called*	PG 7	*ANCL* V/1 (trans. A. Roberts and W. H. Rambaut, 1911)
	Proof; or, Demonstration of the Apostolic Preaching	PO 12.5	ACW 16 (trans. J. P. Smith, 1992)
Origen	*Commentary on the Song of Songs*	PG 13	ACW 26 (trans. R. P. Lawson, 1957)
Polycarp	*Letter to the Philippians*	LCL 24	LCL 24 (trans. B. Ehrman, 2003)
Shepherd of Hermas	*Visions*	LCL 25	LCL 25 (trans. B. Ehrman, 2003)
Tertullian	*Against Marcion*	CCSL 1	*ANCL* XI/3 (trans. E. Evans, 1972)
	Antidote for the Scorpion's Sting	CCSL 2	*ANCL* XI/1

Sources for Ancient Works *(continued)*

Ancient Author	Ancient Works Cited, by English Title	Latin/ Greek Edition	English Translation/s
	Apology	CCSL 1	*ANCL* XI/1
	The Chaplet	CCSL 2	*ANCL* XI/1
	On Baptism	CCSL 1	*ANCL* XI/1
	On Flight in Persecution	CCSL 2	*ANCL* XI/1
	On Modesty	CCSL 2	*ANF* IV (trans. S. Thelwall, 1885)
	On Monogamy	CCSL 2	ACW 13 (trans. W. P. Le Saint, 1951)
	On Prayer	CCSL 1	*ANCL* XI/1 (trans. E. Evans, 1953)
	On the Dress of Women	CCSL 1	FC 40 (trans. E. Quain, 1959)
	On the Flesh of Christ	CCSL 2	*ANCL* XI/2 (trans. E. Evans, 1956)
	On the Shows	CCSL 1	*ANCL* XI/1, *ANF* III/1
	On the Soul	CCSL 2	*ANF* III (trans. P. Holmes, 1978)
	On the Veiling of Virgins	CCSL 2	*ANCL* XI/3
	The Prescription of Heretics	CCSL 1	*ANF* III
	To the Martyrs	CCSL 1	*ANCL* XI/1
	To the Nations	CCSL 1	*ANCL* XI/1

Notes

1. THE CITY AS A WOMAN, FAITH AS A MOTHER

1. E.g., Mark E. Biddle, "The Figure of Lady Jerusalem: Identification, Deification and Personification of Cities in the Ancient Near East," in *The Biblical Canon in Comparative Perspective*, ed. K. Lawson Younger, William W. Hallo, and Bernard Frank Batto (Lewiston, NY: E. Mellen, 1991); Julie Galambush, *Jerusalem in the Book of Ezekiel: The City as Yahweh's Wife* (Atlanta: Scholars, 1992); and Lynn R. Huber, *Like a Bride Adorned: Reading Metaphor in John's Apocalypse* (London: T. & T. Clark, 2007). For a more comprehensive list, see Maggie Low, *Mother Zion in Deutero-Isaiah: A Metaphor for Zion Theology* (New York: Peter Lang, 2014), 54n3. Low and Christl Maier (see n. 6) cite J. Lewy as another author used in the same way as Fitzgerald. See also Aloysius Fitzgerald, "The Mythological Background for the Presentation of Jerusalem as a Queen and False Worship as Adultery in the OT," *Catholic Biblical Quarterly* 34, no. 4 (1972): 403–16.

2. David Christian, *Maps of Time: An Introduction to Big History*, California World History Library (Berkeley: University of California Press, 2004), 245.

3. J. A. Black, "The Babylonian Grammatical Tradition: The First Grammars of Sumerian," *Transactions of the Philological Society* 87, no. 1 (1989): 75–99, at 75.

4. Fitzgerald, "Mythological Background," 405.

5. Peggy Day, "The Personification of Cities as Female in the Hebrew Bible: The Thesis of Aloysius Fitzgerald F.S.C.," in *Reading from This Place: Social Location and Biblical Interpretation in Global Perspective*, vol. 2, ed. Fernando F. Segovia and Mary Ann Tolbert (Minneapolis: Fortress Press, 1995): 283–302.

6. See Christl M. Maier, *Daughter Zion, Mother Zion: Gender, Space, and the Sacred in Ancient Israel* (Minneapolis: Fortress Press, 2008), 68.

7. See Hans Jörg Nissen (Berlin) and Joachim Oelsner (Leipzig), "Mesopotamia," in *Brill's New Pauly*. Antiquity volumes edited by Hubert Cancik and Helmuth Schneider. See http://dx.doi.org/10.1163/1574-9347_bnp_e800690, accessed February 21, 2017.

8. See §30.6 in Edward Lipinski, "Gender," *Semitic Languages: Outline of a Comparative Grammar* (Leuven: Uitgeverij Peeters en Departement Oosterse Studies, 2001), 235–42, at 238. Lipinski explains that this works in the same way as "Hebrew place names beginning with *byt,* 'house,' are masculine since *byt* is a masculine noun in Hebrew."

9. John J. Schmitt, "The Motherhood of God and Zion as Mother," *Revue Biblique* (1985): 557–69, at 568. Schmitt credits David Weisberg (1938–2012), Professor of Bible and Semitic Languages, for this significant piece of information. See 568n48. It is interesting to find the Canaanite scribes perform this gender change given that Martin Worthington says it is more common to write the masculine form than its feminine equivalent in Akkadian. See §3.2.11, "Errors of Gender Polarity," in Martin Worthington, *Principles of Akkadian Textual Criticism* (Boston: De Gruyter, 2016), 109.

10. See Low, who argues similarly in *Mother Zion in Deutero-Isaiah*, 55.

11. Low, *Mother Zion in Deutero-Isaiah*, 73.

12. Low, *Mother Zion in Deutero-Isaiah*, 188.

13. Low, *Mother Zion in Deutero-Isaiah.*

14. Low, *Mother Zion in Deutero-Isaiah.* Low views these descriptions as "locations," but I argue that the descriptions lend to the imaging of Zion as a state of existence, or an "event," as opposed to being simply a geographical place.

15. See Low, who argues that even though Zion is described in unholy terms, Zion as God's dwelling place remains holy, while the people of Zion are the unholy/"whores," who breach their relationship with YHWH by their wrongdoing. Low, *Mother Zion in Deutero-Isaiah*, 188.

16. Maier, *Daughter Zion, Mother Zion*, 151.

17. Maier, *Daughter Zion, Mother Zion*, 2.

18. Maier, *Daughter Zion, Mother Zion*, 2.

19. Judaizers insisted on the conversion of Gentiles to the Jewish faith through circumcision and the observance of regulations concerning diet and moral living.

20. See Bruce Longenecker, "Galatians," in *The Cambridge Companion to St. Paul*, ed. James D. G. Dunn (Cambridge: Cambridge University Press, 2008), 64–73, at 64–66.

21. Low, *Mother Zion in Deutero-Isaiah*, 188.

22. Wes Howard-Brook and Anthony Gwyther, *Unveiling Empire: Reading Revelation Then and Now* (Maryknoll, NY: Orbis Books, 1999), 116.

23. The deuterocanonical/intertestamental period was the time between the writing of the Hebrew Bible and the Christian New Testament. Some of the apocalyptic writings surfacing from that period are the Dead Sea Scrolls (late first century BCE), 2 Baruch (late first century CE), and 4 Ezra/2 Esdras (100 CE).

24. Gordon D. Fee, *Revelation: A New Covenant Commentary* (Cambridge: Lutterworth, 2013), 164–65.

25. See Zeus's birth story and the birth story of his own son in Jenny March, "Creation," in *The Penguin Book of Classical Myths* (London: Penguin, 2009), 21–52; H. J. Rose, "The Children of Kronos-I," in *A Handbook of Greek Mythology including Its Extension to Rome* (New York: Dutton, 1959), 43–77.

26. Brigitte Kahl, "Gaia, Polis and *Ekkl sia* at the Miletus Market Gate: An Eco-Critical Re-imagination of Revelation 12:16," in *The First Urban Churches*, ed. James R. Harrison and L. L. Welborn, vol. 1 (Atlanta: SBL, 2015), 118.

27. Brigitte Kahl, "Gaia, Polis and *Ekkl sia* at the Miletus Market Gate," 118.

28. Paul Figueras, "Legal Status of the Jewish Religion," in *An Introduction to Early Christianity* (Piscataway, NJ: Gorgias, 2014), 19. See also Brigitte W. Kahl, "Reading Galatians and Empire at the Great Altar of Pergamon," *Union Seminary Quarterly Review* 59 (2005): 21–43, at 31, 34.

29. Low, *Mother Zion in Deutero-Isaiah*, 188.

30. Low, *Mother Zion in Deutero-Isaiah*, 188.

31. Low, *Mother Zion in Deutero-Isaiah*, 188–89.

32. Howard-Brook and Gwyther, *Unveiling Empire*, 184.

33. Polycarp was the bishop of Smyrna and a second-century martyr.

34. Polycarp, *Letter to the Philippians* 3:2–3.

35. *Acti Sancti Justini et sociorum* 4, in J. Stevenson and William H. C. Frend, *A New Eusebius: Documents Illustrating the History of the Church to AD 337* (London: SPCK, 1987), 32–34, at 33. On the evidence of the presence of Mater Pistis, see Joseph Conrad Plumpe, *Mater Ecclesia: An Inquiry into*

the Concept of the Church as Mother in Early Christianity (Washington, DC: Catholic University of America Press, 1943), 18–20.

36. Shepherd of Hermas, *Vision* 2.4.1.

37. Shepherd of Hermas, *Vision* 3.3.3.

38. Shepherd of Hermas, *Vision* 3.5.1.

39. Shepherd of Hermas, *Vision* 3.8.2–4.

40. Based especially on Shepherd of Hermas, *Vision* 2.4.1 and 3.3.3, respectively.

41. There were a variety of forms of Gnosticism with differences in beliefs, so it is inaccurate to place them even under the one umbrella called "Gnosticism."

42. For more on the Shepherd of Hermas's Lady in his *Visions,* see D. P. O'Brien, "The Cumaean Sibyl as the Revelation-Bearer in the Shepherd of Hermas," *Journal of Early Christian Studies* 5, no. 4 (1997): 473–96.

43. Eusebius, *Ecclesiastical History* 5.1.55.

44. For further discussion on the authorship of *Letter to the Churches of Vienne and Lyons,* see Denis Minns, *Irenaeus: An Introduction* (London: T. & T. Clark, 2010), 2.

45. See Eusebius, *Ecclesiastical History* 5.1.3–63, esp. 5.1.45–46.

46. "A mother's love" seems a weak translation for μητρικὰ σπλάγχνα since σπλάγχνα can be translated "from the very bowels, a deep pity, compassion, the very seat of one's feelings." The mother here is not just simply loving: she is beside herself with emotion. I thank Denis Minns for pointing this out.

47. Eusebius, *Ecclesiastical History* 5.2.6–7.

48. The threat of Gnostic or unorthodox teachings is evidenced in Irenaeus, *Against Heresies,* where they competed for the attention of Christians. The competing Gnostic cults and philosophies for Irenaeus are listed in *Against Heresies* 1.1–31.

49. Robert M. Grant, *Irenaeus of Lyons* (New York: Routledge, 1997), 25.

50. Irenaeus, *Against Heresies* 3.24.1.

51. Irenaeus, *Against Heresies* 5.20.2.

52. Robert Garland, "Mother and Child in the Greek World," *History Today* 36 (1986): 45.

53. See Irenaeus, *Against Heresies* 3.25.6, where Irenaeus criticizes Gnosticism's version of a "mother" (church).

54. Irenaeus, *Against Heresies* 1.5.3.

55. Irenaeus, *Against Heresies* 1.4.1.

56. Irenaeus, *Against Heresies* 1.5.6; 1.8.4.

57. Plumpe, *Mater Ecclesia*, 40–41.

58. Plumpe, *Mater Ecclesia*, 40. See also Eusebius, *Ecclesiastical History* 5.3.4. The document speaks of the Gallic Christians writing letters to communities in Asia, Phrygia, and Rome, desiring peace from the disputes occurring among the prophets and leaders of Montanism, who were Montanus, Alcibiades, and Theodotus.

59. See, e.g., Karl Shuve, "Irenaeus' Contribution to Early Christian Interpretation of the Song of Songs," in *Irenaeus: Life, Scripture and Legacy*, ed. Sara Parvis and Paul Foster (Minneapolis: Fortress Press, 2012), 81–88, at 84.

60. Shuve, "Irenaeus' Contribution." See also Irenaeus, *Against Heresies* 5.9.4.

61. Irenaeus, *Against Heresies* 4.20.12.

62. Shuve, "Irenaeus' Contribution," 86.

63. Irenaeus also points to the marriage of Moses to the Ethiopian as a prefiguring of the Word's marriage to the church as bride. See also Minns, *Irenaeus*, 106.

64. Shuve, "Irenaeus' Contribution," 86.

65. Shuve, "Irenaeus' Contribution," 86.

66. Shuve, "Irenaeus' Contribution," 81.

67. Shuve, "Irenaeus' Contribution," 81.

68. See Irenaeus, *Against Heresies* 2.30.3. In that work, Mary is called "the virgin with a son" or "virgin." The church is simply called "Church" (e.g., *Against Heresies* 4.19.1; 4.20.12) or "Church of God" (e.g., *Against Heresies* 3.25.7), and her motherhood is implied when Irenaeus attributes "children" to her (*Proof* 94) and describes her as nourishing from her "bosom" (*Against Heresies* 3.24.1; 5.20.2). The Church is called a "virgin mother" in *Proof* 97. But *mother* and *church* are never placed alongside each other in the text.

69. See, e.g., Juan L. Bastero, *Mary, Mother of the Redeemer: A Mariology Textbook* (Dublin: Four Courts, 2006), 34; Brendan Leahy, *The Marian Profile in the Ecclesiology of Hans Urs von Balthasar* (New York: New City Press, 2000), 20; and Joseph Ratzinger, "On the Position of Mariology and Marian Spirituality within the Totality of Faith and Theology," in *The Church and Women: A Compendium*, ed. Helmut Moll (San Francisco: Ignatius, 1988), 74.

70. Irenaeus, *Against Heresies* 3.24.1.

71. Eusebius, *Ecclesiastical History* 5.1.45–46.

72. Irenaeus, *Against Heresies* 3.21.5.

73. Irenaeus, *Against Heresies* 3.22.1.

74. Eusebius, *Ecclesiastical History* 5.1.45–46.

75. Irenaeus, *Against Heresies* 3.24.1.

76. Irenaeus, *Against Heresies* 1.7.2.

77. Irenaeus, *Against Heresies* 3.22.1.

78. Garland, "Mother and Child," 40. I discuss ancient understandings of genetics and parentage, that is, the father's primary role and the mother's secondary role, in more detail in the next chapter.

79. See Irenaeus, *Against Heresies* 1.7.

80. Frances Young, "The Church and Mary," *Ecclesiology* 5 (2009): 276–98.

2. SHE IS MOTHER OF THE FAMILY, WIFE TO ONE MAN ONLY

1. See Ann Ellis Hanson, "Widows Too Young in Their Widowhood," in *I, Claudia II: Women in Roman Art and Society*, ed. Diana E. E. Kleiner and Susan B. Matheson (Austin: University of Texas Press, 2000), 149–65.

2. Rachel Meyers, "Female Portraiture and Female Patronage in the High Imperial Period," in *A Companion to Women in the Ancient World*, ed. Sharon L. James and Sheila Dillon (Malden, MA: Blackwell, 2015), 453–66, at 460. The exception was if she was a vestal virgin, which will be discussed in more detail in chapter 4.

3. Meyers, "Female Portraiture," 460. See also Elizabeth Bartman, *Portraits of Livia* (Cambridge: Cambridge University Press, 1999), 24.

4. Suzanne Dixon, *The Roman Mother* (New York: Routledge, 2015), 51–52.

5. Alan H. Cadwallader, *Fragments of Colossae: Sifting through the Traces* (Hindmarsh, SA, Australia: ATF, 2015), 171.

6. The penalty laws would eventually be repealed in 320 CE by Emperor Constantine to benefit the upper classes of Rome and Christian asceticism—leading to asceticism's growing popularity in the fourth century. Judith Evans Grubbs, *Women and the Law in the Roman Empire: A Sourcebook on Marriage, Divorce and Widowhood* (London: Routledge, 2002), 103.

7. See Laura Betzig, "Roman Monogamy," *Ethology and Sociobiology* 13, no. 5 (1992): 356; Dixon, *Roman Mother*, 72; Judith Evans Grubbs, *Law and Family in Late Antiquity* (Oxford: Clarendon, 1995), 103–4.

8. Andrew T. Bierkan, Charles P. Sherman, and Emile Stocquart, "Marriage in Roman Law," *Yale Law Journal* 16, no. 5 (March 1907): 303–27; and Judith Evans Grubbs, "The Status of Women in Roman Law," in *Women and the Law in the Roman Empire*, 19.

9. Bierkan, Sherman, and Stocquart, "Marriage in Roman Law," 310.

10. Grubbs, "Status of Women," 19.

11. Ulpian in *Justinian's Digest* 50.16.46.1, in Grubbs, "Status of Women," 19.

12. Ulpian in *Justinian's Digest* 43.30.3.6, in Grubbs, "Status of Women," 19.

13. For more on the *univira*, see Dixon, *Roman Mother*, 22. See also Mirielle Corbier, "Family and Kinship in Roman Africa," in *The Roman Family in the Empire*, ed. Michele George (Oxford: Oxford University, 2010), 255–85, at 262–63.

14. Gordon Williams, "Representations of Roman Women in Literature," in *I, Claudia: Women in Ancient Rome*, ed. Diana E. E. Kleiner and Susan B. Matheson (Austin: University of Texas Press, 1996), 126–38, at 128.

15. Gordon Williams, "Representations of Roman Women," 128.

16. Macrobius, *Saturnalia* 2.5.8–9, trans. R. Kaster (Cambridge, MA: Harvard University Press, 2014), 451. See also Rhiannon Ash, "Women in Imperial Roman Literature," in James and Dillon, *Companion to Women*, 442–52, at 451.

17. Ulpian in *Justinian's Digest* 50.16.13, in Grubbs, "Status of Women," 19.

18. For more, see Grubbs, *Women and the Law in the Roman Empire*, 18–20.

19. Service to the vestal virgin cult normally lasted thirty years, after which a woman could decide to remain as a vestal virgin or marry and have a family.

20. See Robin Lorsch Wildfang, *Rome's Vestal Virgins: A Study of Rome's Vestal Priestesses in the Late Republic and Early Empire* (London: Routledge, 2006), 64–67. The topic of vestal virgin is discussed in more detail in chapter 4.

21. See Jane F. Gardner, "The Guardianship of Women," in *Women in Roman Law and Society* (London: Routledge, 1986), 5–29, and especially Grubbs, "Status of Women," 19, 21–46.

22. Tertullian, *On the Shows* 6.2–4.

23. Tertullian, *Apology* 9.16, trans. S. Thelwall, *ANF* III, 26. See also Tertullian, *To the Nations* 1.16.

24. Tertullian, *Apology* 6.9, trans. S. Thelwall, *ANF* III, 23.

25. Dionysius of Halicarnassus, *Roman Antiquities* 2.19.2–5, in Matthew Dillon and Lynda Garland, *Ancient Rome: From the Early Republic to the Assassination of Julius Caesar* (London: Routledge, 2005), 162.

26. Tertullian, *Apology* 9.19, trans. S. Thelwall, *ANF* III, 26.

27. In Suzanne Dixon, "Womanly Weakness in Roman Law," in *Reading Roman Women* (London: Duckworth, 2001), 73–88, at 73. See also Judith Evans Grubbs, "Womanly Weakness," in *Women and the Law in the Roman Empire*, 51–60.

28. Tertullian, *On the Dress of Women* 1.1.1–1.1.2, trans. E. Quain, FC 40, 117–18.

29. Tertullian, *On the Dress of Women* 1.1.2, trans. E. Quain, FC 40, 118.

30. Bonnie MacLachlan, "Cornelia Gracchus: The Ideal *Matrona*," in *Women in Ancient Rome: A Sourcebook* (London: Bloomsbury, 2013), 67–9, at 67. See also Suzanne Dixon, *Cornelia, Mother of the Gracchi* (London: Routledge, 2007).

31. Wildfang, *Rome's Vestal Virgins*, 13. See also Michele George, "Family Imagery and Values in Roman Italy," in *The Roman Family in the Empire*, ed. Michele George (Oxford: Oxford University, 2010), 44–5, 49–50.

32. Tertullian, *On the Dress of Women* 1 and 2. See also Elizabeth A. Clark, "Status Feminae," in *Tertullian and Paul*, ed. Todd D. Still and David E. Wilhite (New York: Bloomsbury, 2013), 127–55, at 143–44.

33. Clark, "Status Feminae," 143–44.

34. *Integritas* can mean any of the following: completeness, soundness, purity, correctness, blamelessness, innocence, or chastity.

35. *Castitas* is purity or chastity.

36. Tertullian, *On the Dress of Women* 1.2.2.

37. Clark, "Status Feminae," 144–45. See also Tertullian, *On Flight in Persecution* 9.4, trans. E. Quain, FC 40, 294–95.

38. Tertullian, *On Baptism* 20.5; *To the Martyrs* 1.1.

39. Tertullian, *On Baptism* 20.5, trans. S. Thelwall, *ANF* III, 679, with my slight adjustment.

40. Tertullian, *On Baptism* 4.1–6.

41. Tertullian, *On Baptism* 8.22–28.

42. Roy Kearsley, "Baptism Then and Now: Does Moltmann Bury Tertullian or Praise Him?" in *Dimensions of Baptism: Biblical and Theological Studies*, ed. Stanley E. Porter and Anthony R. Cross, *Journal for the Study of the New Testament* Supplement Series 234 (London: Sheffield Academic, 2002), 236–52, at 242.

43. Roy Kearsley, "Baptism Then and Now," 238.

44. Roy Kearsley, "Baptism Then and Now," 238.

45. Tertullian, *The Chaplet* 3.3, trans. E. Quain, FC 40, 236–37.

46. Philip Tite, "Nurslings, Milk and Moral Development in the Greco-Roman Context: A Reappraisal of the Paraenetic Utilization of Metaphor in 1 Peter 2.1–3," *Journal for the Study of the New Testament* 31, no. 4 (2009): 381–82.

47. *The Epistle of Barnabas* 6.17, trans. K. Lake, LCL 25.

48. Aulus Gellius, *Noctes Atticae* 12.1.8.9, in Dixon, *Roman Mother*, 94.

49. Dixon, *Roman Mother*, 3, 108. See also Keith R. Bradley, "Wet-Nursing at Rome: A Study in Social Relations," in *The Family in Ancient Rome*, ed. Beryl Rawson (New York: Cornell University Press, 1986), 201–29.

50. Dixon, *Roman Mother*, 119.

51. Dixon, *Roman Mother*, 120.

52. Tertullian, *On the Soul* 19.8, trans. P. Holmes, *ANF* III, 200.

53. Tertullian, *To the Martyrs* 1.1, trans. S. Thelwall, *ANF* III, 693.

54. Geoffrey D. Dunn, *Tertullian* (New York: Taylor & Francis, 2004), 43.

55. In Dunn, *Tertullian*, 44. See Tertullian, *Antidote for the Scorpion's Sting* 1.5–9.

56. Dunn, *Tertullian*, 44.

57. Andrew McGowan, "Discipline and Diet: Feeding the Martyrs in Roman Carthage," *Harvard Theological Review* 96, no. 4 (2003): 455–76.

58. Tertullian, *On Baptism* 20.5; *On Monogamy* 7.8–9.0.

59. Father and son: Tertullian, *On Prayer* 2.3–7; father and children: Tertullian, *On Baptism* 20.5; *On the Flesh of Christ* 7.13.

60. Tertullian, *On Prayer* 2.6, trans. E. Evans, *ANCL* XI/1, 15.

61. George, "Family Imagery," 39.

62. Tertullian, *The Prescription of Heretics* 42.9–10, trans. P. Holmes, *ANF* III, 264, with my adjustments.

63. On ways of recognizing a Roman citizen, see Jane Gardner, *Being a Roman Citizen* (London: Routledge, 1993).

64. Tertullian, *On Monogamy* 16.3–4. trans. W. P. Le Saint, ACW 13 (Mahwah, NJ: Paulist Press, 1951), 106.

65. George, "Family Imagery," 51–52.

66. Everett Ferguson, "Tertullian: Scripture, Rule of Faith, and Paul," in *Tertullian and Paul*, ed. Todd D. Still and David E. Wilhite (London: Bloomsbury/T. & T. Clark, 2013), 22–33, at 24–25; and Eric Francis Osborn, *Tertullian: First Theologian of the West* (Cambridge: Cambridge University, 2003), 37–39.

67. Tertullian, *On Modesty* 19.25, trans. S. Thelwall, *ANF* IV.

68. Tertullian, *On Modesty* 19.9, trans. S. Thelwall, *ANF* IV.

69. Tertullian, *The Prescription of Heretics* 42.9–10, trans. P. Holmes, *ANF* III, 264.

70. Tertullian, *On Modesty* 1.8–9, trans. S. Thelwall, *ANF* IV.

71. See David Rankin, *Tertullian and the Church* (Cambridge: Cambridge University, 2007), 83–84.

72. Osborn, *Tertullian*, 180.

73. Rankin, *Tertullian and the Church*, 82.

74. Rankin, *Tertullian and the Church*, 82.

75. Tertullian, *On Monogamy* 8.2, trans. S. Thelwall, *ANF* IV, with author's changes.

76. Turid Karlsen Seim, "Motherhood and the Making of Fathers in Antiquity: Contextualizing Genetics in the Gospel of John," in *Women and Gender in Ancient Religions: Interdisciplinary Approaches*, ed. Stephen P. Ahearne-Kroll, Paul A. Holloway, and James A. Kelhoffer (Tübingen: Mohr Siebeck, 2010), 99–123, at 100.

77. See Turid Karlsen Seim, "Motherhood," 99–101.

78. Turid Karlsen Seim, "Motherhood," 101.

79. Turid Karlsen Seim, "Motherhood," 101.

80. James G. Lennox, "Form, Essence and Explanation in Aristotle's Biology," in ·*A Companion to Aristotle*, ed. Georgios Anagnostopoulos, Blackwell Reference Online, accessed May 23, 2016, http://www.blackwellreference.com.proxy.bc.edu/subscriber/tocnode.html?id=g9781405122238_chunk_g978140512223825.

81. Seim, "Motherhood," 102.

82. Brendan Leahy, *The Marian Profile in the Ecclesiology of Hans Urs von Balthasar* (New York: New City Press, 2000), 20.

83. Clark, "Status Feminae," 142. See also Tertullian, *On the Veiling of Virgins* 17.1.

84. Clark, "Status Feminae," 144.

85. Tertullian, *On Monogamy* 5.6–7, trans. S. Thelwall, *ANF* IV.

86. Tertullian, *On the Soul* 43.10, trans. P. Holmes, *ANF* III, 222.

87. Marcion was already dead by Tertullian's time. See Judith M. Lieu, *Marcion and the Making of a Heretic: God and Scripture in the Second Century* (New York: Cambridge University Press, 2015), 52.

88. Lieu, *Marcion and the Making of a Heretic*, 53.

89. See Tertullian, *On the Dress of Women* 1.2.2.

90. An exception is the link he makes between holiness and motherhood in *Against Marcion* 5.4.8 to reclaim Gal 4:26 from Marcion.

91. Janet Martin Soskice, *Metaphor and Religious Language* (Oxford: Clarendon, 1985), 64.

3. FROM SEATED MOTHER WITH HER INFANTS TO BRIDE OF CHRIST

1. See Cyprian, *Letters* 7.1; 14.1.2–2.1; 43.4.2.

2. Plumpe says by this time Mother Church was sometimes simply referred to as the "Mother." Joseph Conrad Plumpe, *Mater Ecclesia: An Inquiry into the Concept of the Church as Mother in Early Christianity*, Catholic University of America Studies in Christian Antiquity (Washington, DC: Catholic University of America Press, 1943), 81.

3. Cyprian, *On the Unity of the Catholic Church* 6, in Cyprian, *Cyprian: De Lapsis and De Ecclesiae Catholicae Unitate: Text and Translation*, trans. Maurice Bévenot (Oxford: Clarendon, 1971), 67.

4. Cyprian, *On the Unity of the Catholic Church*, 67.

5. Diana E. E. Kleiner, "Imperial Women as Patrons of the Arts in the Early Empire," in *I, Claudia: Women in Ancient Rome*, ed. Diana E. E. Kleiner and Susan B. Matheson (New Haven, CT: Yale University Art Gallery, 1996), 28–41, at 28, 37.

6. See Diana E. E. Kleiner and Susan B. Matheson, "Her Parents Gave Her the Name Claudia," in Kleiner and Matheson, *I, Claudia II*, 1–16, at 7.

7. For the portrayal of Livia as *justitia* and *pietas*, see Rolf Winkes, "Livia: Portrait and Propaganda," in Kleiner and Matheson, *I, Claudia II*, 29–42, at 38. For the portrayal of Livia as *justitia, salus augusta*, and *pietas*, see Diana E. E. Kleiner, "Family Ties: Mothers and Sons in Elite and Non-Elite Roman Art," in Kleiner and Matheson, *I, Claudia II*, 43–60, at 49. For the portrayal of Livia as *pietas* and *concordia*, see Cornelius C. Vermuele III, "Livia to Helena: Women in Power, Women in the Provinces," in Kleiner and Matheson, *I, Claudia II*, 17–27, at 19.

8. See https://www.cngcoins.com/, accessed May 6, 2017.

9. See Winkes, "Livia," 29–39.

10. Livia is portrayed not only on the Augustan *Ara Pacis* but also on the *Ara Pietatis*, which Kleiner argues was one of the two most significant monuments in Augustan and Julio-Claudian Rome. Kleiner and Matheson, "Her Parents," 37; Kleiner, "Family Ties," 46.

11. Kleiner and Matheson, "Her Parents," 9.

12. Paul Zanker, *Roman Art* (Los Angeles: J. Paul Getty Museum, 2010), 88.

13. Zanker, *Roman Art*, 88.

14. Zanker, *Roman Art*, 88.

15. Diana E. E. Kleiner, "The *Ara Pacis Augustae*," in *Roman Sculpture* (New Haven, CT: Yale University, 1992), 90.

16. Nancy H. Ramage and Andrew Ramage, "Reliefs—*Ara Pacis Augustae*," in *The Cambridge Illustrated History of Roman Art* (Cambridge: Cambridge University Press, 1991), 91.

17. Kleiner, "*Ara Pacis Augustae*," 96; Barbara Spaeth, "The Goddess Ceres in the *Ara Pacis*," *American Journal of Archaeology* 98, no. 1 (1994): 65–100, at 65.

18. Ramage and Ramage, *Cambridge Illustrated History*, 91.

19. Allen Brent, *Cyprian and Roman Carthage* (Cambridge: Cambridge University Press, 2010), 32; Kleiner, "*Ara Pacis Augustae*," 96.

20. For the basis of her argument, see Spaeth, "Goddess Ceres," 93; see also 92–93; Kleiner, "*Ara Pacis Augustae*," 90, 96.

21. Kleiner, "*Ara Pacis Augustae*," 93.

22. Kleiner, "*Ara Pacis Augustae*," 98.

23. For scholarship on the *Ara Pacis* as the original version of the Carthaginian relief, see Barbara Spaeth, "The Goddess Ceres in the *Ara Pacis Augustae* and the Carthage Relief," *American Journal of Archaeology* 98,

no. 1 (1994): 65–100, at 95nn238, 242. Prior to 1960, the Carthage relief was interpreted as a Hellenistic original, possibly from Alexandria.

24. David Rankin, "Cyprian," in *From Clement to Origen: The Social and Historical Context of the Church Fathers* (Aldershot, UK: Ashgate, 2006), 72–80, at 75–77; Alexander Wilhelmus Henricus Evers, "'Post Populi Suffragium': Cyprian of Carthage and the Vote of the People in Episcopal Elections," in *Cyprian of Carthage: Studies in His Life, Language, and Thought,* ed. Henk Bakker, Paul van Geest, and Hans van Loon (Leuven: Peeters, 2010), 165–80; Vincent Hunink, "St Cyprian: A Christian and Roman Gentleman," in Bakker, van Geest, and van Loon, *Cyprian of Carthage,* 29–41; Peter Bingham Hinchliff, *Cyprian of Carthage and the Unity of the Christian Church* (London: G. Chapman, 1974), 15, 17, 22–26, esp. 24–26.

25. Brent, *Cyprian and Roman Carthage,* 23–25.

26. Brent, *Cyprian and Roman Carthage,* 250–89.

27. Hunink, "St Cyprian," 41.

28. Hinchliff, *Cyprian of Carthage,* 27.

29. Hinchliff, *Cyprian of Carthage,* 33.

30. Paul Zanker, *The Power of Images in the Age of Augustus* (Ann Arbor: University of Michigan Press, 1988), 112–13; also 335–39.

31. J. Patout Burns, *Cyprian the Bishop* (New York: Routledge, 2002), 13–14.

32. In Suzanne Dixon, *Cornelia, Mother of the Gracchi* (London: Routledge, 2007), 61.

33. Cyprian, *To Donatus* 8.141–50, trans. R. E. Wallis, *ANF* V, 277, with author changes.

34. Brent, *Cyprian and Roman Carthage,* 30. See also George A. Kennedy, *The Art of Rhetoric in the Roman World, 300 B.C.–A.D. 300* (Princeton, NJ: Princeton University Press, 1972), 378–84, at 381–83.

35. Brent, *Cyprian and Roman Carthage,* 34.

36. J. Patout Burns and Robin M. Jensen, eds., calendar from "Summary of Events," in *Christianity in Roman Africa: The Development of Its Practices and Belief* (Grand Rapids, MI: Eerdmans, 2014), xxxvii–xli, at xxxvii.

37. Burns, *Cyprian the Bishop,* 2. See also Brent on "degrees of apostasy," in Brent, *Cyprian and Roman Carthage,* 8–9.

38. Brent, *Cyprian and Roman Carthage,* 8.

39. Cyprian, *Letters* 16.4.2; 45.1.2; *On the Lapsed* 2; *On the Unity of the Catholic Church* 23.

40. Cyprian, *Letter* 44.3.2.

41. Cyprian, *Letter* 45.1.2.

42. Cyprian, *On the Lapsed* 9.

43. Cyprian, *On the Unity of the Catholic Church* 19.

44. Cyprian, *Letters* 46.1.3; 47.1.1; 71.2.2; *On the Lapsed* 2.

45. Cyprian, *Letter* 41.2.1.

46. Cyprian, *Letter* 48.3.1.

47. Cyprian, *Letters* 15.2.2; 16.3.2; 43.6.2.

48. Cyprian, *Letters* 16.4.2; 45.1.2.

49. Cyprian, *On the Unity of the Catholic Church* 23, trans. M. Bévenot, in *Cyprian: De Lapsis and De Ecclesiae*, 93–94, with my own slight changes. Other examples are found in *On the Lapsed* 2; *Letters* 45.1.2; 16.4.2.

50. Dixon provides examples from Tacitus's *Agricola* 4, *Dialogus* 28, and Cicero's *Brutus* 211. See Suzanne Dixon, *The Roman Mother* (London: Croom Helm, 1988), 130, and 138n38.

51. Dixon, *Roman Mother*, 130.

52. Dixon, *Roman Mother*, 130.

53. The following references are from Dixon, *Roman Mother*, 4: Tacitus, *The Life of Cnaeus Julius Agricola* 29.1; Cicero, *Letters to Friends* 9.20.3; Seneca, *On Consolation to Marcia* 2.3–4, 7.3; See also Plutarch, *Consolation to His Wife* 4.

54. Cyprian, *Letter* 10.4.4, trans. G. Clarke, ACW 43/I, 74.

55. Cyprian, *Letter* 44.3.2. trans. G. Clarke, ACW 44/II.

56. See Jenny March, "Aeneas and the Destiny of Rome," in *The Penguin Book of Classical Myths* (London: Penguin, 2009), 478–97, at 478, 480.

57. Ulpian in *Justinian's Digest* 37.15.1.2. See http://www.thelatinlibrary.com/justinian/digest37.shtml (accessed April 5, 2016).

58. Cyprian, *On the Unity of the Catholic Church* 5, in Bévenot, *Cyprian: De Lapsis and De Ecclesiae*, 66–67.

59. David Rankin, *From Clement to Origen: The Social and Historical Context of the Church Fathers* (London: Routledge, 2016), 74.

60. Rankin, *From Clement to Origen*, 74; Brent, *Cyprian and Roman Carthage*, 4–5.

61. Rankin, *From Clement to Origen*, 75.

62. The purpose of the decree is discussed in Brent, *Cyprian and Roman Carthage*, 6–7; Rankin, *From Clement to Origen*, 72; Burns, *Cyprian the Bishop*, 1.

63. Burns, *Cyprian the Bishop*, 1.

64. George Heyman, "The Sacrifice of the Martyr," in *The Power of Sacrifice* (Washington, DC: Catholic University of America Press, 2007), 161–214, at 162.

65. Heyman, "The Sacrifice of the Martyr," 194.

66. Heyman, "The Sacrifice of the Martyr," 195.

67. Cyprian, *Letter* 15.3.1. See Allen Brent, "Cyprian and the Question of *Ordinatio per Confessionem*," *Studia Patristica* 36 (2001): 323–37, at 325.

68. See Brent, "Cyprian and the Question," 334.

69. See Brent, *Cyprian and Roman Carthage*, 9–10, 257–61; Burns, *Cyprian the Bishop*, 25–27.

70. Brent, "Cyprian and the Question," 325.

71. Brent, "Cyprian and the Question," 325.

72. See Burns, "History of Cyprian's Controversies," in *Cyprian the Bishop*, 1–11; see also the overview in Brent, "Controversies within the Church over the Lapsed in Persecution," in Burns, *Cyprian the Bishop*, 8–14.

73. See Cyprian, *On the Unity of the Catholic Church* 4, in Bévenot, *Cyprian: De Lapsis and De Ecclesiae*, 61, 63. For the two versions, see appendix. 1.

74. For Bevenot's perspectives on the revisions, see *Cyprian: De Lapsis and De Ecclesiae*, 220.

75. See Bradley Peper, *The Development of "Mater Ecclesia" in North African Ecclesiology* (Nashville: Vanderbilt University, 2011), 74–92.

76. Cyprian, *Letter* 47.1.1, trans. G. Clarke, ACW 44/II, 74.

77. Notes on *Letter* 45 and *Letter* 47, in ACW 44/II, 233–34, 249–50.

78. Cyprian, *Letter* 48.3.1, in ACW 44/II, 75.

79. Notes on *Letter* 48, in ACW 44/II, 251.

80. Cyprian, *Letter* 48.3.1.

81. Cyprian, *Letter* 59.13.2, trans. G. Clarke, ACW 46/III, 79–80.

82. Dixon, *Roman Mother*, 157.

83. Compare Song 6:9.

84. Compare Song 4:12; Cyprian, *Letter* 69.2.1, trans. G. Clarke, ACW 47/IV, 33.

85. For a timeline and an overview of the focus for the councils of Carthage, see Burns and Jensen, *Christianity in Roman Africa*, xxxvii–xxxviii.

86. After Easter, April 255 CE.

87. See Cyprian, *Letter* 74.6.2, in ACW 47/IV, 73.

88. See Origen, "Prologue," n. 1, in *Commentary on the Song of Songs*, trans. R. Lawson, ACW 26, 21. See also J. Christopher King, *Origen on the*

Song of Songs as the Spirit of Scripture: The Bridegroom's Perfect Marriage-Song (Oxford: Oxford University, 2005), 11–12.

89. King, *Origen on the Song of Songs*, 14–15.

90. On the reading of the Song of Songs as a journey toward moral and intellectual perfection, see King, *Origen on the Song of Songs*, 28.

91. On kisses as teachings in Origen's reading of the Song of Songs, and on the meanings of the other concepts such as "breasts," "oil," and "spices" in the Song of Songs for him, see King, *Origen on the Song of Songs*, 40.

92. See Origen, "Prologue," n. 4, in *Commentary on the Song of Songs*, ACW 26, 46–47.

93. Kevin M. McGinnis, "Sanctifying Interpretation: The Christian Interpreter as Priest in Origen," in *Religious Competition in the Third Century CE: Jews, Christians, and the Greco-Roman World*, ed. Jordan D. Rosenblum, Lily C. Vuong, and Nathaniel P. DesRosiers (Bristol, CT: Vandenhoeck & Ruprecht, 2014): 60–68, at 65–66. See also R. P. Lawson, "Introduction," for Origen, *Commentary on the Song of Songs*, ACW 26, 9–10; King, *Origen on the Song of Songs*, 12.

94. See King, *Origen on the Song of Songs*, 77–133.

4. THE VIRGIN-MOTHER-BRIDE CHURCH

1. David G. Hunter, "The Virgin, the Bride, and the Church: Reading Psalm 45 in Ambrose, Jerome, and Augustine," *Church History* 69, no. 2 (2000): 281–303, at 285–86; and "Mary Ever Virgin? Jovinian and Marian Heresy," in *Marriage, Celibacy, and Heresy in Ancient Christianity: The Jovinianist Controversy*, Oxford Early Christian Studies (Oxford: Oxford University Press, 2007), 171–205, at 180; and see 197–204; Elizabeth A. Clark, "The Celibate Bridegroom and His Virginal Brides: Metaphor and the Marriage of Jesus in Early Christian Ascetic Exegesis," *Church History* 77, no. 1 (2008): 1–25.

2. Hunter, "Virgin, Bride, and Church," 283.

3. Peter Brown, *The Body and Society: Men, Women and Sexual Renunciation in Early Christianity* (1988; repr. New York: Columbia University Press, 2008), 346. Regarding this line of thought on the Catholic Church as a holy body, cf. Catherine Chin, "The Bishop's Two Bodies: Ambrose

and the Basilicas of Milan," *Church History* 79, no. 3 (September 2010): 531–55.

4. Inge Kroppenberg, "Law, Religion and the Constitution of the Vestal Virgins," *Law and Literature* 22, no. 3 (2010): 418–39, at 419.

5. Theodosius I was the last emperor to rule over the Western and Eastern Roman Empire, and in 380 had issued the "Edict of Thessalonica," together with Emperors Gratian and Valentinian II, making the Nicene trinitarian Christianity the only valid religion throughout the Empire.

6. See Robin Lorsch Wildfang, *Rome's Vestal Virgins: A Study of Rome's Vestal Priestesses in the Late Republic and Early Empire* (London: Routledge, 2006), 1.

7. This meaning contrasts with the current meaning given to *incest,* which is "sexual intercourse between persons so closely related that they are forbidden by law to marry." *Merriam-Webster's Collegiate Dictionary,* 11th ed., s.v. "incest."

8. Kroppenberg, "Law, Religion," 424.

9. Mary Beard, "The Sexual Status of Vestal Virgins," *Journal of Roman Studies* 70 (1980): 12–27, at 14.

10. Beard, "The Sexual Status of Vestal Virgins," 16.

11. Beard, "The Sexual Status of Vestal Virgins," 16–17.

12. Brown, *Body and Society,* 347.

13. J. Warren Smith, "The Soul," in *Christian Grace and Pagan Virtue: The Theological Foundation of Ambrose's Ethics* (Oxford: Oxford University Press, 2011), 11–28, at 12.

14. Smith, "The Soul," 14.

15. Smith, "The Soul," 12. See also Ambrose, *On the Good Death* 3.10; 31.2; 7.27; 9.40; *Isaac* 2.5.

16. Marcia Colish, "Cicero, Ambrose, and Stoic Ethics: Transmission or Transformation?" ch. 5 in *The Fathers and Beyond: Church Fathers between Ancient and Medieval Thought* (Aldershot, UK: Ashgate, 2008), 95–112, at 95.

17. Marcia L. Colish, "Ambrose of Milan on Chastity," ch. 1 in *The Fathers and Beyond,* 1–22, at 1.

18. Colish, "Ambrose of Milan on Chastity," 2.

19. Colish, "Ambrose of Milan on Chastity," 2.

20. Ambrose, *Commentary on the Twelve Psalms,* Psalm 47 §10; *Commentary on the Gospel of Luke 2,* bk. 2 §§7, 57; *Concerning Virgins* 1.31; *Letter* 70.16.

21. Ambrose, *On Repentance* 2.92.

22. Ambrose, *On the Mysteries* 58.

23. Ambrose, *Letter* 41.20.

24. Ambrose, *Commentary on Psalm 118, Sermon* 5 §18.

25. Ambrose, *On the Incarnation of Our Lord* 13.

26. Ambrose, *Concerning Virgins* 1.49.

27. Ambrose, *Concerning Virginity* 1.81; *On Repentance* 2.25; 2.61; *Letter* 21.36.

28. On the ancient Roman mother, see ch. 2 in the present volume.

29. Ambrose, *Commentary on the Twelve Psalms, Psalm 47* §10; *Commentary on the Gospel of Luke 2*, bk. 2 §§7, 57; *Letters* 62.3; 70.16; *Concerning Virgins* 1.31.

30. Ambrose does speak of the church "birthing" members through baptism in *On the Mysteries* 59.

31. Ambrose, *Commentary on the Twelve Psalms*, Psalm 47 §10.

32. Ambrose, *Concerning Virginity* 1.8.

33. Ambrose, *Commentary on the Twelve Psalms*, Psalm 47 §7, pp. 168–69. Colish, too, notes that "following a general trend in the post-Constantinian church, [Ambrose] assimilates martyrdom to the celibate calling." Colish, "Ambrose of Milan on Chastity," 20.

34. I discuss Ambrose's view on virginity later, within the larger context of his views on chastity and the cultivation of virtues.

35. Ambrose, *Commentary on the Gospel of Luke 2*, bk. 10 §24, pp. 28–29.

36. Ambrose, *Commentary on the Twelve Psalms*, Psalm 47 §10.

37. Ambrose, *Commentary on the Gospel of Luke 2*, bk. 10 §24.

38. Ambrose, *Commentary on the Gospel of Luke 2*, bk. 2 §26.

39. Ambrose, *Commentary on the Gospel of Luke 2*, bk. 10 §25, p. 323. Sometimes, though, Ambrose combines the two concepts of conceiving and birthing: "For every soul that believes conceives and brings forth the Word of God and recognizes His works." See Ambrose, *Commentary on the Gospel of Luke 2*, bk. 2 §26, p. 36.

40. Ambrose, *Concerning Virgins* 1.31, p. 368.

41. Hunter, "Virgin, Bride, and Church," 286.

42. Ambrose, *Commentary on the Gospel of Luke 2*, bk. 2 §56, p. 48.

43. As Ambrose says, "Human flesh is inclined by sexual urges to sin. Our minds and souls are weak, and inextricably attached to vice." Ambrose, *Commentary on the Gospel of Luke 2*, bk. 2 §56.

44. Ambrose, *Commentary on the Gospel of Luke 2*, bk. 2 §56.

45. Ambrose, *On Abraham* 1.4.25, trans. M. Colish, "Ambrose of Milan on Chastity," 7.

46. See Jane Gardner, *Women in Roman Law and Society* (Taylor & Francis e-Library, 2009), 41.

47. See Colish, "Ambrose of Milan on Chastity," 1–22.

48. Ambrose, *Instruction for a Virgin* 6.41, in Colish, "Ambrose of Milan on Chastity," 10.

49. Colish, "Ambrose of Milan on Chastity," 6.

50. Pallas was an eastern deity who was brought from Troy to Rome by the ancient Roman hero, Aeneas.

51. See Ambrose, *Concerning Virgins* 1.4.15; Colish, "Ambrose of Milan on Chastity," 16. Ambrose's views on the practice of chastity in widowhood are also reported in Colish.

52. Colish, "Ambrose of Milan on Chastity," 21.

53. Colish, "Ambrose of Milan on Chastity," 20–21.

54. Ambrose, *Concerning Widows* 3.16, in Colish, "Ambrose of Milan on Chastity," 9–10.

55. Factors are adapted from Boniface Ramsey's assessment of the religious milieu of the time. For a fuller assessment, see Boniface Ramsay, *Ambrose* (London: Routledge, 1997), 1–10.

56. See Boniface Ramsay, *Ambrose*, 9.

57. Grubbs, *Women and the Law*, 103.

58. This refers to the First Council of Nicea, a pivotal ecumenical church council held in Nicea, Asia Minor, in 325 CE, condemning Arianism and producing an initial version of the Nicene Creed, which is recited after the homily during Christian Sunday Mass. The creed begins "I believe in one God." Alternatively, the Apostles' Creed can be said at Sunday Mass in place of the Nicene Creed; it begins "I believe in God."

59. Neil B. McLynn, *Ambrose of Milan: Church and Court in a Christian Capital* (Berkeley: University of California Press, 1994), 42.

60. McLynn, *Ambrose of Milan*, 43.

61. Ariel Bybee Laughton, "Virginity Discourse and Ascetic Politics in the Writings of Ambrose of Milan" (PhD diss., Duke University, 2010), 86.

62. See McLynn, *Ambrose of Milan*, 54, 60. Oberhelman also affirms Ambrose's ignorance in Scripture, theology, and functions of the clergy, and that this may have been a reason for Ambrose pursuing virginity as a topic. S. M. Oberhelman, "Jerome's Earliest Attack on Ambrose: On

Ephesians, Prologue (ML 26:469D–70A)," *Transactions of the American Philological Association* 121 (1991): 377–401, at 379.

63. See J. H. W. G. Liebeschuetz, *Ambrose and John Chrysostom: Clerics between Desert and Empire* (Oxford: Oxford University Press, 2011), 59–60, 85–91.

64. In Maria Doerfler, "Ambrose's Jews: The Creation of Judaism and Heterodox Christianity in Ambrose of Milan's *Expositio Evangelii Secundum Lucam*," *Church History* 80, no. 4 (2011): 749–72, at 760.

65. See also David G. Hunter, *Marriage, Celibacy, and Heresy in Ancient Christianity: The Jovinianist Controversy* (Oxford: Oxford University Press, 2009), 201–4.

66. Hunter, *Marriage, Celibacy, and Heresy*, 224. See also Liebeschuetz, *Ambrose and John Chrysostom*, 69. For the ritual itself and its connection to the ritual of marriage, see R. Metz, *La consecration des vierges dans l'Eglise romaine: Etude d'histoire de la liturgie* (Paris: Presses universitaires de France, 1954).

67. See Hunter, *Marriage, Celibacy, and Heresy*, 224–28; and Metz, *La consecration des vierges*.

68. Ambrose, *Instruction for a Virgin* 107, trans. D. Hunter, "Virgin, Bride, and Church," 289. See also Hunter, *Marriage, Celibacy, and Heresy*, 229.

69. See McLynn, *Ambrose of Milan*, 60.

70. McLynn, *Ambrose of Milan*. See also Ambrose, *Concerning Virgins* 2.1–4.

71. McLynn, *Ambrose of Milan*, 60.

72. On Ambrose's theological abilities, see McLynn, *Ambrose of Milan*, 54, 60; and Oberhelman, "Jerome's Earliest Attack on Ambrose," 379.

73. Ambrose, *Instruction for a Virgin* 12.79, trans. P. Brown, *Body and Society*, 356.

74. Brown, *Body and Society*, 343. See also Ambrose, *Concerning Virgins* 1.11.

75. Ambrose, *Concerning Virgins* 1.31, in Hunter, "Virgin, Bride, and Church," 286.

76. Hunter, "Virgin, Bride, and Church," 286–87.

77. Hunter, "Virgin, Bride, and Church," 288. Other celibate Christians were widows and Christian virgins who dedicated themselves to the church from their homes but did not take part in a veiling ceremony.

78. Hunter, "Virgin, Bride, and Church," 287.

79. Hunter, "Virgin, Bride, and Church," 286–87.

80. Elizabeth A. Clark, "The Celibate Bridegroom and His Virginal Brides: Metaphor and the Marriage of Jesus in Early Christian Ascetic Exegesis," *Church History* 77, no. 1 (2008): 1–25, at 2.

81. Clark, "The Celibate Bridegroom," 2.

82. Clark, "Celibate Bridegroom," 8.

83. Brown, *Body and Society*, 343.

84. Ambrose, *Commentary on the Gospel of Luke 2*, bk. 2 §26, p. 36.

85. See Ambrose, *Commentary on the Gospel of Luke 2*, 36.

86. See Ambrose, *Commentary on the Gospel of Luke 2*, §7.

87. Ambrose, *Commentary on the Gospel of Luke 2*, §1.

88. Ambrose, *Commentary on the Gospel of Luke 2*, §43.

89. Ambrose, *Commentary on the Gospel of Luke 2*, §7.

90. Bonosus was bishop of Sardica or Naissus.

91. Hunter, "Virgin, Bride, and Church," 295.

92. David G. Hunter, "Rereading the Jovinianist Controversy: Asceticism and Clerical Authority in Late Ancient Christianity," *Journal of Medieval and Early Modern Studies* 33, no. 3 (2003): 453–70, at 460.

93. Hunter, "Rereading the Jovinianist Controversy," 461.

94. See Mary's motherhood and virginity as an essential statement concerning the mystery of salvation in Hunter, *Marriage, Celibacy, and Heresy*, 201–4.

95. Ambrose, *On Faith* 3.74; *On the Mysteries* 39, 55–57; *On the Death of His Brother Satyrus* 2.118–19; *Letters* 41.18; 63.36; and *Commentary on Psalm 118: Sermons* 1 §16; 2 §§10–11; 4 §18; 5 §§10, 12, 13; 6 §§5–6, 18, 20, 24; 7 §35; 13 §25; 19 §26; 22 §§37, 39.

96. Ambrose, *On Faith* 4.19; *On the Mysteries* 40, 55–58; *On the Death of His Brother Satyrus* 118–19; *Letter* 63.36; *Commentary on Psalm 118: Sermons* 1 §16; 5 §9.

97. Ambrose, *On the Mysteries* 40; *Commentary on Psalm 118: Sermon* 3 §9.

98. Ambrose, *Letter* 63.36.

99. Ambrose, *On the Mysteries* 58; *Commentary on Psalm 118: Sermon* 5 §18.

100. Ambrose, *Concerning Widows* 16; *Letter* 26.5.

101. Ambrose, *On the Mysteries* 40.

102. Ambrose, *On Faith* 4.19.

103. See the earlier chapters on Tertullian's and Cyprian's Mother Church, which outline extensively the portraits of the *materfamilias* and *matrona*.

104. Ambrose, *On Repentance* 2.92.

105. Ambrose, *Concerning Virgins* 1.31.

106. Ambrose, *Letter* 62.3.

107. Ambrose, *On Faith* 4.19.

108. Ambrose, *On Faith* 3.10.74.

109. Ambrose, *On the Mysteries* 7.40.

110. Ambrose, *On the Mysteries* 9.55.

111. Ambrose, *On the Mysteries* 9.55.

112. Ambrose, *Commentary on the Gospel of Luke 2*, bk. 10 §25.

113. Ambrose, *Commentary on the Gospel of Luke 2*, §24.

5. THE FORMIDABLE MOTHER AGAINST THE HERETICS

1. Carol Harrison, *Augustine: Christian Truth and Fractured Humanity* (Oxford: Oxford University Press, 2006), 61.

2. Augustine, *On Christian Teaching* 2.42.63.

3. Augustine, *On Christian Teaching* 2.24.37.

4. Augustine, *On Teaching the Uninstructed* 10.15.

5. Annemaré Kotzé, "The 'Anti-Manichaean' Passage in 'Confessions 3' and Its 'Manichaean Audience,'" *VigChr* 62 (2008): 187–200, at 192.

6. Augustine, *Revisions* 1.20, trans. B. Ramsey, WSA I/2, 86.

7. See *Letter* 23.4, where Augustine describes the Catholic Mother Church as the "most true" church.

8. Carl P. E. Springer, "The Prosopopoeia of Church as Mother in Augustine's *Psalmus Contra Partem Donati*," *Augustinian Studies* 18 (1987): 52–65.

9. Trans. by Springer, "Prosopopoeia," 52.

10. Augustine, *Confessions* 9.9.22, trans. M. Boulding, WSA I/1, 226.

11. Compare Augustine, *Confessions* 1.6.7 and 2.3.6 to *Letter* 89.6.

12. Compare Augustine, *Confessions* 4.16.31 to 3.4.7.

13. Augustine, *Confessions* 3.11.19; 4.4; 5.7.13; 5.8.15; 6.1, as sorrowful Monica; 3.11.19; 4.4; 5.7.13; 5.8.15; 6.1, as interceding/mourning Monica.

14. Augustine, *A Psalm against the Party of Donatus*. See also Springer, "Prosopopoeia."

15. See also Augustine, *Letters* 34.3 and 89.6, for Augustine's Mother Church as despairing, pained, or anxious.

16. Springer, "Prosopopoeia," 60.

17. Alexander Evers, "Augustine on the Church (against the Donatists)," in *A Companion to Augustine*, ed. Mark Vessey (Oxford: Blackwell, 2012), 375–85, at 377.

18. Alexander Evers, "Augustine on the Church," 375.

19. See chs. 2 and 3 of the present volume.

20. See Augustine, *A Psalm against the Party of Donatus*, last section.

21. Augustine, *Letter* 93.6, trans. R. Teske, WSA II/1, 380.

22. Augustine, *Letter* 93.4.

23. See chs. 2 and 3 of the present volume on this matter.

24. James E. Dittes, "Continuities between the Life and Thought of Augustine," *Journal for the Scientific Study of Religion* 5, no. 1 (1965): 130–40, at 133.

25. See Augustine, *On Baptism* 4.10.17, on the worthiness (or otherwise) of a minister or recipient in relation to the effectiveness of baptism as a sacrament. According to Augustine, the necessary elements for a valid baptism are only water and the baptismal invocation. See Augustine, *On Baptism* 3.10.15.

26. R. A. Markus, *Saeculum: History and Society in the Theology of Saint Augustine* (1970; repr. Cambridge: Cambridge University Press, 1989), 116.

27. See Markus, *Saeculum*, 115–17.

28. For an explanation of the unity between Christ and the church, see Aaron Canty, "The Nuptial Imagery of Christ and the Church in Augustine's *Ennarationes* in *Psalmos*," in *Early Christian Literature and Intertextuality*, ed. Craig A. Evans and H. Daniel Zacharias (London: T. & T. Clark, 2009), 225–35, at 227.

29. Aaron Canty, "The Nuptial Imagery of Christ," 230–31. There is a play on the image of the virgin here, since it could mean either Mary or the church or both.

30. Markus, *Saeculum*, 113.

31. See Markus, *Saeculum*, 105.

32. Evers, "Augustine on the Church," 384.

33. Felix Baffour Asare Asiedu, "The Song of Songs and the Ascent of the Soul: Ambrose, Augustine, and the Language of Mysticism," *VigChr* 55, no. 3 (2001): 299–317, at 311–12; Elizabeth A. Clark, "The Uses of the Song of Songs: Origen and the Later Latin Fathers," in *Ascetic Piety and Women's Faith: Essays on Late Ancient Christianity*, Studies in Women and Religion, vol. 20 (New York: Edwin Mellen, 1986), 386–410, at 408; David G. Hunter, "The Virgin, the Bride, and the Church: Reading Psalm 45 in Ambrose, Jerome, and Augustine," *Church History* 69, no. 2 (2000): 281–303, at 283.

34. Asiedu, "Song of Songs and Ascent," 312–13; Hunter, "Virgin, Bride, and Church," 296–302. Hunter refers to Psalm 44 (following the Greek numbering), which corresponds to Psalm 45 (following the Hebrew numbering) in the Vulgate.

35. Augustine, *On Baptism* 5.38.

36. Clark, "Uses of Song of Songs," 408. See Augustine, *To Cresconius, a Donatist Grammarian* 2.15, 18.

37. See van Oort on the Manichean hierarchical church structure. Johannes van Oort, "Augustine and the Books of the Manichaeans," in Vessey, *A Companion to Augustine*, 188–99, at 190.

38. E.g., they have five commandments mimicking Christian Lenten practices and actions based on Catholic social principles. See Samuel N. C. Lieu, "Christianity and Manichaeism," in *The Cambridge History of Christianity*, ed. Augustine Casiday and Frederick W. Norris (Cambridge: Cambridge University Press, 2007), 279–95, at 284.

39. Van Oort, "Augustine and the Books," 189.

40. See Augustine, *Against Faustus, a Manichee* 15.3.

41. Augustine, *Against Faustus*, 15.3.

42. See ch. 3 of the present volume.

43. Augustine, *Sermon* 22.10, trans. E. Hill, WSA III/2, 47–48.

44. Augustine, *Sermon* 72A.8 (also known as *Sermon Denis* 25.8), trans. E. Hill, WSA III/3, 288–89.

45. Augustine, *Letter* 185.11.

46. Augustine, *Expositions of the Psalms* 126.8.19; *Against Faustus, a Manichee* 22.86.

47. Augustine, *On Holy Virginity* 6, trans. R. Kearney, WSA I/9, 71.

48. For more on this, see Asiedu, "Song of Songs and Ascent," 288.

49. Augustine, *On Holy Virginity* 9, p. 72.

50. Augustine, *On Holy Virginity* 10, p. 73.

51. Augustine, *Sermon* 191.3–4, trans. E. Hill, WSA III/6, 43–44.

52. Augustine, *On Holy Virginity* 2, pp. 68–69.

53. Augustine, *Sermon* 192.2.

54. Augustine, *Sermon* 191.2, trans. E. Hill, WSA III/6, 43.

55. Augustine, *Sermon* 191.3, p. 43. The same concepts can be found in Augustine, *Sermon* 188 and *Sermon Denis* 25.

56. Geoffrey D. Dunn, "The Functions of Mary in the Christmas Homilies of Augustine of Hippo," *Studia Patristica* 44 (2010): 433–46, at 439.

57. Dunn, "The Functions of Mary," 444.

58. Augustine, *Sermon* 72A.7, trans. E. Hill, WSA III/3, 287–88.

59. Pelagianism was not singular in its beliefs, and it was upheld by various ascetically minded proponents under the banner of a British monk, Pelagius (350–425 CE).

60. Augustine, *Against Julian, an Unfinished Book* 3.61.

61. Augustine, *Against Julian* 3.51.

62. Augustine, *Against Julian* 3.52.

63. For more on this, see Carol Scheppard, "The Transmission of Sin in the Seed: A Debate between Augustine of Hippo and Julian of Eclanum," *Augustinian Studies* 27, no. 2 (1996): 97–106, at 99–100.

64. For an introduction to Girard's mimetic violence theory, see René Girard, "Are the Gospels Mythical?" *First Things* 62 (April 1996): 27–31.

65. Augustine, *Sermon* 176.2, trans. E. Hill, WSA III/5, 272–73.

66. Mortal sin leads to the death of the soul, whereas venial sins are smaller acts that in a cumulative sense can (but not necessarily) lead a person to eventually commit mortal sin.

67. Augustine, *Against Julian, an Unfinished Book* 3.61.

68. Augustine, *City of God* 20.21, trans. W. Babcock, WSA I/7, 425.

69. Augustine, *Confessions* 1.11.17.

70. Augustine, *Letter* 98.5, trans. R. Teske, WSA II/1, 429.

6. POPE FRANCIS'S *LA CHIESA*

1. Pope Francis, "Address of Pope Francis to Participants in a Seminar Organized by the Pontifical Council for the Laity Celebrating the 25th Anniversary of *Mulieris Dignitatem*," Clementine Hall, Vatican City, October 12, 2013, https://w2.vatican.va/content/francesco/en/

speeches/2013/october/documents/papa-francesco_20131012_seminario
-xxv-mulieris-dignitatem.html.

2. Francesca Ambrogetti and Sergio Rubin, *Pope Francis: His Life in His Own Words: Conversations with Jorge Bergoglio* (New York: G. P. Putnam's Sons, 2014), 13.

3. Ambrogetti and Rubin, *Pope Francis*, 10.

4. Robert Moynihan, *Pray for Me: The Life and Spiritual Vision of Pope Francis, First Pope from the Americas* (New York: Random House, 2013), 137.

5. Robert Moynihan, *Pray For Me.*

6. Ambrogetti and Rubin, *Pope Francis*, 8.

7. See Ambrogetti and Rubin, *Pope Francis*, 24–25.

8. Ambrogetti and Rubin, *Pope Francis*, 14–15.

9. According to the report of the National Commission on the Disappearance of Persons (CONADEP, Argentina), 1984, this was the typical sequence of events for disappeared persons: kidnapping, disappearance, then torture. See http://www.desaparecidos.org/nuncamas/web/english/library/nevagain/nevagain_004.htm (accessed April 26, 2017).

10. Data are from the 1984 report of CONADEP, accessed April 26, 2017, http://www.desaparecidos.org/nuncamas/web/english/library/nevagain/nevagain_209.htm. The report states, though, that there are thousands more unrecorded.

11. John Allen Jr., *The Francis Miracle: Inside the Transformation of the Pope and the Church* (Des Moines, IA: Time Books, 2015), 120–21.

12. Allen Jr., *The Francis Miracle*, 122–23.

13. Allen Jr., *The Francis Miracle*, 122–23.

14. Ambrogetti and Rubin, *Pope Francis.*

15. Jimmy Burns, *Francis: Pope of Good Promise* (London: Constable, 2015), 347.

16. Burns, *Francis*, 242.

17. Burns, *Francis*, 242.

18. Burns, *Francis*, 242.

19. Melody L. Miller, Phyllis Moen, and Donna Dempster-McClain, "Motherhood, Multiple Roles, and Maternal Wellbeing: Women of the 1950s," *Gender and Society* 5 (1991): 565–82; Jessamyn Neuhaus, "The Way to a Man's Heart: Gender Roles, Domestic Ideology, and Cookbooks in the 1950s," *Journal of Social History* 32 (1999): 529–55; Mark G. Toulouse, "Feminist Gains: The Century and Women," *Christian Century* 117 (2000): 1341–43.

20. Miller, Moen, and Dempster-McClain, "Motherhood," 566.

21. Miller, Moen, and Dempster-McClain, "Motherhood," 566.

22. Neuhaus, "Way to a Man's Heart," 543.

23. Neuhaus, "Way to a Man's Heart," 547.

24. Toulouse, "Feminist Gains," 1341.

25. Betty Friedan, *The Feminine Mystique* (New York: W. W. Norton, 1963).

26. Ivy A. Helman, *Women and the Vatican: An Exploration of Official Documents* (Maryknoll, NY: Orbis Books, 2012), 14, 16.

27. Helman, *Women and the Vatican*, 16. See Pius XI, *Castii Connubii*, n. 4.

28. ANROWS, *Fast Facts: Impacts of Family, Domestic and Sexual Violence, 2018*, accessed June 12, 2018, https://www.anrows.org.au/node/1507.

29. Helman, *Women and the Vatican*, 21–23.

30. Helman, *Women and the Vatican*, 22–23.

31. Pope John XXIII, "*Gaudet Mater Ecclesia*: Pope John's Opening Speech to the Council" (October 11, 1962), trans. Joseph Komonchak, https://jakomonchak.files.wordpress.com/2012/10/john-xxiii-opening-speech.pdf.

32. Pope John XXIII, "*Gaudet Mater Ecclesia*."

33. See ch. 3 of the present volume.

34. Pope Francis, "Morning Meditation in the Chapel of *Domus Sanctae Marthae*: Christian Acceptance" (May 25, 2013), http://w2.vatican.va/content/francesco/en/cotidie/2013/documents/papa-francesco-cotidie_20130525_christian-acceptance.html.

35. Pope Francis, "General Audience: Wednesday, 18 November 2015," accessed April 26, 2017, http://w2.vatican.va/content/francesco/en/audiences/2015/documents/papa-francesco_20151118_udienza-generale.html.

36. Ambrogetti and Rubin, *Pope Francis*, 62–63.

37. Pope Francis, *Amoris Laetitia* 138.

38. John XXIII, "*Gaudet Mater Ecclesia*."

39. John XXIII, "*Mater et Magistra*: Encyclical of Pope John XXIII on Christianity and Social Progress" (May 15, 1961), http://www.vatican.va/holy_father/john_xxiii/encyclicals/documents/hf_j-xxiii_enc_15051961_mater_en.html.

40. John XXIII, "Pope John XXIII Convokes the Second Vatican Council" (apostolic constitution *Humanae Salutis*, December 25, 1961), trans. Joseph Komonchak, http://jakomonchak.files.wordpress.com/

2011/12/humanae-salutis.pdf. Latin text: *Acta Apostolicae Sedis* 54 (1962): 5–13.

41. Paul VI, *Gravissimum Educationis* 7.

42. *Sacrosanctum Concilium* 14. See also John O'Malley: "What, then, were the most important issues at the council? The desire to recognize the dignity of lay men and women and to empower them to fulfill their vocation in the church was certainly among them." John W. O'Malley, *What Happened at Vatican II* (Cambridge, MA: Belknap Press of Harvard University Press, 2008), 5.

43. See *GS* pt. 2, ch. 2, and other Vatican II documents: *Sacrosanctum Concilium* 14, *Gravissimum Educationis* 7, *Optatam Totius* 19, *Presbyterorum Ordinis* 6, *Lumen Gentium* 65, and *Apostolicam Actuositatem* ch. 6.

44. Pope Francis and James P. Campbell, *The Joy of Discipleship: Reflections from Pope Francis on Walking with Christ* (Chicago: Loyola, 2016), 7.

45. See Pope Francis, "General Audience, St. Peter's Square," September 10, 2014, http://w2.vatican.va/content/francesco/en/audiences/2014/documents/papa-francesco_20140910_udienza-generale.html.

46. *GS* 61.

47. Pope Francis, "Address of Pope Francis to the Participants in the Plenary Assembly of the International Union of Superiors General (I.U.S.G.)," Paul VI Audience Hall, Vatican City, May 8, 2013, http://w2.vatican.va/content/francesco/en/speeches/2013/may/documents/papa-francesco_20130508_uisg.html.

48. See Pope Francis, *Amoris Laetitia* 138, accessed April 27, 2017, http://w2.vatican.va/content/francesco/en/apost_exhortations/documents/papa-francesco_esortazione-ap_20160319_amoris-laetitia.html. See particularly Francis's affirmation of Paul VI's idea of "integral human development," which concerns the desire to abolish division, binary thinking, an "us" and "them" mentality, and large gaps between the poor and rich, individuals and communities, the body and soul, etc., in Pope Francis, "Address of His Holiness Pope Francis to the Participants in the Conference Organized by the Dicastery for Promoting Integral Human Development, Marking the 50th Anniversary of the Encyclical *Populorum Progressio*," Synod Hall, Vatican City, April 4, 2017, http://w2.vatican.va/content/francesco/en/speeches/2017/april/documents/papa-francesco_20170404_convegno-populorum-progressio.html.

49. Helman, *Women and the Vatican*, 13.

50. *GS* 60, *AA* 9.

51. Paul VI, Second Vatican Council Closing Speech, *Papal Encyclicals Online*, accessed October 20, 2014 http://www.papalencyclicals.net/Paul06/p6closin.htm.

52. See Helman, *Women and the Vatican*, 16.

53. See http://www.vatican.va/roman_curia/congregations/cfaith/documents/rc_con_cfaith_doc_19761015_inter-insigniores_en.html (accessed April 27, 2017).

54. Its complete title was "Sacred Congregation of the Universal Inquisition," for it saw "its duty was to defend the Church from heresy." See http://www.vatican.va/roman_curia/congregations/cfaith/documents/rc_con_cfaith_pro_14071997_en.html (accessed April 27, 2017).

55. John Paul II, *Man and Women He Created Them: A Theology of the Body* (Boston: Pauline Books & Media, 2006).

56. Paul VI, "Address to Participants at the National Meeting of the Centro Italiano Femminile (December 6, 1976)," *Insegnamenti di Paolo VI*, 14 (1976): 1017.

57. "Apostolic Journey to Rio de Janeiro on the Occasion of the XXVIII World Youth Day: Press Conference of Pope Francis during the Return Flight," July 28, 2013, http://w2.vatican.va/content/francesco/en/speeches/2013/july/documents/papa-francesco_20130728_gmg-conferenza-stampa.html.

58. See "Address of Pope Francis to Participants in a Seminar Organized by the Pontifical Council for the Laity on the Occasion of the 25th Anniversary of 'Mulieres Dignitatem,'" accessed April 27, 2017, http://w2.vatican.va/content/francesco/en/speeches/2013/october/documents/papa-francesco_20131012_seminario-xxv-mulieris-dignitatem.html.

59. See http://w2.vatican.va/content/francesco/en/speeches/2013/october/documents/papa-francesco_20131012_seminario-xxv-mulieris-dignitatem.html (accessed April 27, 2017).

60. See Pope Francis, "Prayer Vigil for the Festival of Families, Address of the Holy Father," in *The Allure of Goodness and Love: Pope Francis in the United States; Complete Texts* (Collegeville, MN: Liturgical, 2016), 77–92, at 82.

61. Pope Francis, "The Family in the Light of the Aparecida Document," *Family and Life: Pastoral Reflections; From His Years as Archbishop of Buenos Aires, 1998–2013* (New York: Paulist Press, 2015), 37–50, at 42.

62. Francis, *Amoris Laetitia* 40.

63. See https://archive.org/details/CNNW_20150927_000000_CNN _Special_Report_The_Peoples_Pope/start/1440/end/1500 (accessed April 3, 2017).

64. Francis, *Amoris Laetitia* 36.

CONCLUSION

1. For more on this, see my article, "From Infants to Mothers: Recovering the Call to the People of God to Become Mother Church," *Ecclesiology* 11, no. 1 (2015): 34–64.

2. *The Writings of Saint Francis of Assisi,* trans. Paschal Robinson of the Order of Friars Minor (Philadelphia: Dolphin Press, 1906), 50.

Index